Career Diplomacy

Career Diplomacy

Life and Work in the US Foreign Service

Second edition

Harry W. Kopp
Charles A. Gillespie

GEORGETOWN UNIVERSITY PRESS | WASHINGTON, DC

Library of Congress Cataloging-in-Publication Data

Kopp, Harry.
    Career diplomacy : life and work in the US foreign service /
Harry W. Kopp, Charles A. Gillespie. — 2nd ed.
        p.   cm.
    Includes bibliographical references and index.
    ISBN 978-1-58901-740-5 (pbk. : alk. paper)
    1. United States. Foreign Service. 2. Diplomatic and consular service,
American. 3. United States—Foreign relations administration.
I. Gillespie, Charles A. II. Title.
    JZ1480.A5K67 2011
    327.73—dc22   2010037042

∞ This book is printed on acid-free paper meeting the requirements
of the American National Standard for Permanence in Paper for Printed
Library Materials.

15 14 13 12 11   9 8 7 6 5 4 3 2 First printing
Printed in the United States of America

In Memoriam
Charles A. Gillespie
1936–2008

Contents

Illustrations

Preface

Career Diplomacy: Life and Work in the US Foreign Service began as a gleam in a general's eye. In 2005 retired US Army General John R. Galvin joined the policy committee of the Una Chapman Cox Foundation, a private foundation dedicated to a strong, professional foreign service. General Galvin, a soldier-diplomat who commanded allied forces in Europe and was dean of the Fletcher School of Law and Diplomacy, wondered out loud whether the foreign service had a book that would guide him through the basics. There is no such book, he was told. "Well, there should be," he said, and Tony Gillespie, another member of the committee, agreed. Tony, the Charles A. Gillespie whose name is on the cover, recruited former foreign service officer Harry Kopp to work with him on the project, and the Cox Foundation provided some seed money. Tony died in 2008, before publication of the first edition.

Whether America's diplomacy succeeds or fails depends to a large extent on its foreign service professionals. *Career Diplomacy* describes the foreign service as an institution, a profession, and a career. It provides a full picture of the organization, its place in history, its strengths and weaknesses, and its role in American foreign affairs. It is not a polemic. The authors have (mostly) resisted the temptation to tell the world what is wrong and how to set it right.

Readers of this book will come to understand who America's professional diplomats are, what they do, the behavior they reward, and the culture in which they operate. If you are in, or interested in, the service, *Career Diplomacy* will teach you things you did not know. If you are thinking about joining the service, this book will help you make a wise decision.

The first edition of *Career Diplomacy: Life and Work in the US Foreign Service* was published in 2008, from a manuscript that was essentially completed in 2007. This 2011 edition, from a manuscript completed in the first half of 2010, brings the facts and figures up-to-date and addresses three great changes that occurred in the intervening years. The first of these is the increasingly important—and increasingly competent—work of foreign service personnel alongside the US military in fragile states threatened with or emerging from combat. The second is the rapid growth of the foreign service in the US Agency for International Development, and the close integration of that agency's budget and mission with those of the US Department of State. The third, closely tied to the other two, is the arrival late in 2008 of a golden moment, which may have passed by the time this book is published, when Congress and the administration found a common determination to improve the foreign service by adding people, training them better, and giving them more money to work with. These changes are captured in Secretary of State Hillary Clinton's slogan "Diplomacy 3.0," or the three D's—shorthand for diplomacy, defense, and development—treated as equally important pillars of American foreign policy.

The website www.careerdiplomacy.com will try to keep readers informed when information in the book becomes outdated. Comments and questions are welcome via the website.

Acknowledgments

The authors are grateful to the many men and women who assisted in this project. We thank those whose names appear in the list of interviews, and equally those interviewed whose names have been withheld.

The Una Chapman Cox Foundation (www.uccoxfoundation.org), a remarkable institution with a remarkable history, provided support and seed money. The foundation and its principals—chairman Margo Branscomb; president Dian VanDeMark; executive directors Clyde Taylor and Lino Gutierrez; and trustees Harvie Branscomb Jr., Shannon Wilde, and Elizabeth Jones—are stalwart friends of the foreign service.

Librarian Sara Schoo and Bill Sullivan of the Ralph Bunche Library at the Department of State made the stacks accessible and the facilities available. Dan Geisler, Alec Watson, Harry Geisel, John Naland, Tony Motley, Charles Gillespie IV, Lew Allison, Ellen Guidera, Susan Johnson, and other friends and colleagues read ungainly drafts and offered corrections and improvements from which the book greatly benefited. Georgie Ann Geyer helped get the whole thing started. Richard Brown and the staff of Georgetown University Press gave the project their full support.

State Department officials gave us encouragement but the department did not request or receive any control over the final product. The authors are jointly responsible for the contents of the book, and Harry Kopp is solely responsible for any mistakes that appear in the second edition, despite the efforts of so many to make sure we got things right.

Part I

The Institution

1

What Is the Foreign Service?

"Look," he said. "What do we need them for? Especially so many of them." He was talking about members of the US Foreign Service. "What we need to know," he said, "is mostly in the news. What we need to say should come from people in tune with the president, not from diplomats in tune with each other."

The speaker was a businessman with international interests. His listener was a former foreign service officer. His question was serious and deserves a careful answer.

Why does the United States need its foreign service, professionals who spend the bulk of their careers in US embassies and consulates around the globe? Does the work they do need to be done, and if so, could others do it better or more efficiently?

The United States is engaged in regional and global conflicts that are at least as political as they are military. Over 12.5 percent of our population, more than 38 million people, are foreign born. Foreign trade is one-quarter of our economy. Environmental changes, epidemic and pandemic diseases, and financial panics sweep across borders. They cannot be controlled unilaterally.

We need to make sense of this world, and we need to make sure the world makes sense of us. We need to understand, protect, and promote our own interests. Whenever and wherever we can, we need to shape events to our advantage. That is why we have a foreign service.

The foreign service is the corps of more than 14,000 professionals who represent the US government in more than 260 missions abroad and carry out the nation's foreign policies. Its members serve mainly in the Department of State, but also in the Department of Commerce, the Department of Agriculture (USDA), the US Agency for International Development (USAID), and wherever else in the US government that the mission requires civilian service abroad.

Like the army, the navy, the air force, and the marines, the US Foreign Service is a true service. Its officers are commissioned by the president, confirmed by the Senate, and sworn to uphold and defend the US Constitution. Rank is vested in the person, not in the job. Members of the foreign service, with a very few exceptions, are available for assignment anywhere in the world. On average, they spend two-thirds of their careers abroad.

The Mission

The foreign service has a triple mission. The first is representation. In US government jargon, representation often refers to official entertaining, for which the government provides a famously small allowance. But diplomacy is not a dinner party, and representation, as used here, is not so much something a diplomat does as a condition of foreign service life abroad. A member of the foreign service on overseas duty not only acts on behalf of the US government but lives as a representative of the country as well. On behalf of the United States, the foreign service talks, listens, reports, analyzes, cajoles, persuades, threatens, debates, and above all negotiates. The foreign service reaches into other societies across barriers of history, culture, language, faith, politics, and economics to build trust, change attitudes, alter behaviors, and keep the peace.

The second mission is operations. The foreign service is on the ground, dealing every day with host governments and populations, running US programs, executing US laws, giving effect to US policies, offering protection to American citizens, and supporting the full US official civilian presence overseas.

The third is policy. Members of the foreign service, through their long engagement with foreign societies, are well placed to predict the international consequences of what we say and do. They are the government's experts on how America's national interests, defined by our political process, can be most effectively advanced abroad. The service is the government's institutional memory for foreign affairs and is able to place policy in historical perspective and project risks, costs, and benefits over the long term.

All three missions are essential. A foreign service that sees its mission as diplomacy, with no role for policy, will wait passively for instructions that may come too late, or not at all. A service that believes it should set policy as well as carry it out will lose the trust of the president and the Congress and become an irrelevant annoyance. A service that neglects hands-on operations will exhaust its energy in bureaucratic exercises and forfeit its ability to act to more nimble and aggressive organizations.

Representation, operations, and policy are all essential to the grand task the country has asked its diplomats to perform. At her confirmation hearings, Hillary Clinton told the Senate Foreign Relations Committee that "if I am confirmed, the State Department will be firing on all cylinders to provide forward-thinking, sustained diplomacy in every part of the world; applying pressure and exerting leverage; cooperating with our military partners and other agencies of government; partnering effectively with NGOs, the private sector, and international organizations; using modern technologies for public outreach; empowering negotiators who can protect our interests while understanding those of our negotiating partners. There will be thousands of separate interactions, all strategically linked and coordinated to defend American security and prosperity."[1] Her approach, she said, was "what has been called 'smart power': [using] the full range of tools at our disposal—diplomatic, economic, military, political, legal, and cultural—picking the right tool, or combination of tools, for each situation. With smart power, diplomacy will be the vanguard of foreign policy."[2]

An Institution, a Profession, a Career

This book is descriptive, not prescriptive. Readers looking for polemics for or against smart power, or a program for reform of America's foreign policy, or a reconstruction of its foreign policy establishment should go elsewhere. What we have produced here is a guide to the foreign service as it is, with a look back at what it was and a look ahead at what it may become. We treat the service three ways: as an institution, as a profession, and as a career.

The Institution

The institution is the men and women, and their predecessors and successors, who serve the United States under the Foreign Service Act. But the people and the institution are not the same. Presidents often distrust the foreign service as an institution—President Nixon vowed to ruin it—even as they promote individual members of the service to positions of confidence. Yet the spirit and culture of the service shape its members and, in turn, are gradually shaped by them.

Seven events and decisions have played an especially large role in making the foreign service what it is today. They are, in chronological order,

- the nineteenth-century split between diplomats, responsible for state-to-state relations, and consuls, who took care of commercial matters and citizens abroad;
- the reliance, until well into the twentieth century, on the well-heeled and well-connected;
- the wall, until the 1950s, between officers of the foreign service, who spent their entire careers abroad, and officers of the Department of State, who served only in Washington;
- the marginalization of the foreign service during World War II;
- the attacks, in the late 1940s and early 1950s, on the loyalty of the foreign service to the United States, and the absence of a defense;
- the rigor of the competitive entrance examination; and
- the control by existing members of the service of their own promotions and the admission of new members.

These factors have led to a service that, until recently, has been elite and clubby, hierarchical, cautious, strong in analysis but less so in operations, deeply patriotic, deferential to the status quo, and respectful of the weight of history. Over the past few years the service has grown in numbers and become more diverse, more skilled in languages, less desk-bound, and less obeisant to rank. The depth of patriotic feeling is unchanged.

The Profession

The profession of the foreign service is diplomacy. Among professions it is an odd one, more like journalism than like law or medicine. It is open to all. Specialized training is available but not required. The skills needed to practice diplomacy at a high level are difficult to master but they are not esoteric. They can be acquired in many fields, including politics, business, the military, and academia. Some of the best practitioners (and also some of the worst) are outsiders who start at the top.

Virtually every country that has a department of foreign affairs also has a professional diplomatic service, and almost none but the United States employs amateurs in large numbers. Most governments recognize that diplomatic skills are most surely gained through diplomatic experience. A diplomatic service, with ranks gained by merit, also serves to identify the best talents and temperaments as it weeds out the worst.

Diplomatic professionals are skilled in negotiation, communication, persuasion, reporting, analysis, and management. They recognize ambiguity and dissembling and can practice both when necessary. They know foreign languages, cultures, and interests, and they have learned, with respect to at least some parts of the world, how other governments make decisions and carry them out and what moves societies to action and change. Equally important, they have learned how their own government works—its politics, laws, and bureaucratic processes. They know where diplomacy fits in the array of tools the nation can deploy to assert its interests, and they can work effectively with military and intelligence professionals in pursuit of common objectives.

One need not be a member of the foreign service to be a skilled diplomat, or even a great one. Outsiders can bring new ideas and new energy. Most important in the US system, they can bring to diplomacy a relationship with the country's political leadership that nonpartisan career diplomats rarely attain. But gifted amateurs and revolving-door diplomats are not enough to do the work the nation demands around the world and around the clock. This book will show that the administration of US laws and programs with international reach, the management of the official US civilian overseas establishment, and the daily negotiation of relationships with foreign governments on matters large and small require a dedicated, professional service.

The Career

A foreign service career is like a good limerick: It has unpredictable content in a predictable form.

The content of a career is a function of specialized knowledge, personal preference, and luck. In the Department of State, knowledge places officers in one of five tracks—(in alphabetical order) consular affairs, economic affairs, management, political affairs, and public diplomacy—and specialists in one of seven categories that cover nineteen kinds of jobs. Most if not all assignments will be in that track or category. Of course, regional knowledge and language skills heavily influence the location of assignment—except when the opposite occurs, and the assignment drives language instruction and the development of regional expertise. Members of the foreign service by law must be available for assignment worldwide. Two-thirds of a career is likely to be spent abroad—and more than that for foreign service officers in agencies other than the Department of State.

Within these parameters there is plenty of room for surprise. The next post, the next job, the next boss are rarely predictable. Change is constant, but it is not random. The needs of the service impose constraints, but foreign service personnel make many of the choices that determine the progress of their careers. When you are in the service, the positions that are open when you are ready to move are the luck of the draw, but the preferences you express among them weigh heavily on the outcome.

The form or trajectory of a foreign service career has less variation: Four or five years in entry-level positions, about twenty years in midlevel positions of increasing responsibility, and, for a few people, several more years in the senior ranks. Retirement is mandatory at age sixty-five, so officers and specialists who begin at the bottom in their fifties face truncated prospects. Pay and benefits are fixed by Congress, and managers are able to intervene only at the margins. The checkpoints for an officer's passage from entry level to midcareer to the senior ranks and eventual retirement are well established, though the requirements for passing through the checkpoints change from time to time and have recently grown more rigorous.

Foreign service takes over a life in a way that few occupations do. Where you live, the food you eat, the languages you hear and use, even the diseases you contract come with the job. If you have a family, the service is a family affair. Children experience the benefits and the challenges of frequent moves and exposure to many cultures. Opportunities for a spouse to work will be erratic. Hazardous duty is likely to impose a separation of a year or more at some point, or at several points, during a career. Nevertheless, retention rates are high. "In for two, in for twenty" is a fair summation, except where "in for three, in for thirty" is more appropriate.

The personnel system gives strong guidance to new recruits but it has declining influence as a career progresses. After two or three tours a member of the foreign service should know how assignments come about (this book will help) and should take responsibility for his or her career. The service is small. In all probability, once you have finished three or four tours, which will take about ten years, anyone interested in you will likely know you, or will know someone who does.

The career is changing. Secretary Clinton likes to alliterate three components of US foreign policy: diplomacy, development, and defense. The Department of State, she says, is responsible for two of the three. Diplomacy and development are "on a par with the military and defense functions of our foreign policy" and with each other.[3] Her formulation shifts the center of gravity of the foreign service away from the conduct of strictly government-to-government relations toward the deeper involvement of diplomats with all elements of the societies in which they work.

It is a shift that began under Secretary Clinton's predecessor, Condoleezza Rice, who often described the challenge facing the foreign service as transformational. "The greatest threats now emerge more within states than between them," she said, referring to the world after September 11, 2001.[4] "This time of global transformation calls for transformational diplomacy. More than ever, America's diplomats will need to be active in spreading democracy, reducing poverty, fighting terror, and doing our part to protect our homeland."[5]

The novelty of this shift away from traditional diplomacy can be exaggerated. At least since the end of World War II, American diplomats have followed American foreign policy beyond official relations. From negotiation of the Universal Declaration of Human Rights in 1948 and implementation of the Point Four aid program in 1949, American diplomats have worked to move foreign societies toward reduced poverty, economic growth, democratic government, the rule of law, and respect for basic human freedoms. What is new since September 11, 2001, is the degree of emphasis and the commitment of resources to these endeavors, the shift of focus from mature industrial countries to more volatile societies, and the rising importance of operations and program management, relative to reporting and analysis. The stars of the foreign service in the years ahead will be those who take on hard jobs in lonely places, master difficult languages, and get things done, not just written.

2

History

Like the US Congress, the US Foreign Service has rarely enjoyed the esteem as an institution that its members have enjoyed as individuals. Foreign service personnel are widely respected for their intellect, honesty, energy, courage, and patriotism. The service itself, and the Department of State with which it is so closely identified, have often been held in what the late Arizona congressman Mo Udall called "minimum high regard."

Dean Acheson, secretary of state under President Harry Truman, noted that many Americans did not want to hear too much about the complexities of foreign affairs or the stubborn refusal of foreigners to see the world as we do. When world events fail to follow American desires, he wrote, the "believers in American omnipotence, to whom every goal unattained is explicable only by incompetence or treason," were quick to blame the department and the foreign service.[1] Robert F. Kennedy exemplified the paradox. Traveling abroad in 1962 as attorney general in his brother Jack's administration, he "made little connection between the Foreign Service people he met overseas, whom he by and large admired, and those working in a State Department he disparaged."[2]

President Nixon loathed the foreign service. Henry Kissinger wrote that Nixon "had very little confidence in the State Department" and did not trust the foreign service, which he felt "had disdained him as Vice President and ignored him the moment he was out of office."[3] Indeed, Nixon said he intended "to ruin the foreign service. I mean ruin it."[4] Yet many young foreign service officers, several of whom went on to high office, played critical roles on his White House staff.[5]

Mistrust of the foreign service and the State Department is, as Acheson noted, partly a function of American suspicion of foreigners and, by extension, of those who deal with them. It is also a product of the history of the foreign service. Only in the past twenty years or so has the foreign service really begun to reflect Main Street America, and only in the past few years have American attitudes toward the service begun to recognize that shift.

Amateurs and Entrepreneurs

American diplomacy, like the American military, is older than the federal government. Even before adopting a declaration of independence, the Continental Congress established armed forces to fight against the British and commissioned envoys to seek support from other countries. American diplomats, notably Benjamin Franklin, secured French support that proved vital to military victory and then negotiated favorable terms of peace with Britain. The Constitution later provided not only for raising an army and a navy but also for naming ambassadors, ministers, and consuls.

The paths of the military and diplomatic establishments quickly diverged. The American military developed a professional structure at West Point in 1802 and at the Naval Academy in 1845. Military service became for many young men an attractive career. American diplomacy, however, remained a part-time and largely amateur affair.

Throughout the nineteenth century, Washington maintained two kinds of representatives. The diplomatic service handled state-to-state relations. The consular service, established in 1792, dealt with commercial matters and the problems of individual American citizens abroad. The diplomats were nearly all men of wealth who served with only token pay and rarely sought or received more than one assignment. Consuls, more numerous and socially less privileged, were typically American businessmen living in foreign ports who had political connections strong enough to secure an appointment.[6] Working without salary (Congress authorized the first consular salaries in 1856, but payment was spotty), they were entitled to pocket the fees they collected for their services, largely related to merchant shipping. Many found ways to use their official positions to advance their private interests—behavior that was scandalous even by the standards of those days. Other than the spoils system by which they were appointed, members of the diplomatic and consular services had little to do with each other.[7]

In the 1850s, in the days of Horace Greeley, the *New York Herald Tribune* wrote, "Diplomacy is the sewer through which flows the scum and refuse of the political puddle. A man not fit to stay at home is just the man to send abroad."[8] A consular inspector sent out by the Department of State reported in 1882 that the service was riddled with "incompetency, low habits, and vulgarity," and so much corruption that "the most cold and indifferent citizen would blush."[9] The nineteenth-century writings of Henry Adams, Richard Harding Davis, O. Henry, and others established the pompous ambassador and the spoils-system consul as popular stereotypes.[10] President Theodore Roosevelt complained that "our ambassadors . . . seem to think that [their] life work is a kind of glorified pink tea party."[11] Ambrose Bierce, noting that defeated candidates of the president's party were often consoled with a consular appointment, defined consul as "a person who, having failed to secure an office from the people, is given one by the Administration on condition that he leave the country."[12] Early in the McKinley administration, Secretary of State John Hay complained that the president "will have promised all the consulates in the service; the senators will come to me and refuse to believe me disconsulate; I shall see all my treaties slaughtered, one by one."[13]

Public familiarity bred public contempt and built support for change. Reforms that had begun in the 1880s created a merit-based civil service and a Civil Service Commission that rolled back the use of the spoils system in most domestic federal employment. Between 1895 and 1915, legislation and executive action applied civil service rules to the still separate consular and diplomatic services. Consular salaries were much improved, and salaried consular officials were prohibited from engaging in private business. Consular officials came to be better paid, and by and large were more capable, than their diplomatic counterparts. A 1909 executive order instructed the secretary of state to identify to the president those career diplomats with the potential to serve as chiefs of mission. Subsequent legislation established a personnel classification system and the principle of promotion by merit.

Toward a Professional Service

By the end of the nineteenth century the United States was a formidable world power with an inferior diplomatic establishment. As late as 1910 the United States had only 121 diplomats stationed abroad but more than 1,000 consuls (see table 2.1). Domestic State Department employees numbered 234.

In 1913, Woodrow Wilson named as his first secretary of state a political rival within his own Democratic Party, the venerable prairie populist William Jennings Bryan. Wilson installed him in the weirdly ornate State, War, and Navy Building (now the Eisenhower Executive Office Building), and

Table 2.1
State Department Posts and Staffing, 1781–2010

	Diplomatic and Consular Posts		State Department Personnel	
	Diplomatic[a]	Consular[b]	Domestic[c]	Overseas[d]
1781	4	3	4	10
1790	2	10	8	20
1800	6	52	10	62
1810	4	60	9	56
1820	7	83	16	95
1830	15	141	23	153
1840	20	152	38	170
1850	27	197	22	218
1860	33	282	42	281
1870	36	318	65	804
1880	35	303	80	977
1890	41	323	76	1,105
1900	41	318	91	1,137
1910	48	324	234	1,043
1920	45	368	708	514
1930	57	299	714	633
1940	58	264	1,128	840
1950	74	179	8,609	7,710
1960	99	166	7,116	6,178
1970	117	122	6,983	5,865
1980	133	100	8,433	5,861
1990	143	100	10,063	6,783
1999	160	83	12,232	7,158
2010	177	94	14,674	8,199

Source: Author's compilation; Trask, *Short History*.

[a] Embassies and other overseas posts headed by a chief of mission.

[b] Includes overseas posts not headed by a chief of mission.

[c] Includes civil service and foreign service.

[d] Civil service and foreign service, excluding foreign service nationals.

then ignored him. Wilson ignored the rest of the Department of State as well, and continued to do so even after Bryan had been replaced. Key foreign policy decisions—to remain neutral when war broke out in Europe in 1914, to join the Allied cause in 1917, and to try to dictate terms of the peace negotiated in 1918—were all made without regard for the secretary of state or his department. Robert Lansing, Bryan's successor, complained in a 1920 letter to Republican congressman John Jacob Rogers of Massachusetts that the government's organization for foreign affairs, though it served well when "the world [was] free from the present perplexities," needed reform and modernization. Rogers took up the challenge and drafted a bill for sweeping change.[14]

Hearings on the bill made it clear that business and shipping interests, American travelers, and academicians were all dissatisfied with the quality of representation abroad. Testimony drew invidious comparisons between polished, efficient, European professionals and untrained, ineffective, and sometimes venal American representatives. State Department officials complained that pay was so low that only people of private wealth could enter the diplomatic service. Hugh Gibson, a foreign service professional who was at the time ambassador to Poland, declared that "we are the only great power which consistently excludes from competition for [senior diplomatic] posts any but men of independent means." The language he used set a stereotype that lingers ninety years later: "You hear very frequently about the boys with the white spats," he said, "the tea drinkers, the cookie pushers. . . . Our great problem now is to attract enough men so that we will have a real choice of material and crowd out these incompetents and defectives."[15]

The modern foreign service began with the enactment of the Rogers Act on May 24, 1924. This legislation merged the diplomatic and consular services and set appointments by competitive examination, promotion by merit, and pay comparable to other government jobs. It established a retirement system, home leave, and other benefits. Subsequent legislation authorized the government to buy or build and operate facilities overseas as missions and consulates, which made it possible for citizens without extraordinary wealth to serve as chiefs of mission.

Postwar Promise and Persecution

The department was not a strong agency during World War II. Franklin Roosevelt distrusted the judgment of the foreign service, whose members, he told Secretary of State Henry Stimson, were "entirely out of touch with American affairs."[16] Wartime policy, wrote one historian, "required coordination of political ends and military means." The Department of State, he continued, might have understood political ends, but it was unfamiliar with military means, and so it lacked "the expertise and institutions [needed] to exert dominant influence on the shaping of grand strategy."[17] White House planners rarely consulted the State Department, and President Roosevelt left Secretary Cordell Hull out of most of the conferences where the Allies planned the conduct of the war and the shape of the postwar world. The department also created political problems for the president by seeking draft deferments for its officers. That could not have helped its standing.[18]

The end of the war should have changed the department's fortunes. President Harry Truman, who assumed office in 1945, looked to the department for advice. In 1947 he named General George C. Marshall, the army's chief of staff, as secretary of state. Marshall was, with Dwight Eisenhower, one of the country's most respected soldiers, and one of its most admired citizens as well. Under Marshall (1947–49) and his successor Dean Acheson (1949–53), the State Department recognized the Soviet challenge in Europe and reacted vigorously with a coherent strategy brilliantly executed: the Marshall Plan, the North Atlantic Treaty Organization (NATO), aid to anticommunist forces in Greece and Turkey, and the Berlin airlift. In the decade from 1940 to 1950, the State Department's Washington-based staff, who served only in Washington, grew from 1,128 to 8,609. At the same time, its foreign service personnel, who served only overseas, increased from 840 to 7,710.

For broad sectors of the American public, however, the story of the day was communist victory, not Western defense.[19] The detonation of the first Soviet atomic bomb in September 1949, the flight of the Chinese Nationalist government to Formosa (Taiwan) in December 1949, and North Korea's attack on South Korea in June 1950 all suggested to many that the United States was losing a global battle. In the atmosphere of extreme partisanship that followed the unexpected Democratic sweep of the White House, the Senate, and the House in the elections of 1948, the State Department became the target of a violent political attack.

State was especially vulnerable to an anticommunist witch hunt because it harbored a number of actual witches. George Kennan, a career foreign service officer generally regarded as the country's leading authority on the Soviet Union, wrote this on the subject: "The penetration of the American governmental services by members or agents (conscious or otherwise) of the American Communist Party in the late 1930s was not a figment of the imagination of the hysterical right-wingers of a later decade. . . . The Roosevelt administration was very slow in reacting to this situation and correcting it."[20]

In 1945 and 1946, the Department of State dismissed almost three hundred employees for security reasons, including forty who were said to have "close connections or involvement" with foreign powers. Ten more were dismissed in the first half of 1947. One of these was Alger Hiss, alleged to be an agent of the Soviet Union.[21]

In a speech in West Virginia on February 9, 1950, the recklessly ambitious Senator Joseph McCarthy, Republican of Wisconsin, blamed the department for Communist gains and accused it of treason. "I hold in my hand," he said, "a list of 205 that were known to the Secretary of State as being members of the Communist Party and who, nevertheless, are still working and shaping policy in the State Department."[22] The State Department, he later told the Senate, was "thoroughly infested with Communists." On the Senate floor, a McCarthy supporter, Republican Senator William Jenner of Indiana, called Secretary of State Dean Acheson a "Communist-appeasing, Communist-protecting betrayer of America."[23]

The attacks came to focus on the Communist takeover in China and on the performance of a small group of foreign service officers known as the China hands. These officers, many of them sons of missionaries, were fluent in Chinese. Most had spent time during the war with Communist forces in China. Over a period of years in the 1940s, they had reported the deteriorating capacity of the Nationalist government and the near certainty of a Communist victory in the civil war that followed the collapse of the Japanese occupation. They recommended that the United States drop its support for the Nationalists and develop a relationship with the Communists, to keep the Communists from turning to Moscow for support.[24]

McCarthy and his supporters charged the China hands with working to bring about the Communist takeover they predicted. In the words of one of their accusers, "the professional foreign service men sided with the Chinese Communist Party."[25]

State had praised the work of the China hands when they were performing it but did not defend either the officers or their work when they were attacked. Instead, it opened secret investigations and denied the China hands access to their own classified reporting, which was considered evidence against them. George Kennan, who was peripherally involved in these events, described the department's attitude as "pious detachment" that in effect said to the accused, "'Here's what people say about you. Defend yourself if you can. We won't lift a finger on your behalf.'"[26]

In the end, two of the China hands were fired, two were forced to resign or retire, and nearly all of the others were assigned outside of Asia for the remainder of their careers.[27] McCarthy lost his grip on the public imagination, and on political power, when he shifted his target from State to the army and provoked resistance from President Dwight Eisenhower. The Senate censured McCarthy in December 1954. He died of complications of alcoholism three years later.

The foreign service suffered as much from the failure of State's leadership to offer a defense as from McCarthy's attacks. An aide recorded the views of Secretary of State John Foster Dulles (1953–59): "With the responsibilities I have now, I need broad support in Congress. I regret if injustice must be done to a few Foreign Service officers, but as secretary I must be guided by the larger national interest."[28] Officers drew the lesson that their careers depended on political caution and conventional thinking. These habits of mind entered the culture of the service and persisted for many years. Even now, if a senior foreign officer is publicly attacked, other officers do not necessarily rally around. For the foreign service, wrote one observer, "McCarthy was like a flash bulb witnessed up close, seen much later when one's eyes were closed."[29]

Growing Pains

The absence of trust between the State Department's leadership and its employees affected—or afflicted—the management of both the department and the foreign service. The expansion of America's international power, responsibilities, and presence after World War II presented challenges to management that were unevenly met.

As the United States entered the postwar world, foreign service personnel, who spent virtually their entire careers abroad, had little to do with the civil service personnel who staffed the State Department's domestic positions. One noncareer ambassador complained that foreign service posts, with their "fantastic network of men, women, and typewriters," sent reports to Washington, where "they are placed in files." Then "the home team, having properly disposed of the information from the field, proceeds to write its own endless reports to go forward to the same ultimate fate in the embassies throughout the world."[30]

Blue-ribbon commissions in 1949 and 1954 called for integrating the department's civil and foreign service personnel. Foreign service traditionalists objected, but Secretary Dulles acted on most of the proposals. By the end of the 1950s, about 1,500 civil service employees had transferred into the foreign service, and roughly the same number of positions in Washington were designated for foreign service employees. The service as a whole gained in numbers, and foreign service officers, though not foreign service staff (today's foreign service specialists), began to expect to spend about one-third of their careers in domestic assignments. These changes, called Wristonization after Henry Wriston, author of the 1954 report, improved communication between the department and the field and gave foreign service personnel a much-improved understanding of how policy is formed in Washington.

The service was less successful in meeting the demands of the postwar world for specialized expertise in trade promotion, labor affairs, science and technology, cultural affairs, public relations, international finance, development assistance, international law, and other areas beyond the ken or outside the experience of the typical foreign service officer. Congress hoped to solve this problem by creating, in the Foreign Service Act of 1946, a corps of specialists who would enter the foreign service for limited periods without competitive examination. The concept may have been sound, but its execution was flawed. The reserve officers, as they were called, were haphazardly recruited and poorly integrated into the service.[31] Planning for long-range personnel requirements became increasingly divorced from recruitment and training and then collapsed.

Eventually State's personnel system fell into crisis. The Vietnam War was a contributing factor. The Civil Operations and Revolutionary Development Support (CORDS) program, which combined military, Central Intelligence Agency (CIA), and USAID counterinsurgency programs under a single, CIA-dominated management, sent civilians into rural areas of South Vietnam and created a huge demand for linguists with political skills and physical energy. The State Department stepped up recruitment to supply CORDS with foreign service officers. At the height of the program, more than four hundred foreign service officers were in the field in CORDS, and about one hundred more were in language training.

CORDS was a turning point in the lives and careers of many of the foreign service officers who served in the program. A number of CORDS officers were thoroughly dismayed by US policies and left the service. For those who stayed, the experience taught management, leadership, and operational skills that sometimes led to rapid advancement. CORDS veterans faced a problem, though, as they moved up through the ranks: There were not enough positions to accommodate them all.

By the mid-1970s, the discipline of *up or out*, which the foreign service had borrowed from the US Navy and renamed *selection out*, had grown lax.

Officers in higher grades almost never lost their jobs for substandard performance. Without selection out and with an attractive, inflation-indexed retirement package that encouraged at least a twenty-year career, the service came to have more senior diplomats than places to put them. "At the worst point," according to one of the department's managers, "as many as a hundred and thirty senior officers were unassignable, and thus reduced to 'walking the halls.'"[32] Midgrade officers, many of them veterans of CORDS, resented the senior glut that frustrated their chances for promotion.

Dissatisfaction built pressure for change that coincided with President Carter's efforts to reform the civil service. Immediately following passage of the Civil Service Reform Act in October 1978, the State Department's undersecretary for management gathered a small group of insiders to work closely with key members of Congress (including Senator Claiborne Pell of Rhode Island, a former foreign service officer) to draft what became the Foreign Service Act of 1980. The 1980 act gave the service the shape and structure it has today.[33]

The act created a senior foreign service, a top echelon comparable to the senior executive service that the Civil Service Reform Act had just established. To reduce the surplus of senior officers, it introduced mandatory retirement at sixty-five and cut the time allowed in the senior grades from twenty-two to sixteen years. It placed foreign service officers and specialists on a single pay scale more comparable to the one used by the civil service.

Fragmentation and Consolidation

The act also tried to deal with a question that the Rogers Act had failed to resolve: whether the Department of State could represent all US interests abroad, or whether each government agency with an international interest needed a separate overseas presence. The Rogers Act had made the service more professional but not much less patrician. Many members of the old diplomatic service resisted change, looked down on the consular corps, and failed to acquire the specialized skills that America's rapidly complicating and expanding international interests demanded. Government agencies and private interest groups, feeling ill served, pressed for change. The newly unified service quickly fractured, and in the 1920s and early 1930s many government agencies, including the Treasury, the Commerce Department, the Department of Agriculture, and the Bureau of Mines, sent their employees overseas to work outside the foreign service. The bureaucratic fragmentation of American representation abroad continued until the late 1930s, when the approach of war brought a reduction in the US overseas presence and a consolidation of functions in the Department of State. In the postwar period, however, the hiving off of various functions to other agencies resumed. The Foreign Service Act of 1980 addressed this situation by creating a single Foreign Service of the United States that could be used by any agency to "carry out functions which require service abroad." The head of the service, called the director general, was to be a senior foreign service career officer in the Department of State, but each agency that employed members of the foreign service retained control over its employees.

The approach taken by the act had little practical effect on the conduct of American diplomacy or on the struggles among federal agencies and congressional committees over who runs what. The lust for reorganization that periodically sweeps across the executive and legislative branches has proven irresistible. Consolidation and fragmentation follow in successive waves, with a heavy cost in bureaucratic turmoil at each turn of the cycle. Three areas of policy have been especially affected: trade, information, and foreign assistance.

Trade

Trade had been a shuttlecock between the Departments of State and Commerce from the earliest days. The State Department's Bureau of Statistics, which compiled and published commercial reports, became the Bureau of Foreign and Domestic Commerce in 1897 and was transferred to the newly established Department of Commerce and Labor in 1903. At the same time, the Department of State established a Bureau of Trade Relations, and consular officers were assigned the task of gathering and reporting useful information to it. The Consular Commercial Office was set up in 1921, but a few years later Congress established a separate Foreign Commerce Service (FCS) in the Department of Commerce and a separate Foreign Agricultural Service (FAS) in the Department of Agriculture. As war approached in 1939, these agencies were closed and their functions returned to State. Congress restored the Foreign Agricultural Service in 1954 and the Foreign Commercial Service in 1980.[34] The Foreign Service Act of 1980 specifically authorized the Departments of Agriculture and Commerce to use the foreign service personnel system.

The Foreign Commercial Service and the Foreign Agricultural Service were concerned primarily with promotion of US exports, not with development of trade policy or conduct of trade negotiations. Those responsibilities moved in the 1960s and 1970s from the Department of State to the Office of the US Trade Representative (USTR), a White House agency established by Congress in 1962.[35] This change was not a typical turf battle, as power struggles between departments are called in Washington. The transfer of trade policy from the State Department to an agency that reported, uniquely, to the president and to Congress represented the domestication of what had previously been treated as primarily a matter of foreign relations. As US international trade grew with postwar prosperity at home and recovery abroad, competition touched more industries and workers and became an increasingly important political issue. Congress, which under the Constitution has the power to regulate foreign commerce, wanted domestic considerations to weigh more heavily than concern for foreign relations in the shaping of trade policy and the negotiation of trade agreements. Unlike the diplomats in the State Department, the FCS, or the FAS, the diplomats in the Office of the USTR were and remain civil servants, outside the foreign service system.[36]

Information

The United States had no systematic approach to dissemination of information before World War II. The Office of War Information, established in 1942 as a clearinghouse and control point for dissemination of war news, was quickly dissolved when the war ended in 1945. Its domestic operations were closed and its foreign operations, called the US Information Service (USIS) in most countries, were transferred to the State Department. In 1953, President Eisenhower transferred USIS and other overseas information activities from the Department of State to a new United States Information Agency (USIA), whose director reported to the secretary of state. USIA personnel were brought into the foreign service as foreign service information officers by an act of Congress in 1968. Cultural activities, including the Fulbright program, were transferred in 1978, when President Carter renamed USIA the United States Information and Communications Agency (USICA). President Reagan restored the USIA name in 1982.

In 1996, President Clinton vetoed legislation to abolish USIA and return its functions to State. Two years later, however, he signed the Foreign Affairs

Reform and Restructuring Act of 1998, which abolished USIA (except for the Broadcasting Board of Governors and the International Broadcasting Bureau) and moved its functions to the State Department, effective October 1, 1999. Those functions have lately received new urgency, new resources, and a new name, public diplomacy.

Foreign Assistance

Foreign assistance has plenty of enemies and a handful of allies. The general public hates foreign aid.[37] In Congress the program has a few strong supporters and as many strong opponents. The president, the secretary of state, and the national security agencies see it as an essential tool of foreign policy, whatever the domestic political complications. Foreign aid accounts for less than 1 percent of the federal budget, but it generates more passionate debate per dollar spent than almost any other federal activity.

Perhaps as a defensive reaction, the executive and legislative branches, consecutively or serially, have repeatedly reorganized, restructured, renamed, and generally kicked around the agencies they have entrusted with the program. Foreign aid has been in, then out, then in, then out, then half in and half out of the Department of State. Where in the foreign affairs bureaucracy foreign aid fits today is not entirely clear. The history bears recapitulation.

Today's US Agency for International Development is a direct descendent of the Economic Cooperation Administration (ECA), set up in 1948 to administer the Marshall Plan for aid to postwar Europe. As the Marshall Plan wound down, the ECA closed and was succeeded by the Mutual Security Agency (1951) and later the Foreign Operations Administration (1953) and the International Cooperation Agency (1955). The Foreign Operations Administration had been outside the Department of State, but the International Cooperation Agency was part of it. With passage of the Foreign Assistance Act of 1961, still the basic authorizing legislation for most US foreign assistance programs, the International Cooperation Agency became the US Agency for International Development (USAID or AID).

USAID was set up as an independent agency, though its administrator reported to the secretary of state. Its staff was not part of the career foreign service until passage of the Foreign Service Act of 1980. In 1979, President Carter issued an executive order that placed USAID under a new International Development and Cooperation Agency (IDCA), established outside the Department of State, though State retained control of security-related assistance programs. The Reagan administration, however, allotted no staff or funds to IDCA, which effectively ceased to exist. It was formally abolished by the Foreign Affairs Reform and Restructuring Act of 1998.

USAID survived an existential challenge in 1996 when President Clinton vetoed legislation that would have abolished the agency and transferred its functions to the Department of State. But the agency has seen other organizations encroach on its area of competence. In 2004, Congress created the Millennium Challenge Corporation (MCC), a government corporation outside USAID, to administer up to $5 billion annually in foreign assistance funds appropriated to promote good governance and economic freedom. That same year Congress placed a provision in the National Defense Authorization Act that allowed the Department of Defense to receive and disburse foreign assistance directly. (Indeed, the Department of Defense, which has had a role in foreign assistance since the days of the Marshall Plan and its own founding in 1947, was so deeply involved in assistance programs in Iraq and Afghanistan that by 2009, by some measures, it accounted for about one-quarter of all US spending on official development assistance.)[38] Also in 2004 the administration and Congress worked together to set up the US President's Emergency Program for AIDS relief (PEPFAR) outside USAID.

In January 2006 administratively imposed reforms linked USAID more tightly to State and made the USAID administrator a deputy secretary of state. Many observers, and certainly many USAID foreign service and civil service employees, expected further consolidation of programs in the Department of State (see chapter 3). In 2010, however, the Department of State and the White House completed separate strategic reviews of development policy that left the relationship between State and USAID basically unchanged.[39]

Gender and Race

Congress put this instruction on the first page of the Foreign Service Act of 1980: "The members of the Foreign Service should be representative of the American people." The mandate was so prominent because the need for change was so great.

In the 1970s the department and the foreign service were wrestling, generally unsuccessfully, with the treatment of women and minorities. The foreign service in the first half of the twentieth century was very much a white man's organization. As late as 1970 the corps of foreign service officers was 95 percent male (2,945 of 3,084) and only 1 percent African American (34 of 3,084). All female foreign service officers were single and, until 1971, required to resign if they wed. The service would almost never assign single women to communist or Islamic countries, for fear in the former case of vulnerability to sexual blackmail, and in the latter of giving offense to the host government. African American officers were typically and disproportionately assigned to posts in Africa.[40]

Foreign service spouses—that is, wives—were regarded as adjuncts. Only in 1972 did the department recognize in a formal statement called Policy on Wives of Foreign Service Employees that "the wife of a Foreign Service employee who is with her husband at a foreign post is an individual, not a government employee." The same statement reversed long-standing practice by prohibiting, instead of requiring, consideration of a wife's activities in evaluating her husband's performance.

An internal task force in 1977 worried that women and minorities might not seek foreign service careers because of the image of the service as "elitist, self-satisfied, a walled-in barony populated by smug white males, an old-boy system in which women and minorities cannot possibly hope to be treated with equity in such matters as promotions and senior level responsibilities."[41] Maybe this language wasn't strong enough. The department did little to bring about change until employee grievances escalated into litigation.

The impetus came first from Alison Palmer, who had joined the foreign service in 1958 and began to complain of discrimination in assignments and promotions in 1965. The department rebuffed or ignored her until 1972, when she took her complaints to sympathetic senators, who blocked an ambassadorial confirmation for the department's director of personnel.[42] She then received a promotion.

In 1976, Palmer initiated a class action lawsuit that charged the Department of State with discrimination against women in hiring, assignments, and promotions. Like the suit in Dickens's *Bleak House*, the case threatened to outlast the plaintiffs, but she won judgments in 1989 and 2002 that forced the department to give new assignments and revised performance ratings to about six hundred women foreign service officers and to revise entry test scores for another four hundred.

African American officers followed the path the women had blazed. In 1985, Walter Thomas, a black foreign service officer, filed a complaint of discrimination with the Equal Employment Opportunity Commission (EEOC), an independent agency charged with enforcement of equal opportunity across the federal government. The EEOC, whose chair at the time was future Supreme Court Justice Clarence Thomas, found that the State Department "typically" discriminated against black officers in assignments, performance evaluations, and promotions. After ten years of litigation, the department agreed to compensate plaintiffs with money and retroactive promotions.

Litigation was not the only pressure brought to bear on State's practices. In the 1980s the EEOC repeatedly criticized the department's affirmative action plans as inadequate. In 1988, Congress directed the General Accounting Office (GAO), renamed the Government Accountability Office in 2001, to report on the department's recruitment, appointment, assignment, and promotion of women and minorities.

The report was broadly unfavorable. The GAO found that in 1987, of a total of 9,432 foreign service officers and specialists, about 65 percent were white men, fewer than 25 percent were white women, 6 percent were black, and 3 percent were Hispanic, and the officers were paler and maler than the specialists (see table 2.2). Recruitment efforts were failing to attract increased numbers of minority candidates to take the entrance exam, and those who did were failing at relatively high rates. After four years of service, minority junior officers were much more likely to be denied tenure than their

Table 2.2
Foreign Service Officers (Generalists)

Year	Total	Female Total	Female %	Black Total	Black %	Hispanic Total	Hispanic %	Other Total	Other %
1970	3,084	139	4.5	34	1.1	NA	NA	NA	NA
1987	5,163	1,114	21.6	286	5.5	196	3.8	84	1.6
1994	4,877[a]	1,186	26.1	249	5.5	206	4.5	148	3.3
2005	6,293[b]	2,299	36.5	313	5.0	280	4.5	348	5.6
2010	7,458	2,908	39.0	350	4.7	290	3.9	539	7.2

Source: Author's compilation based on data from Bacchus, Staffing for Foreign Affairs; US General Accounting Office, State Department: Minorities and Women Are Underrepresented in the Foreign Service; US Department of State, Bureau of Human Resources, private communication to the author.

[a] Of these, 337 are not specified by gender or race ethnicity and were therefore excluded from the calculation of race-ethnicity percentages.

[b] Of these, 88 are not specified by race ethnicity and were therefore excluded from the calculation of race-ethnicity percentages.

white male or female counterparts. Assignments were skewed, with white men overrepresented in political and economic jobs, white women in consular work, and minority officers in administrative positions. Promotions, however, seemed color blind and gender neutral.[43]

In response to the GAO report, the department, not for the first time, pledged increased efforts to recruit and promote women and minorities. By the late 1990s, changes in policies and attitudes began to work their way through the system and have an impact on the numbers.

The expansion of the foreign service under Secretary Colin Powell's Diplomatic Readiness Initiative (DRI) from 2001 to 2004 was an opportunity to increase minority hiring. According to a former senior official in the Bureau of Human Resources, minorities had been failing the foreign service written exam in greater proportions than whites, though minorities tended to fare as well as whites in the oral assessment. So, the official said, "we made sure the cut score on the written exam was set low enough to give us a representative sample of minorities at the orals." The change had the desired effect. "Minority intake through the foreign service exam rose from about 12.5 percent to 19 percent in thirty-six months."[44] By 2005, 49 percent of foreign service entrants were women, and 22 percent were racial or ethnic minorities.

For women, the changes that began in the 1970s are now reaching the highest levels of the service. By 2010, 30 percent of chiefs of mission were women, a number certain to grow over time. The *Washington Post* reported in January 2010 that the United States is seen as a world leader in bringing women into positions of leadership in diplomacy. The "Hillary effect," said the *Post*, has led other countries to send female ambassadors to Washington in record numbers.[45]

Minorities are still underrepresented in the foreign service. The situation is improving at the bottom but not at the top. Minority officers hired under affirmative action programs in the 1970s and early 1980s are now approaching retirement. Affirmative action programs diminished in the 1980s and 1990s as a matter of both policy and law, and as a result there are not enough minority officers in the middle grades to replace the retirees. One retiring officer called this change "decolorization." The diversity visible in the junior grades in 2009 will take fifteen or twenty years to reach the upper ranks.

Luis Arreaga-Rodas, head of recruitment, examination, and employment, acknowledges that hiring for diversity is challenging. "We look not only for ethnic and national-origin diversity, but geographic diversity as well. We're trying to stay away from the coasts, where we have plenty of applicants. We're working on the smaller colleges. We work with professional organizations that are diversity oriented. We spend a lot of time with midcareer professionals, people with more experience who are looking for a change. But the share of applicants from diversity backgrounds hasn't increased much."[46]

Marc Grossman, director general of the foreign service in 2000 and 2001, said in 2005 that "the Alison Palmer lawsuit was one of the best things that happened to the State Department, because it forced the department to change its hiring and promotion practices." Without losing focus on the recruitment and promotion of women, Grossman said, additional effort is going into recruiting and retaining minorities. In particular, the department wants to increase the number of Hispanic Americans, who Grossman said are "woefully underrepresented" in the service. Building a foreign service that is "representative of the American people," as the Foreign Service Act requires, takes constant effort. "We work at this," said Grossman, "every single day."[47]

The Iranian Hostage Crisis

The Iranian hostage crisis of 1979 to 1981 put the foreign service in the public eye as it had not been since the McCarthy era. The attention this time was wholly favorable and deeply sympathetic, but a lasting impact of the crisis on the foreign service is hard to discern. The story bears retelling.

The shah of Iran, Reza Pahlavi, ascended to the Peacock Throne in 1941. US support, and especially arms sales and military cooperation, helped to sustain him in that position for almost forty years. By the late 1970s, however, his grip on power was increasingly uncertain. In early 1978 demonstrations in support of Ruhollah Khomeini, an exiled Shiite cleric, brought thousands and then hundreds of thousands of Iranians into the streets. The shah abandoned his throne and fled to Egypt on January 16, 1979. Khomeini arrived in Tehran on February 1.

The revolution came as no great surprise to the foreign service officers serving in the Tehran embassy, nor to those in Washington who read their reports. L. Bruce Laingen, who took up the post of chargé d'affaires (the person responsible for running an embassy in the absence of an ambassador) in Tehran in June 1979, said that embassy reporting on the shah's deteriorating position had been consistent and correct. In Laingen's view, the White House ignored or discounted foreign service reporting in favor of its own sources, who were closer to the shah than to the situation.[48] The memoirs of Cyrus Vance, then secretary of state, support Laingen's position in a backhanded way. Vance wrote that on November 9, 1978, two months before the shah fled to Egypt, "[Ambassador William] Sullivan sent a message that brought home how far the situation had deteriorated. . . . Sullivan's message corroborated the analysis of some State Department advisers, but caused consternation in the White House."[49]

In the chaos that followed the collapse of the shah's regime, the State Department acted quickly to reduce the American presence in the country. Embassy staff was cut from more than 1,400 to about 70. Private Americans were urged to leave, and more than 45,000 did so.[50] Ambassador Sullivan left the post in April.

In late October, the shah, suffering from lymphoma, entered the United States for medical treatment. Large demonstrations against the US embassy began in Tehran a week later. On November 4, 1979, the embassy was overrun. Two days later the provisional government, which might have provided help, itself collapsed. Khomeini, who may or may not have directed the seizure of the embassy, was pleased to keep his prize. Fifty-two hostages were held for 444 days, not for ransom (though the hostage takers demanded the return of the shah for trial in Iran), but to humiliate the United States. Most of the hostages were members of the foreign service. Many of the rest were members of the US armed forces.[51]

The seizure of the embassy in Tehran was not the first assault against American diplomats. In the ten years leading up to the taking of the American hostages, ten American diplomats had been murdered in eight incidents, and almost fifty more had survived thirty-seven incidents of kidnapping or kidnap attempts.[52] The Tehran attack, however, was different in scope, duration, and drama. The American Broadcasting Company gave extended daily late-night coverage to the story under the caption "America Held Hostage." The program found and held a large and grimly fascinated audience for fourteen months.

A frustrated Carter administration launched a military rescue mission in April 1980 that ended in disaster, aborted in the Iranian desert with the loss of eight servicemen. Secretary Vance, who had opposed the mission, resigned. Tehran released the hostages the moment the administration left office, but only after the United States, in a complex negotiation conducted through intermediaries, had unwound most of the sanctions it had imposed and renounced all present and future legal claims by US persons, including the hostages, arising from the affair.[53]

The hostages acquitted themselves throughout the crisis with courage and grace. Many members of the foreign service believed that the stalwart behavior of the hostages and the outpouring of public support would change public and congressional attitudes toward the foreign service. They looked forward to a period of growth in the prestige and policy role of foreign service professionals, and to an increase in the budget of the Department of State. Former foreign service officer Andy Steigman wrote in 1985 that "the Iranian hostage crisis suddenly and dramatically made Americans aware of the Foreign Service as they never had been before. By the time the 444 days of captivity were at an end, the United States had a new set of heroes—and the Foreign Service had a new image."[54]

Steigman was right about the heroes but wrong about the image. The public and Congress embraced the hostages as individuals, but admiration for the way they had borne their ordeal did not carry over to the foreign service as an institution or to diplomacy as a profession. In the Hostage Relief Act of 1980, Congress provided benefits that came to a bit more than $50 per hostage per day, about what the presidential Commission on Hostage Compensation had recommended. The hostage crisis played no role in the legislative history of the Foreign Service Act of 1980, the most fundamental overhaul of the service since its creation in 1924.

Security: From Tehran to Beirut to East Africa

The hostage crisis did lead to increased attention to physical security at posts abroad. The department launched a security enhancement program in 1980 to reduce the vulnerability of American overseas facilities to mob violence. Congress gave the department pretty much what it asked for in money and positions, $136 million and the equivalent of thirty-two positions over the six years from 1980 to 1985, levels that seemed quite high at the time but in retrospect were far too modest.

Any sense that the programs in place were adequate to the job ended in 1983. In April of that year, a suicide bomber drove a truck with a ton of explosives into the Beirut embassy, destroying the building and killing sixty-three people, including thirteen members of the foreign service. Six months later, in a similar attack, a suicide bomber drove a truck through wire barriers into the front of the US Marine barracks near the Beirut airport, killing 241 American servicemen.

The Inman Report and the 1986 Act

Policies changed in response. Secretary of State George P. Shultz asked retired Admiral Bobby Ray Inman, a former deputy director of the CIA, to lead a panel of experts to make detailed recommendations for improving embassy security. The Inman report, published in 1985, led directly to passage of the Omnibus Diplomatic Security and Antiterrorism Act of 1986 (the 1986 act), which provided nearly $2.5 billion for upgrading the physical security at American posts around the world.[55] Secretary Shultz also created, in 1985, the Overseas Security Advisory Council (OSAC), which brought private-sector organizations with an overseas presence (mainly commercial, but also religious, educational, and charitable groups) together with government representatives to address security concerns. OSAC today has more than 3,500 member organizations.[56] Congress in 1984 established the Rewards for Justice Program, now administered by the department's Bureau of Diplomatic Security (DS), to provide reward money to those who provide information leading to the prevention or resolution of acts of terrorism and related crimes.

The Inman report led the department to create the Bureau of Diplomatic Security (DS) and the Diplomatic Security Service (DSS).[57] DS took on responsibility for the security of the people, the buildings, and the information at all State Department facilities, whether overseas or in the United States, and for the protection of foreign diplomats and high-level official visitors in the United States. The special agents of the DSS quickly became by far the largest group of specialists in the foreign service.[58] Unlike their predecessors in the State Department's old Office of Security, DSS special agents are federal law enforcement officers. Their arrest powers, however, do not extend overseas, where they rely on local police and other agencies with which they have built cooperative relationships.[59]

In addition to the DSS special agents, the Bureau of Diplomatic Security has foreign service specialists who are not law enforcement officers. They are the engineers and technicians who develop, install, manage, and maintain the department's technical security programs, and the diplomatic couriers who move classified material securely around the world.

The 1986 act made the secretary of state—and by extension the ambassador or chief of mission—responsible for protecting US citizens abroad, and for the security of US government personnel on official duty in his or her country.[60] To carry out that mandate, beginning in the late 1980s the department sent DSS agents overseas to take charge of security under the chief of mission's authority in virtually every American embassy. These agents kept the title regional security officer (RSO), a holdover from the days when professional security officers were so few in number that each had to cover several posts in several countries. By 2009 the DS bureau had about 480 special agents assigned to embassies, consulates, and other posts in more than 150 countries worldwide.[61]

Marine Security Guards

One element of post security did not change. The agents working as RSOs could continue to rely on a unique and splendid resource, the marine security guards. Marines have had a role in protecting American diplomats and diplomatic property abroad since the early nineteenth century (William Eaton, American consul in Tunis, played a central role in the war that brought marines to the shores of Tripoli in 1804), but the modern relationship between the State Department and the marine corps began after World War II, formalized in the Foreign Service Act of 1946. Marine guards protect classified material and provide a last, armed line of defense for the embassy and its personnel in the event of attack. They are assigned to most but not all embassies and to a few large constituent posts. They do not provide bodyguard security for the ambassador or other officials, and they have no authority or right to operate outside embassy grounds. The size of a detachment depends on the size of the facility it protects: There must be enough marine guards to cover critical embassy locations around the clock. All members of the detachment are noncommissioned officers or enlisted personnel, and all are volunteers.

Marines have a vital and visible role in foreign service life. A marine guard on duty is the first American an embassy visitor sees. Marines raise and lower the embassy's flag at sunrise and sunset in a brief, emotionally powerful ceremony that brings those within sight of it to a halt. They also bring to the embassy traditions of the corps, including the annual Marine Corps ball (dress blues, black tie) that celebrates the anniversary of the founding of the corps on November 10, 1775. Where security permits, the marines, all of whom except for the detachment commander must be single, often entertain American and foreign service national personnel at their quarters, the marine house, with barbecues, softball games, and parties. But they don't stick around. A marine guard ordinarily spends three years in the program, one year at each of three different posts.

Many more marines volunteer for this duty than positions are available, and the corps applies high standards to make its selection. The exotic nature of the work does not make it cushy. Fourteen marines have died in the line of duty as marine security guards.

Accountability

The general acclaim that greeted the Inman commission led Congress to look for ways to ensure that any future terrorist attacks or security failures would be followed by determinations of what went wrong and efforts to set it right. In the 1986 act, Congress required the secretary of state to convene an accountability review board (ARB), a temporary, ad hoc, independent group of experts armed with subpoena powers, to investigate and report on serious breaches of security at missions abroad involving loss of life and other incidents defined in the act.

ARB members come from a roster maintained by State's management bureau, and each has an executive secretary, normally a senior foreign service officer. Because ARB members need high-level security clearances to do their work, and because "only in exceptional circumstances" may they be federal employees, they are most often recent retirees from the foreign service, the intelligence community, or the military, or former senior noncareer officials with a background in security affairs. Each ARB sends a report to the secretary with its findings and, at its discretion, recommendations on policy and personnel. The secretary then reports the recommendations and the department's response to them to Congress. The ARB report and findings do not go to Congress.

Ambassador Langhorne A. Motley served as chairman of an ARB that examined a 1987 bombing at the embassy in Lima, Peru. "We were able to figure out where the weaknesses were in that case," he said. "We had the independence we needed. Because we had a mandate from Congress, we could deal effectively with the highest levels at State and with the other agencies involved. An ARB is a painful exercise, but it's a way to learn from failure."[62]

An amendment enacted at the end of 2005 made the ARB optional in the case of incidents involving loss of life at missions in Iraq and Afghanistan.

Ambassador Gib Lanpher chaired three ARBs that investigated incidents in Iraq that occurred before the amendment became law. He was disappointed that the department initiated the amendment, even though the recommendations of his boards were not all adopted: "My boards believed that ARBs would still be useful in the case of Iraq because they bring an independent perspective to security issues outside the normal chain of command," he said. "We heard a lot of dissent and different perspectives that would not have surfaced in-house. Folks really let their hair down with us—and we assured them they would not be named in our reports. The DS people we worked extensively with valued our work and fully cooperated. They saw our effort as enhancing their ability to carry out their mandate."[63]

Worldwide Security Upgrades

Throughout the 1990s Congress continued to appropriate large sums to implement the Inman report, even as funds for other diplomatic purposes were cut and the ranks of the foreign service depleted by attrition (see table 2.3). The construction and retrofitting of embassy buildings to Inman standards, including the recommended setback of at least one hundred feet from roadways, proved more difficult and more expensive to accomplish than anticipated.

Car bombs struck the embassies in Nairobi and Dar es Salaam on August 7, 1998, killing 220 and injuring many more. Both embassies were older buildings that had not been brought up to Inman standards. Following those attacks, Congress funded an ongoing program of worldwide security upgrades. The program cost well above $9 billion through fiscal year 2009 and is budgeted at well over $800 million a year in fiscal years 2010 and 2011.

Security demands have changed the face of American diplomacy. Embassies were once typically located in city centers, close to pedestrian and vehicular traffic. The US Information Agency ran libraries and cultural centers easily, even eagerly, accessible to the public. After the Inman report, the department began to move embassies from downtown to suburban areas, which were easier to protect but harder for people to reach. Libraries and cultural centers were closed, partly for security reasons and partly for lack of funding. Whenever possible, buildings were set back from roadways and guarded by walls, moats, and other barriers. Access was restricted by identity checkpoints and metal detectors, similar to that of the State Department building in Washington. In some places diplomats who lived scattered

Table 2.3
Outlays on International Affairs (Function 150)

Year	$ Billions	Year	$ Billions
1980	12.7	1996	13.5
1981	13.1	1997	15.2
1982	12.3	1998	13.1
1983	11.8	1999	15.2
1984	15.9	2000	17.2
1985	16.2	2001	16.5
1986	14.1	2002	22.3
1987	11.6	2003	21.2
1988	10.5	2004	26.9
1989	9.6	2005	34.6
1990	13.8	2006	29.5
1991	15.8	2007	28.5
1992	16.1	2008	28.9
1993	17.2	2009	37.5
1994	17.1	2010 (estimate)	51.1
1995	16.4		

Source: White House, Office of Management and Budget, *Historical Tables*, Table 3.1, "Outlays by Superfunction and Function."

Note: Amounts in current dollars. Office of Management and Budget adjusted the data to provide consistency with the 2011 budget request and to provide comparability over time.

around the city were moved into compound housing adjacent to embassy offices.

Foreign service officers often complain that high levels of security make their work more difficult: It is harder for them to get to where they need to be—in the middle of the political, economic, and cultural life of the country—and it's harder for people—visa applicants, students, importers, members of the media—to get to them. The complaint is valid, but no one disputes the need to reduce the risk of another Beirut or Nairobi. The 1998 East Africa embassy bombings resolved the tension between security and convenience in favor of the former, and spending on security personnel and worldwide security upgrades has reflected that priority. But the balance may be shifting. At the end of 2010, the department announced its intention to establish "a new global standard for risk management" that would accept, for State and USAID, "a greater level of mitigated risk, commensurate with the expected benefits."[64]

Decline and Rise: The Diplomatic Readiness Initiative

Over the two decades following the Iranian hostage crisis, the motto for management in the foreign service was "do more with less." Especially in the 1990s, the administration's search for budget cuts and the desire to realize a "peace dividend" at the end of the Cold War led to reductions in spending on international affairs and national security. Looking back on the period, Defense Secretary Robert Gates saw "the gutting of America's ability to engage, assist, and communicate with other parts of the world."[65] Foreign service responsibilities grew, but foreign service ranks did not. The Department of State, each year from 1993 to 2001, brought in too few new foreign service officers to replace departures. Staffing gaps became chronic, especially in the middle grades, and performance declined. In USAID, staffing levels that had reached fifteen thousand during the Vietnam War fell to around three thousand. The USIA was closed down entirely in 1999, its functions and personnel folded unhappily into the State Department.

The political fission of the Soviet Union and then Yugoslavia in the 1990s left twenty countries where there had been only two. The strain of opening and staffing posts in these newly independent states left vacancies and exposed weaknesses throughout the service. By 2001 the staffing deficit left empty desks at more than seven hundred foreign service and six hundred civil service positions.[66] Training and leave were routinely curtailed.

Recruiting seemed unlikely to repair the damage. Primarily for budgetary reasons, entering classes in the 1980s and 1990s were small. Candidates who passed the exams faced a wait of two years or more to receive an appointment—and, of course, some of the best candidates found other things to do with their lives. Twice in the 1990s the foreign service canceled what was then a once-a-year written exam. In 2000 the exam attracted only about eight thousand candidates, about half the usual number. The management consulting firm McKinsey and Company, in a widely read report titled *The War for Talent*, warned the department that the foreign service had lost much of its attraction. McKinsey predicted that increasing numbers of officers would leave for private-sector employment. A blue-ribbon Overseas Presence Advisory Panel (OPAP), convened by Secretary of State Madeleine Albright in 1999, found "insecure and decrepit facilities, obsolete information technology, outmoded administrative and human resource practices, poor allocation of resources, and competition from the private sector" that placed America's diplomatic representation "near a state of crisis."[67]

Marc Grossman, then director general of the foreign service and head of human resources for the Department of State, remembered this period well. "There were gaps everywhere. We were spending huge amounts of time arguing over transfers—when you were going to leave post and when I was going to come. I couldn't send you to training because you had to be at post on such-and-such a day. The military didn't have this problem. I learned that our military colleagues have built a 15 percent float into staffing levels in every unit to cover transfers and training. I knew we had to do the same thing."[68]

Twenty years earlier a small group of insiders had put together the early drafts of the Foreign Service Act of 1980. In 2000 Grossman assembled a similarly small group to draft the reforms that became the Diplomatic Readiness Initiative. With encouragement from Secretary Albright, Grossman and what he called his skunk works developed a plan for a rapid and dramatic increase in the size of the foreign service.[69] Then came the election.

"I was driving with a carful of kids through Bull Run Park to see the Christmas lights," Grossman recalled, "when Secretary-designate Powell called my cell phone. He said, 'I'm coming into the building tomorrow, and after I call on the secretary I want to call on you.' I said, 'If you call on me, there'll be a riot, so I'll call on you.'"

Grossman laid out the problem and his proposed solution: an increase in staffing to eliminate vacancies and provide a 15 percent float for training and transfers, 1,158 additional people, at a cost of $100 million per year.[70] Powell was enthusiastic. "'This is great,' the secretary-designate told me. 'We'll do it over three years.' And he took up the idea in his confirmation hearing and kept at it throughout his term. At the end of the three years we had all the positions we asked for."[71]

The DRI began to rebuild the foreign service. "I never liked 'do more with less,'" Grossman said. "'Do more with more' had greater appeal." The number of candidates taking the foreign service exam rose from eight thousand to more than twenty thousand. The average hiring delay fell from twenty-seven months to nine months, and refusals of job offers fell from 25 percent to 2 percent. New testing procedures reduced the mismatch in skills between entrants and jobs and gave greater weight to critical languages like Arabic, Urdu, and Chinese. A boost in funding for the Foreign Service Institute, the State Department's training facility, added time for training in tradecraft, hard languages, and new courses in leadership and management. Measured by student hours, training expanded by 25 percent between 2000 and 2004.[72]

The DRI added 1,069 new foreign service personnel and created and filled more than 200 new civil service positions. In addition, Congress approved the hiring of another 561 consular officers and 608 specialists in diplomatic security. By 2005 the service was bigger by more than 2,000 than it had been four years earlier.[73]

But the DRI had begun before September 11, 2001. Planning did not include the extraordinary demands of Afghanistan and Iraq or the need for heightened security and more intense scrutiny of visa applicants. By 2007 the department's managers found that keeping the most important posts fully staffed left gaping holes elsewhere: Even with training time reduced to keep as many active-duty officers as possible in the field, 20 percent of overseas positions were vacant.

A new wave of expansion began in 2007–8 and accelerated in 2009 as a new administration took over. "On August 6, 2007," said Harry Thomas, "I got a call from Secretary Rice's chief of staff, asking me to be one of seven people coming to Camp David the next day. I had been nominated and was waiting for confirmation as director general of the foreign service, and the former DG had retired. I went up there with Henrietta Fore, John Negroponte, Richard Boucher, Nick Burns, Chris Hill, Brian Gunderson. The vice president was there, and Bob Gates, General Pace, Admiral Giambastiani, and several others.[74]

"We explained to the president that 22 percent of the foreign service had already served in Iraq or Afghanistan, which surprised him. Admiral Giambastiani praised what the foreign service was doing in Iraq but said there weren't enough of them. We asked for seven hundred foreign service officers and three hundred specialists and civil service. The president turned to Secretary Rice and said, 'What do you want me to do?' She said to him, 'Mr. President, when OMB [Office of Management and Budget] says no, I want you to say yes.' The president said OK, and that's what got it started."[75]

President Obama and his team were even more ambitious, planning to add 3,600 officers and specialists to the work force over five years (fiscal years 2009 through 2013), a 25 percent increase.[76] The details for this hiring plan, and its prospects in Congress, are discussed in chapter 10.

The new hires flowing into the foreign service are changing the institution. They lower the age and lift the quality. Recruitment has not been a problem. The service benefited from a surge of interest in national security following September 11, 2001, and in personal financial security following the collapse of the dot-com boom in 2003 and the financial crisis in 2007. As

Marc Grossman put it, "Suddenly a shot at a pension didn't seem so bad." Of the new entrants from 2001 through 2008, more than two-thirds had master's degrees or higher, and more than 10 percent had law degrees.

"They came to us with new thoughts," Grossman continued. "They have a different sense of hierarchy. They want a flatter organization. They have a different sense of training—they think it's the employer's responsibility to provide a professional education. They speak more languages, they've been to more places. They have a very different sense of the balance of work and family. And they are much more technologically adept. They bring huge pressure on us to modernize. They will be our revolutionaries, throughout the system. They will insist that we change."[77]

3

The Foreign Service Today

This book opened with a question: "What do we need them for?" The answer in the Foreign Service Act of 1980 is dry but clear. The foreign service, it says, exists to "represent the interests of the United States in relation to foreign countries and international organizations," to "provide guidance for the formulation and conduct of programs and activities of the Department [of State] and other agencies," and to "perform functions on behalf of any agency or other Government establishment (including any establishment in the legislative or judicial branch) requiring their services."[1]

The Department of State is the government's lead agency in foreign affairs, and the secretary of state is the president's chief foreign policy adviser (to be sure, on any given issue they both have plenty of competition). The Foreign Service Act says that "the Secretary of State shall administer and direct the Service," but other agencies, including USAID, the Department of Agriculture, and the Department of Commerce, "may utilize the Foreign Service personnel system."

No matter what agency they work for, all foreign service personnel are paid on the same salary scale and have access to the same retirement, insurance, and other benefits. An interagency Foreign Service Board set up in 1982 is supposed to ensure "maximum compatibility" among the personnel systems of the foreign service agencies. But within the limits of the law, each agency establishes its own rules and policies for recruitment, hiring, training, assignment, and promotion. Exchanges of personnel between foreign service agencies are rare, and personnel transfers from one agency to another rarer still.

The foreign service and the civil service are civilian institutions established by law to ensure that the work of government is carried forward professionally, without partisanship or taint of corruption. Their similarities of purpose and design are great, but the differences in their missions lead to important differences in the rights and obligations that each service offers to and demands of its members. Four features in particular distinguish the foreign service.

First is *rank in person.* Members of the foreign service, like members of the military, have a personal rank that determines base pay. Rank in the regular foreign service is designated by a number, starting at nine and rising to one. Members of the senior foreign service have ranks designated with titles: counselor, minister-counselor, and career minister. Rank is in the person and pay is linked to rank. In the civil service, however, rank and pay are in the position, not in the person. The Office of Personnel Management (OPM) maintains a general schedule (GS) of pay grades, and each civil service position in the federal government has a pay grade associated with it. A civil service employee who changes jobs may end up with a pay raise or a pay cut, depending on whether the new job has a higher or lower pay grade than the old one; a foreign service employee who changes jobs keeps the same base salary.[2]

Second is *worldwide availability.* Members of the foreign service may be sent anywhere in the world. They can expect to spend about two-thirds of their careers abroad. They have a voice in choosing their assignments, but in the end they must respond to the needs of the service. Civil service personnel, however, are routinely assigned to domestic positions only; overseas assignments are voluntary and exceptional. Of the nearly 2 million civil servants in the federal government, only a few hundred work abroad.

Third is *up or out.* After a certain number of years in grade without promotion, or years in service without advancement to the senior ranks, a foreign service officer faces mandatory retirement. Officers may also be forced to retire for substandard performance (selection out). Civil servants face no such requirements.

Fourth is *early retirement* at the option of the employee. Foreign service personnel may retire as early as age fifty with twenty years' service. The earliest retirement in the civil service is ordinarily at age fifty-five with thirty years' service, or at sixty with twenty years' service. In congressional testimony over many years, the foreign service has defended its more generous retirement benefits by pointing to the hardship of worldwide availability and the insecurity of *up or out.* Congress has agreed.

The Department of State

Understanding the foreign service begins with the Department of State. The two organizations are distinct but inseparable.

There is no better introduction to the Department of State than a visit to the building that has housed it since 1947.[3] Over the years, the building and the department, like a pet and its owner, have come to resemble each other. Like the department, the Harry S Truman Building, more often called Main State, is somewhat removed from Washington's federal center. It stands about two miles west of the White House, in a part of town called Foggy Bottom, a name beloved of columnists looking for an easy joke. The building covers more than two city blocks, but there is nothing grand about it. Like a diplomatic communiqué, it is featureless and forgettable in shape, color, and material. Inside, the building is a grid in which visitors and even employees routinely lost their way until 1974, when Nancy Maginnes Kissinger, wife of the secretary, asked that each corridor be blazed in a different color. The windows do not open.

Approach the department from any direction and you will encounter tiers of Jersey walls, concrete planters, steel bollards, and dragon's teeth that force pedestrians to choose between a slalom course around the barriers or a mogul course over them. Visitors pass through metal detectors even before they enter the marble lobby, where they queue twice, once to check in with a receptionist and again to wait for an escort. When a VIP shows up, protocol officers and security personnel clear a path through the crowd.

The security is not excessive. The State Department is an obvious target for terrorists looking for symbols of America's international reach, and it has been repeatedly stung by spectacular security failures. In 1985, even though security had been tightened following the attacks on the US embassy and marine barracks in Beirut two years earlier, a visitor managed to bring a rifle into the building and murder his mother, a secretary, near the office of Secretary of State George P. Shultz. In 1998 a recording device, believed to have been planted by a Russian agent, was found in a conference room used by the secretary of state and other senior officials. In 2000 a laptop computer containing highly classified information disappeared from a conference room in a secure area. Neither the computer nor the culprits were ever found. Early reports indicate, however, that the department is blameless in the 2010 Wikileaks affair. The security breach that exposed some 250,000 classified State Department messages appears to have occurred at the Department of Defense.

At either end of the department's lobby are memorials to foreign service personnel who lost their lives in the line of duty. A plaque on one wall bears the names and dates and places of death of 103 officers who died while on active duty "under heroic or tragic circumstances," from William Palfrey, lost at sea in 1780, to Robert Little, killed in Vietnam in 1968. A newer plaque on the opposite wall bears, as of May 2010, the names of 131 persons "serving their country abroad in foreign affairs" who died "under heroic and inspirational circumstances," from Robert P. Perry, murdered by Palestinian terrorists in Jordan in 1970, to Victoria DeLong, who died in the Haitian earthquake of 2010. Most died in warfare or terrorist attacks. Seven of those listed since 2003 died in Iraq or Afghanistan.[4] A similar plaque honoring fallen employees of USAID is displayed at the agency's headquarters in the Ronald Reagan Building.

Physically as well as bureaucratically, the State Department is hierarchical. Vertical location in the building is a rough indication of vertical location in the department's chain of command (see appendix A):

- Secretary
- Deputy secretary
- Undersecretary
- Assistant secretary (who heads a bureau)
- Deputy assistant secretary
- Office director (whose office may have more than one division)
- Deputy office director
- Division chief

Offices of the secretary of state, the deputy secretary, and the undersecretaries are on the seventh floor, with the highest-ranking officials in the offices closest to the secretary. The operations center, a 24/7 hub for crisis management, is there as well. "The trick to this place," said one old hand, "is to get as close as you can to the center of power without stepping inside the circle of abuse."

For practical purposes, the seventh is the top floor. For ceremonies, however, the eighth floor offers a balcony with a magnificent view and reception rooms that private donors have furnished with artifacts of America's early diplomatic history: the desk on which John Adams, Benjamin Franklin, and John Hay signed the Treaty of Paris in 1783; a Houdon bust of Franklin dated 1778; an 1816 portrait of John Quincy Adams painted when the future president was minister to Great Britain.

Most assistant secretaries are on the sixth floor. Surrounded by their deputies, they occupy office suites with conference rooms, sitting areas, and, for the boss, a private washroom. Proximity counts. The front offices of the six geographic bureaus, and the office of the foreign service's director general, are directly below the offices of the secretary of state and the other principals. Assistant secretaries who lead other bureaus make do with less prized territory.

Most office directors and below are on floors five, four, and three. The second floor holds the department's press and public affairs operations and much of the machinery and equipment that service the rest of the building. The first floor holds the protocol office, the cafeteria, two large auditoriums, several smaller conference rooms, and the family liaison office.

Washington jargon gives buildings human powers and characteristics: The White House says, the Pentagon wants, Treasury insists, Commerce drags its feet. In the Department of State, this kind of language is applied to floors—and to letters. Letter codes designate all State Department offices. The secretary of state is S. S/ES is the executive secretariat, which manages information flow to seventh-floor principals such as P, the undersecretary for political affairs, or M, the undersecretary for management. The Bureau of East Asian and Pacific Affairs is EAP, the Office of Japanese Affairs (also called the Japan desk) is EAP/J, and so forth. It is quite possible for the seventh floor to be furious when S/ES bounces a memo that P tasked to EAP back to J, because the sixth floor did not sign off.[5]

Readers with a sense of geometry may now be wondering how the pyramid of State's hierarchy fits into the cube of the main State building. The question has a three-part answer.

First and most obvious is that high-ranking officials have larger offices. The office of the secretary of state would probably hold some two dozen employees if it were on the third or fourth floors.

Second and most important is that State's pyramid is not steep. The department is seriously top heavy. In Washington, it has about sixty officials with the rank equivalent to assistant secretary or above—roughly one for every 360 employees.[6] The Treasury Department, by contrast, has only thirty such officials—roughly one for every 4,500 employees. The big-shot-to-small-fry ratio at State is affected by the large number of high-ranking officials with narrowly defined jobs and relatively small staffs. State has, for example, an assistant secretary for verification, compliance, and implementation (of arms control agreements); an assistant secretary for democracy, human rights, and labor affairs; an assistant secretary for population, refugees, and migration; a senior coordinator for international women's issues; a global AIDS coordinator; a special envoy to the Organization of the Islamic Conference; and others. Some of these posts were created at high levels in response to public or congressional pressure, or to provide the incumbents with the rank needed to deal on an equal footing with foreign counterparts. One organizational result of the proliferation of assistant secretaries is the proliferation of even higher officials to oversee them. State has six undersecretaries and three deputy secretaries, to Treasury's three undersecretaries and one deputy secretary.

Third and most promising is that the building simply isn't big enough. Offices are a jumble of cubicles and warrens, and some spill out into the corridors. Many offices are outside the building entirely, in the forty-five State annexes around the city. C. Northcote Parkinson, the British aphorist and student of large organizations, once observed that a bureaucracy that fits in its building is in serious trouble. "Perfection of planned layout," he wrote, "is achieved only by institutions on the point of collapse." By this standard, the Department of State is full of vigorous good health. The hierarchy of the building, like the hierarchy of the foreign service, keeps breaking down under pressure from below.

As of October 2009, seventeen of the department's fifty top officials were career members of the foreign service. The highest ranking were Undersecretary for Political Affairs William Burns and Undersecretary for Management Patrick Kennedy. Ambassador Burns's post is traditionally reserved for a member of the career foreign service.

Three members of the career foreign service have served as deputy secretary of state: Walter Stoessel (1982–83), Lawrence Eagleburger (1989–92), and John Negroponte (2007–9). Lawrence Eagleburger was nominated as secretary of state and confirmed by the Senate in time to serve six weeks in that position, from December 1992 to January 1993. He is the only foreign service officer to hold that office.

The Foreign Service, the Civil Service, and Foreign Service Nationals

State employs about sixty-six thousand people, including about twenty-three thousand US citizens and forty-three thousand foreign staff. Of the Americans, about fifteen thousand work in Washington and eight thousand, almost all of them members of the foreign service, work overseas. Essentially all of the forty-three thousand non-Americans work abroad. These are locally employed staff (LES), a term that includes foreign service nationals

(FSNs), who are US government employees directly hired by US missions abroad, as well as local citizens hired under personal-service agreements (PSAs). Locally engaged staff are almost always nationals of the country in which they live and work, but a US mission overseas may also hire third-country nationals, locally resident Americans, and family members of American employees at the mission.

State's foreign service personnel are either generalists (about 7,500) or specialists (about 5,400). *Generalist* is a term devised and used by the State Department's Bureau of Human Resources; the rest of the world calls them *officers*. Foreign service officers, or FSOs, get most of the public's attention. In an embassy they are the political, economic, public affairs, consular, and management officers. The specialists handle communications and information, take care of the money, maintain the buildings, organize and provide security, manage the personnel system, and in general keep things running and humming.

Not included in any of these numbers are foreign service retirees who return to work and still receive their pension plus salary up to their last salary level. Because they are paid a salary only "when actually employed," they carry the acronym WAE. At the beginning of 2007, State had about 700 of these WAE personnel back in harness, more than 5 percent of the work force, and about half of the 1,400 retirees who had notified the department of their availability for assignment.

State also employs close to ten thousand members of the civil service. Inside the department, foreign service and civil service employees do the same kind of work in the same bureaucratic structure. A foreign service officer or specialist may report to a civil service boss, or vice versa—but they operate under different personnel rules, with different rights and obligations. The foreign service is governed by the Foreign Service Act of 1980.[7] The civil service is covered by the Civil Service Reform Act of 1978, as amended. The director general (DG) of the foreign service is also the director of human resources for State, and so has responsibility for the department's civil service as well foreign service employees. But when the DG makes decisions that affect the department's civil servants, he or she must follow the regulations and policies of the Office of Personnel Management (OPM), an independent federal agency that administers nearly 2 million civil service employees throughout the federal government. The DG has a freer hand with the foreign service.

The leadership of the Department of State likes to refer to the department's staff as "the foreign service, the civil service, and foreign service nationals." Repetition of this phrase is intended to emphasize the integration of these three categories of employees into a single team. The phrase is hard to say, but it is easier said than done. The prejudices and resentments that marred the conversion of civil service employees to foreign service status in the 1950s and 1960s are long gone, but the real differences in the personnel systems constrain managers and affect attitudes.

Other Agencies

The Department of State is not the only place where members of the foreign service work. As of mid-2010, USAID employed about 1,600 foreign service officers and 4,500 foreign service nationals in its worldwide operations. The US Department of Agriculture's Foreign Agricultural Service, which promotes the export of American food and agricultural products, has about 175 foreign service officers working in US embassies and consulates as agricultural counselors and attachés.[8] The US Commercial Service, the trade promotion arm of the Department of Commerce, includes about 230 foreign service officers—the Foreign Commercial Service—who staff positions abroad as commercial counselors, senior commercial officers, and attachés, and more than one thousand foreign service nationals. The Peace Corps and the Broadcasting Board of Governors (BBG), which operates the Voice of America, Radio Marti, Radio Sawa, and all other US official civilian international broadcasting, employ a handful of foreign service personnel. Many active-duty members of the foreign service work under various arrangements elsewhere in government or in the private sector for the National Security Council staff, the Department of Defense, other federal agencies, the US Congress, state and local governments, and for-profit and nonprofit corporations, but they remain employees of their home agencies, to which they normally return.

The Foreign Service Act of 1980 lays down a few basic rules that apply to all foreign service agencies, among them rank-in-person, worldwide availability, up or out, and early retirement. The American Foreign Service Association (AFSA) is both the professional association of the US Foreign Service and the union that represents foreign service employees in collective bargaining with their employers—the departments of State, Commerce, and Agriculture; AID; and the BBG. AFSA is one of the few unifying elements in a service whose agency employment rules and personnel systems have little in common beyond the basic structures of the 1980 act. For example, the Department of State hires mainly through competitive examination and requires a period of probation before granting full employment, called tenure. Other agencies do things differently. Part III of this book describes the career paths open to the State Department's foreign service personnel in detail. The foreign service in other agencies is dealt with in summary in the following section.

The four major foreign service agencies—State, AID, the FCS, and the FAS—have all been growing with bigger budgets and more people. For State and AID, the increases are an integrated effort to place diplomacy and development on a par with defense as tools of American foreign policy. For the departments of Commerce and Agriculture, the increases are linked to an initiative of the Obama administration aimed at doubling US exports between 2010 and 2015.[9] But plans for growth will face severe pressure from budget cutters in fiscal year 2011 and beyond.

Agency for International Development

After the State Department, the Agency for International Development employs the largest number of foreign service personnel—about 1,600 foreign service officers and about 4,500 locally employed staff. About 60 percent of the American foreign service staff are overseas. The agency has about 2,000 positions in the United States, filled by 1,500 civil service and 500 foreign service personnel.[10]

AID is the most operational of the foreign service agencies. In 2009, spending on employee salaries and other direct operating costs was about 6 percent of appropriations; the rest went to programs.[11] Its foreign service officers run programs, manage budgets, and supervise contractors. Some foreign service people in State do similar work, but at AID programs and operations are the rule rather than the rarity.

When President Kennedy established AID in 1961, its personnel were not part of the career foreign service. AID was created as a temporary agency, and most people working for it were not expected to stay for the length of a career. Foreign assistance, though, evolved into a permanent feature of US foreign policy. By 1980, when the Foreign Service Act was rewritten, AID clearly needed a permanent staff of skilled professionals ready to serve throughout the developing world. The extension of the foreign service to AID in the 1980 act provoked no controversy.

Not so the agency's mission. The battles in Congress and within the administration over how much to spend on foreign aid and how and where to spend it make the agency vulnerable to sharp swings in funding and frequent reorganization (see chapter 2). Douglas Broome, the AID senior labor management adviser at the AFSA, saw scores of these battles during his career in AID.

The budgets for programs and for operations—for the staff and infrastructure needed to manage the programs—are rarely synchronized, especially given how quickly operating funds are expended, in the year they are appropriated, with program funds frequently staying in the pipeline, to be spent only over several years. Programs may be expanding while the capacity to manage them is shrinking, which can lead to poor management and waste. Or programs may be shrinking while staff is growing, which can lead to reorganizations, hiring freezes, and other dislocations. The administrators who come in to run this agency have an impossible task.[12]

Like the foreign service in the Department of State, AID's foreign service lost positions in the mid-1990s. State let its foreign service ranks shrink through attrition, hiring fewer new officers than needed to replace retirements and resignations. AID stopped hiring entirely in 1995 and then laid off about two hundred active-duty civil service and foreign service personnel, and as many as eight hundred foreign service nationals. Government workers call layoffs a reduction in force, or RIF. In 1996, AID riffed 10 percent of its American employees and pulled out of more than twenty-five countries. In the federal government, a 10 percent RIF is carnage. Around the same time, AID's Washington headquarters moved from crowded but comfortable offices in the Harry S Truman Building to spartan cubicles in the new Ronald Reagan Building. Many in AID worried that the agency was in terminal decline.

Not so. The National Security Strategy issued in September 2002, the document that presented the doctrine of the preventive war, also defined development as a component of national security. It assigned to development the most ambitious national security goals: shoring up weak states such as Afghanistan that might (again) become safe harbors for terrorists, supporting strategic states such as Pakistan that are allies in the war on terrorism, transforming vulnerable states through support for the infrastructure of democracy and free markets, responding to humanitarian needs and crises, and addressing global concerns such as the spread of HIV/AIDS. Between 2001 and 2004, US foreign aid budgets doubled.

The Obama administration continued to move in the same direction, but more aggressively. The National Security Strategy paper released in May 2010 declared that "Development is a strategic, economic, and moral imperative"[13] and said that "Our diplomacy and development capabilities must be modernized."[14] A President Policy Directive signed a few months later called for organizational changes to "raise the importance of development in our national security policy decision-making and generate greater coherence across the US government."[15]

After nearly two years of work, the State Department and USAID completed the first Quadrennial Diplomacy and Development Review (QDDR), released in December 2010 with the title *Leading through Civilian Power*. The QDDR outlines steps needed to "[re-establish] USAID as the world's premier development agency"[16] and to "elevate development and integrate the power of development and diplomacy."[17]

To many in USAID, the word "integrate" suggests an unwelcome subordination to State. "We're operational. We go out there and implement programs," said Francisco Zamora, the AID vice president at AFSA. "We do long-term stuff, we have a five-year, a ten-year horizon. When we come under the control of people at State, with their short-term outlook, our programs suffer."[18] Secretary Clinton is aware of this resistance and addressed it forthrightly in a major speech at the Center for Global Development:

> Now, I know that the word *integration* sets off alarm bells in some people's heads. There is a concern that integrating development means diluting it or politicizing it—giving up our long-term development goals to achieve short-term objectives or handing over more of the work of development to our diplomats or defense experts. That is not what we mean, nor what we will do. What we will do is leverage the expertise of our diplomats and our military on behalf of development, and vice versa. The three Ds must be mutually reinforcing.[19]

Integration of State and USAID, and of the foreign services of the two agencies, certainly has its supporters. Ambassador L. Craig Johnstone, who handled budgets and resource allocation at the State Department in late 1990s, observed that AID people have learned how to run big programs.

That's a skill the State Department generally lacks, he said, and in an era of transformational diplomacy, one it badly needs. Closer integration of AID and State, Johnstone observed, could make both agencies stronger.[20] Frank Almaguer, a USAID senior foreign service officer who retired in 2002, said, "I have been leaning more and more toward full integration, because what we're doing now," with State in charge of the budget but USAID in charge of implementing the programs, "doesn't work well."[21] Luis Arreaga-Rodas, State's director of recruitment, examination, and employment, is especially qualified to address the issue—he spent the first eleven years of his foreign service career in USAID before moving to the Department of State. Arreaga would like to see more personnel exchanges between the agencies: "We [at State] have everything to gain. AID is much more operational than we are. We need to have those skills. We need to understand the long term better."[22] A cross-assignments program allows foreign service officers from one agency to take assignments in the other, but the program is small, with most of the swaps in the management area. The QDDR would sharply expand this program and provide more joint and cross training as well.

The foreign service in AID is growing even faster than the foreign service in State. The first director of foreign assistance, Henrietta Fore (who gave her initial to State's F bureau), drew on Colin Powell's Diplomatic Readiness Initiative to launch USAID's Development Leadership Initiative (DLI). The DLI aimed to increase the agency's staff of foreign service officers by 30 percent, from 1,000 to 1,300. Then, in 2009, with USAID's foreign service officer work force at about 1,200, the Obama administration called for doubling the number to 2,400 within five years. "That requires hiring about 1,600 new officers, given normal attrition," said Deborah Kennedy-Iraheta, the agency's director of human resources, in early 2010. "We've already brought on 420, and we have funds to hire another 300, so we'll be asking for money for some 700 to 800 more officers in fiscal years 2011–12. And 60 or 70 percent of our workforce are foreign service nationals. We plan to expand their capabilities and their numbers, from 5,000 to 9,000, over the same period. We have about 1,800 civil servants, and we'll be adding to their numbers too."[23] Of course, the pace of growth will depend on budgets and appropriations. Kennedy-Iraheta acknowledged that the original plan may well take more than five years to complete.

During this expansion USAID's work force is likely to change in several respects. It will become younger as senior officers leave: In 2010 about 80 percent of the agency's two hundred senior officers are eligible for retirement, and in 2011 that number will rise to nearly 90 percent. The work force will have different skills. "We're changing our model in several ways," Kennedy-Iraheta explained.

> We'll be programming more resources through host governments and working more with other donor countries in multi-donor forums. And we're breaking up some of our big contracts with big companies, moving to more and smaller contracts with smaller firms, which Congress wants to see. So we'll be hiring more contract professionals, legal specialists, financial analysts—people who can work with host governments to bring them up to standard. Congress wants us to design more of our programs in-house, so we'll be hiring people who can do that, who can design a program and assess its implementation. And we want to make our demographics work for us by setting up a policy bureau to work on issues like donor engagement, knowledge management, continuous learning, science and technology in development—a place where the old can teach the young but the young can teach the old as well.[24]

AID's foreign service personnel system differs from State's in several respects. There is no written entry exam. Candidates for AID's foreign service positions respond to job offers published on the agency's website, and if their paperwork looks good they will be interviewed. Successful candidates—the agency takes about one in ten applicants—have five years to achieve tenure, a decision made, as at State, by a tenuring board. Like FSOs in the Department of State, tenured officers can expect to spend about twenty years in the middle grades. The most successful will then go on to the senior foreign service. Some will become chiefs of mission—by tradition, the State Department recommends to the White House, and the White House nominates, career FSOs in USAID to three ambassadorships, one each in Latin America, Asia, and Africa.

Unlike State, but like the Foreign Commercial Service (FCS), AID brings some people in at the middle grades in the rank structure. Most of these midlevel appointments are noncareer officers who serve no more than five years, but a few with skills in short supply are regular career officers whose career starts in the middle, not at the bottom.

Although AID hires people with specialized skills—agricultural economists, sanitation engineers, health care professionals, experts in small business finance, to name a few—AID does not divide its foreign service into generalists and specialists. That is both a problem and an opportunity for some seeking promotion into the senior foreign service. "We draw our mission directors [directors of USAID missions in foreign countries] and deputy directors from all different professions, with the result that we have gutted our senior technical ranks," said Kennedy-Iraheta. "We're trying to change the system, to provide incentives that will bring people who are the best at what they do into the senior foreign service, without making them take management positions. We want to open things up, maybe bring in more people from academia for one- or two-year assignments, and let more of our people go out to a semester or two at a university. We want to make USAID a risk-taking environment and culture."[25] The QDDR followed the same path, promising a new path to the top for technical specialists, greater intake of outside expertise, and reduced reliance on contractors.

Historically, promotions have come a bit faster for AID officers than for their counterparts at State. Despite the increasing integration of the two entities, this pattern may persist for a number of years. AID has an acute shortage of midlevel officers—a legacy of the hiring freeze of the mid-1990s—and that vacuum will be filled by the junior officers who now make up 40 percent of AID's foreign service. If Craig Johnstone and Luis Arreaga-Rodas are right, the demand for foreign service officers who have run complex programs and managed large budgets is likely to rise. That should mean increased responsibilities and professional opportunities for AID's best people.

Commerce and the Foreign Commercial Service

The Commerce Department is a giant grab bag of an agency. Domestic functions that have no obvious relationship to each other account for the great bulk of the department's $9 billion budget and its forty-four thousand employees. The largest unit, with 30 percent of the staff and over 60 percent of the budget, is the National Oceanic and Atmospheric Administration, which includes the National Marine Fisheries Service and the National Weather Bureau. Twenty-five percent of the staff work in the Patent and Trademark Office, which in budget scoring costs nothing, because its revenue from fees covers its outlays.

The lack of coherence among the department's agencies and administrations made it briefly a target of fiscal conservatives. In 1995, Republican members of the House of Representatives, in the majority for the first time in fifty years and feeling their oats, proposed closing the Commerce

Department, killing some of its functions and assigning the rest elsewhere. Their effort failed but Commerce management ran scared for years, devoting considerable effort to documenting and justifying the department's performance. The department more recently has regained its confidence and its standing. The budget for the FCS, and for the department's other activities in international trade, is expanding.

Inside the Commerce Department, the FCS operates out of the International Trade Administration (ITA), which has about 6 percent of the department's budget and 5 percent of its staff. The FCS is headed by a director general with the rank of assistant secretary, one of four reporting to the head of ITA, the undersecretary for international trade. The FCS, which operates in about 120 overseas posts in about 90 countries, is part of the US and Foreign Commercial Service, which also maintains 107 US offices staffed by members of the civil service.[26] The president's fiscal year 2011 budget request for the entire commercial service, foreign and domestic, is about $320 million, an increase of more than 20 percent from the year before.[27]

The FCS has a dual mission to protect US commercial interests and to promote US exports of goods and services. Its overseas locations are chosen to cover the regions that offer the best prospects for US trade and investment. Where the FCS is absent, foreign service officers from State handle commercial work.

The Commerce Department and its FCS have a sometimes difficult relationship. Commerce's foreign service personnel are a bit lost among the forty thousand members of the civil service that staff the agency's domestic positions, including the domestic field offices of the US Commercial Service. There are about 230 foreign service officers at Commerce, including about twenty noncareer officers brought in outside the regular examination process on time-limited contracts. Nearly two hundred work overseas. There are only eight positions for FSOs at FCS Washington headquarters. New officers typically start with a two-year tour in a domestic field office, but after that opportunities for service in the domestic field offices are rare. The Commerce Department frequently waives rules that limit consecutive years of service overseas, simply because it lacks stateside positions for its foreign service personnel.

"Generally you serve only once or twice domestically in the course of a twenty-five year career," said Keith Curtis, a senior foreign service officer in the FCS.

Our tours are normally four years, and people often go back for multiple tours in the same country or region. But it's a different life than at State. We put our people where business is being done. We rarely send officers to posts where dependents are not allowed. Like the State Department, we've been shifting positions into China, India, Brazil, Mexico. We have more resources in China than any other country, by far, but London, Brussels, Moscow, and other traditional commercial centers are still important. In some way we have a more comfortable life than our colleagues from State. Housing, schools, hospitals, they're usually pretty good wherever we go. And we like staying overseas. We like our independence—most of us don't like bureaucracy, we'd rather ask forgiveness than permission. And we like being close to the boss. In Washington, even a senior officer is pretty far from the top, but at an embassy you're only one or two levels below the ambassador.[28]

The FCS has had some difficult years. Ambassador Charles Ford, a member of the FCS from its inception, wrote in 2005 that "the foreign Service has yet to find a comfortable coexistence with the Civil Service culture of the Commerce Department and its International Trade Administration." In contrast to the foreign service components of AID, Agriculture, and of course State, Ford said that senior FSOs at Commerce "have no real opportunity to serve in program and policy positions in Washington."[29]

The Commercial Service in the George W. Bush administration went through a long budget squeeze that fell especially hard on the FCS. From fiscal year 2001 to fiscal year 2009, annual spending on the Commercial Service rose from $192 million to $238 million, an increase of $46 million. But costs rose even faster. Contributions to the cost of security improvements in the overseas posts, the FCS share of Commerce Department information technology upgrades and other overhead, and mandated but not fully funded pay raises added about $62 million in costs over the same period. To cut costs and stay within the budget, FCS had to cut people.

Between 2004 and 2009, the agency reduced its work force from more than 1,700 to fewer than 1,500, mainly through attrition. The cuts fell most heavily on the agency's roughly 800 non-American staff overseas, whose cost, because of a falling dollar, was rising rapidly.

By 2008, Keith Curtis said, the FCS was "at the breaking point," at risk of being unable to perform core functions. "We started fiscal year 2009 with a $29 million deficit, which for us is very difficult. We cut training basically to

zero, beyond absolutely necessary language training. But there's a big shining light at the end of the tunnel now, with the National Export Initiative the president announced in his [January 29, 2010] state of the union address." The fiscal year 2011 budget request calls for a $59 million increase in the budget for the commercial service, the largest increase since the creation of the service in 1981. "The FCS is hiring again."

The FCS brings in new officers with no written exam. Candidates who successfully complete an online screening process are invited to a daylong oral assessment exercise. In early 2010, of 460 applicants 128 were selected to participate in an assessment. Sixty passed and were placed on a register to receive job offers as positions became available. "Usually we do an assessment every other year," said Curtis, "but with the step-up in hiring under the export initiative, we may have to make this an annual exercise."

In recruitment and hiring, experience counts. "We look for people with five to ten years of international work experience, including schooling," Curtis said. As a result, new recruits to the FCS on average begin their careers at a higher pay grade than new FSOs at the Department of State. The shortage of positions at the lowest grades is matched by a shortage at the top. "The FCS is informally held to one ambassadorship at a time," Curtis said. "And to my knowledge no FCS officer has ever served as a deputy chief of mission, although a number of us have been consuls general." Even so, he added, "if you're a person of ability, you have no particular problem making it into the senior foreign service." But because the FCS has relatively few junior or senior positions, a career in the foreign service at Commerce is likely to begin at a slightly higher level and end at a slightly lower one than a career at State.

Agriculture and the Foreign Agricultural Service

The FAS in the US Department of Agriculture shares a number of characteristics with the FCS and USAID. Like the FCS, the FAS has a small foreign service operating in a large domestic agency. The Department of Agriculture has more than one hundred thousand employees. Only some eight hundred work in the FAS, and of these, only about 175 are FSOs.[30] Like USAID, the FAS administers billion-dollar programs on a million-dollar budget. To be precise, in fiscal year 2010 the FAS had an operating budget of about $180 million. FAS programs, including export credits and credit guarantees, market development programs, and food aid, were budgeted at nearly $8 billion.

The FAS represents American agriculture, and, increasingly, the US food industry, around the world. The central mission is exports but the work goes well beyond trade promotion. "Traditionally we think of our job in three parts," said Chuck Alexander, a thirty-year veteran of the service. "We do policy, reporting, and market development. All of these are changing now."[31]

The work is more technical than it was a generation ago. "It's biotechnology, avian influenza, bovine spongiform encephalopathy [mad cow disease]. We used to recruit agricultural economists, mostly midwestern farm boys like me," said Alexander. "Now we need a different kind of expertise." FAS no longer insists on a farming background. "If you're overseas talking to farmers, you'd better know something about farming. But if you're going to spend your career in Brussels or Geneva negotiating trade rules and talking to bureaucrats, you don't have to be all that familiar with production agriculture." Many younger officers have a background in law, economics, or public administration.

Even apparently straightforward export promotion and market development have a strong technical element. Genetically modified varieties account for most of the major crops in the United States, including 85 percent of the corn, 90 percent of the soybeans, and 55 percent of the cotton. Promoting US agricultural exports requires an understanding of the biotechnology involved in developing these strains and ensuring their safety. It requires as well constant diplomatic efforts to ensure that national and international standards, labeling requirements, and testing at the border are grounded in science and protection of health rather than in fear or protectionism.

The technical nature of the work requires training that so far the department has largely failed to provide. "When I went to my first post in Argentina twenty years ago," Henry Schmick, a senior FSO, said, "I could go out to a soybean field and understand what I was seeing and report. But I couldn't say anything about biotechnology or phytosanitary standards. We have to do a better job training people so they know what the WTO is, what the Codex is, the OIE, the IPPC. We don't have an A-100 class. We should."[32]

The service's recruitment and hiring practices mitigate the lack of training. A foreign service aspirant must first be hired by the FAS as a civil servant and spend at least eighteen months on the job before taking a written exam for entry into the foreign service. Those who pass the written test are invited to take an oral assessment. Those who succeed in the orals must still undergo a physical exam and a security background check before they receive a job offer. Even then, there may be a delay of another year or two

before an appropriate overseas assignment opens up and a commission as an FSO is finally awarded.

The long incubation means that first-tour officers are already agency veterans, with exposure to the USDA bureaucracy and culture and with the beginnings of a network of colleagues and associates. Even so, first-tour officers are never left on their own at a small post. A first-tour officer is always sent to a post where he or she has an FAS supervisor—a senior officer posted as an agricultural attaché or counselor—as a mentor. Tours, including the first tour, usually last four years. An officer can expect to spend two-thirds of a career overseas and one-third in FAS positions in Washington.

When Henry Schmick went to Argentina, reporting meant data—crop conditions, market trends, changes in land use. Maintaining the famed USDA database is still important, but so increasingly is the kind of analysis that gives direction to policy. Chuck Alexander offered an example: "What do rising oil prices mean for global demand for ethanol, and what does that mean for sugar prices, and what does that mean for US policy? Can we get rid of our sugar quotas? We need to look at these global connections. It's pretty interesting stuff."[33] Reporting on climate change—not the weather, but laws, regulations, and practices in foreign countries that bear on the issue—is a new requirement that fits into this category. How does the European Union take secondary land-use effects into account when calculating the carbon balance of corn-based ethanol production or soybean-based biodiesel? What information does the price of carbon permits traded on European exchanges convey, and how can that information be useful to American agricultural producers and exporters? These are challenging questions, whose answers affect billion-dollar decisions.

The FAS stands out among foreign service agencies in several ways. It's small: "Everybody knows everybody. Nothing we do is ever impersonal," said Alexander. It's focused: "We know exactly what we're supposed to do, and we do it." It's well supported: "We have a constituency, American agriculture, that historically has gotten pretty much what it wants on Capitol Hill. And we serve them well." That view is shared by other agencies and by American ambassadors around the world. "In my experience," Alexander said, "no ambassador has ever opposed the addition of an agricultural officer to his staff, or has ever called for a cut. We're highly valued members of the embassy team."

Given this record of success, how has it happened that the service has diminished in size and budget over the past fifteen years? Export promotion—the core function—changed faster than the service did, and now FAS is playing catch-up. The commodity groups with which the service works most closely—representatives of producers and processors of corn, wheat, soybeans, cotton, rice, poultry, pork, beef, and scores of other export products—no longer need the kind of assistance from the US government that they required in the 1960s, 1970s, and 1980s, or at least they no longer need as much of it, or in the same places. "The cooperators [as the commodity groups are known, after a market development program enacted in 1954] are more independent. They know their way around. They don't need an embassy attaché to hold their hands in Tokyo or Paris," said Schmick. "We need to adapt, to improve our relationships with our stakeholders." Doing so entails a higher priority for trade policy and market access issues, if necessary at the expense of database reporting.

The FAS will need to rebuild its personnel, not only to perform its traditional tasks, but also to carry out duties related to development assistance and food security, work that acquired new emphasis after the 2001 attacks and the 2006–7 global shortages and price spikes in basic commodities such as rice and corn. "When the service was part of the State Department [in 1939–53], we did a lot of agricultural development work, under the Marshall Plan," Henry Schmick pointed out. "But when the service returned to the Department of Agriculture in 1953, and the focus turned to exports, many of the people who had been working in development eventually migrated to USAID."[34]

They never came back. The Department of Agriculture today has experts in every area related to farming, but they are civil servants with domestic jobs in extension services, the soil conservation service, the farm service agency, the animal and plant health inspection service, and other parts of the sprawling agency, not in the FAS. The FAS is now limited to a managerial role, overseeing contractors and the USDA component of the State Department's Civilian Response Corps (see chapter 10). "In Afghanistan," said Schmick, "what's the first thing you need to get the economy going? Agriculture. We're putting people into the country, into the provincial reconstruction teams, but they're not from FAS. We do have foreign service people in Kabul to supervise the activity."

The foreign service in FAS needs to grow in number and shrink in age. With 160 FSOs, the service is more than 25 percent below its 1992 peak, and almost half of the officers are eligible for retirement. In fiscal years 2007, 2008, and 2009, new hires failed to keep up with attrition; the foreign service component of FAS lost personnel. Redeployment is a short-term fix, to move officers where they are most needed. Of the fifty-six posts where FAS has American personnel, the post with the most positions is Beijing, which has five, and positions are being cut in Western Europe to add to the China contingent. Other new positions are opening in India, Vietnam, and Central America. More fundamental repairs are also under way. In fiscal year 2010, as part of the National Export Initiative that has raised hopes also in the FCS, hiring will exceed attrition. Hiring will need to expand just to stay even as retirements, optional at fifty years of age and mandatory at sixty-five, grow in number. The internal goal of growth to 190 foreign service officers by 2015 will be hard to achieve.

Table 3.1
The Foreign Service in Round Numbers, 2010

Agency	US Personnel	Remarks
Department of State	12,900	7,500 generalists (officers) 5,400 specialists
Agency for International Development	1,500	
Department of Commerce	230	Foreign Commercial Service
Department of Agriculture	225	175 Foreign Agricultural Service 50 Animal and Plant Health Inspection Service
Total	14,855	9,455 officers, 5,400 specialists

Source: Author's compilation.

Part II
The Profession

4

Form and Content

Members of the foreign service like to say that they are professionals, and not just in the sense that they are paid for their work. They see diplomacy as a profession—a set of skills to be mastered through apprenticeship and training, with restrictions on entry, advancement by merit, and codes of behavior.

But diplomacy is different from other professions. Unlike the law, medicine, teaching, or preaching, amateurs are allowed to participate. There are no sanctions against being diplomatic without a license.[1] Anyone formally designated by a sending state and accredited by a receiving state is a certified diplomat, with rights and obligations under international law. In the United States there are only two credentials for service in a high diplomatic position: nomination by the president and confirmation by the Senate.[2]

Professionals are proud of their craft, and when elected officials name political friends as ambassadors or assistant secretaries, career diplomats fret and pout. Career foreign service personnel tend to presume that political appointees, especially those without a distinguished record in academia or public service, are incompetent until proven otherwise. The ratio of career to political appointees under President Kennedy was about two to one, and that rough standard has prevailed ever since. The Obama administration, which in its first year awarded fewer than half of its ambassadorial nominations to career foreign service officers (FSOs), said it would over time move back toward the historic 2:1 ratio. That ratio is not good enough for the AFSA, which is simultaneously the professional society for American diplomats and the collective bargaining agent for American foreign service personnel, or for the American Academy of Diplomacy, a group of eminent retired career and noncareer ambassadors. These two organizations want the administration to fill no more than 10 percent of ambassadorial positions with noncareer appointments.[3] They have no prospect of success.

The numbers game has its silly side. After all, the foreign service is a career. It is diplomacy that is the profession, and you don't have to belong to the foreign service to be a professional diplomat, or eminently qualified for an ambassadorial assignment. Zalmay Khalilzad, American ambassador to Afghanistan (2003–5), Iraq (2005–7), and the United Nations (2007–9), moves between think tanks, such as the Center for Strategic and International Studies, RAND, and Cambridge Energy Research Associates, and government service with the National Security Council staff, the Department of State, and the Department of Defense; he is not a member of the foreign service but diplomacy has become his profession. Peter Galbraith left the staff of the Senate Foreign Relations Committee to become the first US ambassador to Croatia (1993–98), where he is credited with putting together the agreement that ended the Muslim-Croat war. He later worked for the United Nations in East Timor and in Afghanistan. Robert Gallucci, who led the nuclear negotiations with North Korea during the Clinton administration, was a State Department civil servant with no overseas experience; he later became dean of the Georgetown University School of Foreign Service.

The late Richard Holbrooke, who in 2009 was named special representative to Afghanistan and Pakistan, was ambassador to Germany (1993–94) and to the United Nations (1999–2001), and twice assistant secretary of state (for East Asian affairs, 1977–81, and for European affairs, 1994–96). Ambassador Holbrooke joined the foreign service in 1962 but resigned a decade later; the Department of State considers him a noncareer appointee.[4] Is Dennis Ross a professional diplomat? He came to government from an academic background and served presidents of both parties as the chief US negotiator on Middle East issues from 1988 to 2000, and he served as special adviser to the secretary of state for the Persian Gulf and southwest Asia in 2009.

Military officers with international experience are often asked to take on diplomatic roles. Colin Powell's deputy secretary of state, Richard Armitage, was a US Navy veteran who under presidential assignment in the 1990s handled diplomatic missions in the Philippines, the Middle East, and the former Soviet Union. Major General Scott Gration (USAF, Ret.), a Swahili speaker who grew up in Congo and Kenya and served in the Pentagon as the air force assistant deputy undersecretary for international affairs, was named in 2009 as the president's special envoy to Sudan. Lieutenant General Karl Eikenberry (USA, Ret.) commanded coalition forces in Afghanistan in 2005–7 before his appointment as ambassador to that country in 2009.

Under the last nine secretaries of state, from Haig to Clinton, three of the eleven undersecretaries for political affairs, traditionally the highest post held by a career FSO, came from outside the service and served with distinction.[5]

This long list is intended to show that noncareer does not necessarily mean nonprofessional. But there is no denying that many noncareer ambassadors have been incompetent, an embarrassment to the president who appointed them and to the senators who voted to confirm them. Too often, when weighed against ability to make political contributions, ability to perform is not an essential requirement for nomination to high diplomatic office. The United States is one of the few countries to go routinely outside its career service to fill high diplomatic posts. The Philippines does so, perhaps as a legacy of American colonial rule. Poland also sometimes does. Presidents in some Latin American, and especially Central American, countries from time to time offer foreign embassies to military and political figures, usually to get them out of the way. Nearly everywhere else, however, the top diplomatic jobs go to people who devote their lives to diplomatic service.

If you don't have to be a professional to be a diplomat, you also don't have to be a diplomat to practice diplomacy. When Hu Jintao, the president of China, came to the United States in April 2006, his first stop was Washington State, not Washington, D.C. He spent his first evening at dinner with Bill and Melinda Gates. "Increasingly," wrote the *Seattle Post-Intelligencer*, "the Microsoft billionaire and his palatial Medina estate serve as an extension of the State Department. Sort of a White House West."[6] Hu's second day in the United States began with a Boeing plant tour and a speech to Boeing employees. President Hu certainly had a diplomatic purpose in arranging these meetings: He intended to confront American protectionism by showing how important China is to companies that create jobs and wealth for hundreds of thousands of Americans. Bill Gates and Jim McNerney, CEO at Boeing, were practicing diplomacy as well, trying to influence Chinese policies and purchasing decisions and inevitably affecting the Chinese leader's view of the United States.

Diplomatic Traditions and Protocol

Diplomacy is an ancient practice, but as a profession it is merely old. Harold Nicolson, the British diplomat and scholar, says that the origins of diplomacy "lie buried in the darkness" of prehistory. Modern diplomacy, however, he traces to the France of Louis XIV and Cardinal Richelieu. The French system, as Nicolson named it, replaced the opportunistic scheming of

Byzantium and Machiavelli's Italian states with permanent negotiations that aimed at "solid and durable relations" that furthered "national interests" and had support in "national opinion." Richelieu and his disciple François de Callières taught that successful negotiation depends on building confidence, which in turn depends on avoidance of lies. Callières urged that diplomacy be treated as a profession, with appointments and advancement according to talent and regular payment.[7]

Emerging nation-states in Europe followed the French example. They set up ministries of foreign affairs to centralize policy and sent and received permanent resident embassies to conduct negotiations with other states. The formulation of policy in foreign ministries, and the pursuit of policy through resident embassies, dominated diplomatic practice from the eighteenth century well into the twentieth century.

Diplomats operating in the French system confronted a number of problems that continue to bedevil foreign service professionals today. Receiving states often regarded embassies with deep suspicion, as nests of spies and agents of subversion. They kept diplomats physically isolated in compounds and socially isolated in endless and expensive rounds of official obligations. (Even when receiving states are less hostile, American FSOs today complain that security requirements keep them in compounds, and reporting requirements, often of dubious value, keep them at their desks.) Diplomats also provoked suspicion in their native lands, where their long sojourns among foreigners left them out of touch with domestic matters and vulnerable to charges that they lacked, if not patriotism, then patriotic fervor.

Cut off or estranged from the local population and thrown into each other's company, diplomats gossiped and pooled information and found that they had much in common. The sense of shared hardships produced what Callières called a "freemasonry of diplomacy," a professional bond that operated without regard to country of allegiance.[8]

Immunity

The maligned practice of diplomatic immunity enhances the sense that diplomats of different countries belong to the same odd guild. When private persons, or for that matter most officials, visit or live in a foreign country, they submit themselves to that country's laws and regulations. If they fail to conform, they risk punishment. Diplomats, however, once named by the sending state and accepted by the receiving state, travel in a legal bubble.

They are subject to the laws of the state that sends them but are exempt from the laws of the state that receives them. This is called diplomatic immunity.

Diplomatic immunity may have begun with the pragmatic battlefield custom of providing safe passage to envoys offering terms of surrender. When adhered to, the practice reduced carnage on both sides. Adherence from the Greeks forward was erratic. The adage "don't shoot the messenger" is evidence that messengers were sometimes shot. The messengers—the diplomats—had to rely on the uncertain mercy of their enemies. They were eager to find a stronger basis for their security.

By the seventeenth century, as nation-states gained power across much of Europe, the aristocrats and churchmen who carried out most diplomatic missions developed a theory that justified their protection. According to the theory, a diplomat represents a sovereign who rules by divine right as a power independent of all other earthly powers. "In medieval Europe," writes Professor Paul Sharp, "ambassadors did not merely represent the interests of their sovereigns. . . . Rather, they literally stood for or in the place of those being represented."[9] One sovereign cannot exercise authority over another, and so a diplomat who is properly accredited must be immune from arrest, prosecution, taxation, and all other forms of coercion by the government that receives him. This theory, which became doctrine, facilitated negotiation, flattered the sovereigns, and not incidentally protected the lives and property of the diplomats.

At the Congress of Vienna, the multilateral peace conference that ended the Napoleonic wars in 1815, diplomatic immunity found a home in treaty law. One hundred and fifty years later, the 1961 Vienna Convention on Diplomatic Relations and the 1963 Vienna Convention on Consular Relations codified the rights and obligations of sending and receiving states, and of their envoys. These conventions have been ratified by nearly every country in the world.[10]

Under the Vienna conventions, an accredited diplomat, called a "diplomatic agent" in the language of the conventions, is immune from any form of arrest or detention. His home and its contents are as inviolable as the embassy itself. He is immune from the criminal and, with a few exceptions, from the civil and administrative jurisdiction of the host country. Administrative and technical staff have the same immunities, except from civil and administrative jurisdiction for acts committed outside the course of their duties. Immunities extend to family members, which can present difficulties for spouses who seek employment outside the embassy.

Immunity is not a license to break the law or a get-out-of-jail-free card. It is a right balanced by an obligation. According to the Vienna Convention, "It is the duty of all persons enjoying such privileges and immunities to respect the laws and regulations of the receiving State. They also have a duty not to interfere in the internal affairs of that State."[11]

The sending state may always waive the immunity of any of its diplomats, and the diplomat has no role or recourse with regard to that decision.[12] When a diplomat commits a crime, sometimes the sending state waives immunity, as the Republic of Georgia did when its deputy chief of mission killed a woman in a drunk-driving incident in 1997 in Washington, D.C. Sometimes it does not, as Brazil did not when the son of its ambassador shot a man in a bar in 1992, also in Washington, D.C.

Accreditation, Rank, and Precedence

History and tradition weigh heavily on the diplomatic profession, as well they should. The use of Latin and French terms to describe certain diplomatic practices testifies to their early origins. When one state prepares to send an ambassador to another, it asks the receiving state for *agrément*, not for agreement. *Agrément* involves a confidential message from the sending state to the receiving state: "If we name Smith, will you accept him?" If the answer is no, Smith is never named and therefore never suffers rejection. In American practice today, when the president's choice seems controversial, the Department of State may ask an even more hypothetical question: "If we were to ask you whether, should we name Smith, you would accept him, how would you reply?" If the answer is "we would say yes," then a formal request for *agrément* will follow.[13] A receiving state recognizes the right of a consular officer accredited to it to perform consular functions by granting an *exequatur*, often in the form of an elaborate stamp or seal on the officer's consular commission.

A receiving state that wants to rid itself of a diplomat it has accredited may declare that person unwelcome, or persona non grata (PNG). No reason need be given, but governments often cite "activities incompatible with diplomatic status," meaning espionage. The US government covers the basic costs of transferring an American diplomat who is declared PNG (or "pinged"). Some insurance companies offer PNG policies that will cover out-of-pocket expenses.

A similar patina of age appears in the terminology and practice of diplomatic rank and precedence, codified in 1815 at the Congress of Vienna and scarcely changed since.[14] The forms and titles in use in the American foreign service, and in foreign ministries around the world, have a comic-opera quality that contribute to the popular image of the diplomat as a twit with table manners. Diplomats may be ambassadors (in most cases, ambassadors extraordinary and plenipotentiary); chargés d'affaires; ministers; minister-counselors; counselors; first, second, or third secretaries; attachés; or assistant attachés. Consular officials may be consuls general, consuls, or vice consuls. The pope's representative to a country that has diplomatic relations with the Vatican carries the title of *nuncio* and is equivalent to an ambassador. *Chargé d'affaires* denotes an officer in charge of an embassy who is not an ambassador; if he is in charge only temporarily, the words *ad interim* are tacked on, a Franco-Latin twofer.

For members of the American foreign service, diplomatic rank will be (but should not be) confused with personal rank, which determines pay (see chapter 7). The senior foreign service has three ranks, or grades, called counselor, minister-counselor, and career minister. An officer with the personal rank of counselor may have the diplomatic rank of minister-counselor, or one with the rank of career minister may be sent abroad as an ambassador. A member of the foreign service may be most proud of his personal rank, but to the outside world, it is the diplomatic rank that counts. Diplomatic rank establishes precedence, which may determine where one sits at dinner, or stands in line to greet a dignitary, or—more important—whom one calls upon in host government offices. For diplomats of equal rank, precedence depends on seniority at post, determined by the date of accreditation. In US practice, ties are broken by pay grade.

Precedence is a central element of social protocol, an often mocked but necessary set of written and unwritten rules of behavior for diplomats abroad. American embassies and the foreign service have become less protocol conscious over the years, but they are hierarchical institutions and rank matters. Officers and staff still rise when the ambassador enters a room, respond promptly and almost always positively to invitations to functions, and remain at those functions until their ambassador leaves or gives them permission to do so.[15]

Accreditation is the recognition by the receiving government of the diplomatic status of the envoy of the sending government. It is the final step in establishing the privileges, immunities, and precedence that a diplomat is accorded under the Vienna conventions. For most diplomats, accreditation is routine. The embassy of the sending state sends a note with names and particulars to the foreign ministry of the host government, which replies with approval and often with identity cards (*carnets*) that diplomats are expected to carry at all times. For ambassadors, however, accreditation usually involves the presentation of credentials, the in-person delivery of a letter from the head of the sending state to the head of the receiving state.

The accreditation ceremony can be elaborate. In the United Kingdom, according to the official website of the monarchy, a new ambassador "is collected from the embassy or residence by a State landau from the Royal Mews" and "escorted by the Marshal of the Diplomatic Corps." During a twenty-minute "audience with The Queen" the ambassador "presents his or her Letters of Credence," and the Queen also greets "his or her suite," which has followed in a separate state landau.[16] In the United States, the president holds a simpler ceremony for newly arrived ambassadors about three or four times a year. Until they have presented their credentials ("letters of credence"), ambassadors are properly called ambassadors-designate.

Local staff, including foreign service nationals (FSNs), are not accredited but are normally reported to the host government. FSNs receive no immunities or diplomatic privileges. On the contrary, in some countries they are targets of harassment.

Foreign ministries ordinarily maintain and publish a diplomatic list identifying by name and title all accredited diplomats in the country, just as the State Department does.[17] The embassy tells the ministry where an individual diplomat fits on the list of that embassy's diplomatic personnel. Family members over the age of eighteen are also listed. In the US foreign service, nearly all generalists (officers) have diplomatic status when posted abroad, as do many foreign service specialists and most civil servants assigned to embassies from non–foreign service agencies. Those without diplomatic status are ordinarily recognized as officials, a title of courtesy that confers no immunity.

Diplomatic accreditation is not automatic. A government may reject any request for accreditation either through a declaration of persona non grata or through denial or withdrawal of a visa. Some governments formally or informally limit the number of people they will accredit or prohibit access by diplomats to parts of the country.

The Secret Handshake

As it was in the days of Richelieu, so it is today. Men and women in foreign service, regardless of the country or government they serve, belong to the same profession. They share a secret handshake with their colleagues. It is a blessing and a curse.

Most diplomats acquire, along with foreign languages, cuisines, customs, and diseases, a certain broadmindedness and tolerance, a ready sympathy for foreigners and their points of view. Knowledgeable diplomats, with their common professional ideals and similar experiences, are less likely than amateurs to misunderstand each other. Negotiations between them are thereby facilitated. Professor Paul Sharp posits that good diplomats share a theory of international relations that embraces "ambiguities and complexities" and that resists framing disputes in moral terms.[18] But political leaders and public opinion generally prefer clarity, especially moral clarity, to ambiguity, and, as Sharp warns, "Diplomats are the servants of their masters rather than of their profession."[19] A professional diplomat who brings an agreement home carries a heavy burden of proof: Did he or she achieve the maximum advantage for national interests and cede as little as possible to the other side? Especially after it is reached, an agreement negotiated by someone who sees an issue from more than one point of view may be suspected of failing this test.

Secretary of State George Shultz made it a practice to receive newly appointed American ambassadors in his office before they left Washington to take up their posts. He would take them over to a large globe that stood near the secretary's desk and ask them to "show me your country." When they did, Shultz would correct them. "No, that is the country to which you are assigned. Your country is here, the United States of America."[20]

No diplomat can afford to forget, even for a moment, for whom he works and whose interests he serves. It is not the country to which he is accredited, nor the world in general, nor the cause of peace. A diplomat serves his country, his people, and his government, and them only.

What Diplomats Do

As old as it is, the diplomatic profession is hard to pin down. Definitions of a diplomat range from the waggish ("an honest man sent to lie abroad for his country"), to the pompous ("the voice of their state in foreign lands . . . the peaceable heralds of its power"), to the mundane ("a person appointed by a national government to conduct official negotiations and maintain political, economic, and social relations with another country or countries").[21]

To complicate the question, the American foreign service defines its personnel by the department they work for, their job description, and their rank or pay grade. The matrix generates scores of pigeonholes but produces more confusion than enlightenment. In fact, just as the foreign service has a triple mission, the diplomatic profession has just three corresponding areas of practice: representation, operations, and policy (see chapter 1).

Representation

Representation is the efficient, precise, and persuasive transmission of information from the United States to foreign audiences, and from foreign sources to the US government. Four verbs define the work: talk, listen, report, negotiate. The craft—and occasional craftiness—involved can be learned and will improve with practice, but a lively curiosity and high level of social energy are essential to success.

The representational work of the foreign service is often described by analogy: Reporting is like journalism, public diplomacy is like advertising, negotiation is like law or business. These are all misleading.

Foreign service reporting is not journalism. It cannot and should not compete with the mainstream media in speed, immediacy, or shock value, but it can and should provide context and analysis that journalism does not.

Unlike journalists, foreign service reporters are actors, not observers. Their work is not done when they hit the Send button. Unlike journalism, foreign service reporting has direct implications for policy. It may generate replies in the form of instructions that the reporter then acts upon and carries out. If reports that seek action are merely sent and forgotten, however, they may be merely received and ignored. A foreign service reporter who wants to be heard must make some noise. "In Washington," wrote Henry Kissinger, "ideas do not sell themselves. Authors of memoranda who are not willing to fight for them are more likely to find their words turned into ex post facto alibis than guides to action."[22]

"Accurate reporting," said Ambassador Ron Neumann, "is a core skill of professional Foreign Service officers, but it needs constant emphasis and teaching to balance quality and speed."[23] Elegance of style is overrated. The value is in the work behind the text. Effective reporting that leads to action is grounded in hard-won experience, based on information not available from other sources, and persuasively presented. Despite the lingering fascination with George Kennan, whose eight-thousand-word telegram from Moscow in February 1946 shaped America's cold war policies for forty years, extended analysis is not what Washington wants from the field.[24] Policymakers can consult scores or hundreds of analysts in and out of government, but foreign service work has special value. "The most effective embassies," said Ambassador Barbro Owens-Kirkpatrick, "are those that put a robust list of suggestions for action at the end of every reporting cable, to help Washington know what it should be considering as a course of action."[25] Former National Security Adviser Brent Scowcroft said, "I want to know what our ambassador thinks," because the embassy is best able to interpret events on the ground.[26]

Public diplomacy is not advertising, or marketing, or brand management, and when it strays too far in those directions it often loses its effectiveness.[27] To influence public opinion abroad, the techniques and ethical norms of journalism and education, with their emphasis on information and truth seeking, have proven more successful than those of Madison Avenue, with their emphasis on repetition, hyperbole, and emotional manipulation. Over the years, the flow of personnel into and out of public diplomacy has been primarily with the news media and cultural organizations. However, after the creation of the position of undersecretary of state for public diplomacy in 1999, its first three occupants came from the fields of marketing, government relations, and political consulting (undersecretaries Charlotte Beers, Margaret Tutwiler, and Karen Hughes, respectively). The appointments of journalist James K. Glassman in 2008, and of Discovery Channel CEO Judith McHale in 2009, marked a return to earlier practice.

The comparison of diplomatic negotiations to law and business has some validity. Like negotiations between buyers and sellers, employers and employees, or litigants seeking a settlement, diplomatic negotiations are an effort to adjust relationships through compromise. Skills developed in one type of negotiation are transferable to another. George Shultz wrote that "a sense of strategy is critical in any negotiation: when to make concessions, when to hold firm, when to let things cool off, when to be intransigent." Shultz considered his training and experience as a labor economist and negotiator excellent preparation for diplomacy.[28]

But diplomatic negotiations present special problems. The gaps between the parties may be unusually wide. Differences of language, history, and culture mean that the parties to a negotiation may have different views of what they are talking about and why. And regardless of the issue under discussion, every country has its own style, its own negotiating behavior, shaped by the institutions of its government, its geopolitical position, and its unique culture. The scope for misunderstanding and miscalculation is quite broad.[29]

Professional diplomats who can bridge these gaps may come to understand each other but lose touch with their domestic masters who make the final decisions. Robert Gallucci, former dean of Georgetown University's School of Foreign Service and a negotiator of the 1994 nuclear agreement with North Korea, said that many Americans will attack any negotiated agreement because they are skeptical of negotiation. "It's an easy sophistry to go from 'We can never compromise our national security,' to 'We can never compromise where national security is concerned,' which means that any negotiation is suspect. I tell students, you have to get the support of the people for your enterprise."[30]

International negotiations often break down between negotiating rounds because, though the parties at the table want agreement and move toward each other, domestic interests in each country, typically not at the table, harden their positions and prevent compromise. Diplomats who do not maintain communication and credibility with domestic interests waste their cross-cultural skills, their training, and their time. Their work will end in failure.[31]

Unlike other talks, diplomatic negotiations are rarely grounded in a body of law accepted by all sides and enforceable by courts of justice armed with police powers. Instead, even the most genteel diplomatic negotiations generally take place in a lawless realm where the final agreement is enforced only by mutual self-interest. There are no courts, no police, and no certain compulsion short of war to ensure that the parties fulfill their obligations. A diplomatic agreement endures only as long as the parties consider it better than the alternatives.

Operations

Operations involve running systems, projects, and programs. The skills required are primarily technical and managerial. Foreign service specialists who run the communications, manage the money, maintain the buildings,

and protect the health, welfare, and security of official (and often unofficial) Americans abroad, are operational personnel. So are the consular officers, customs and border protection personnel, drug enforcement agents, and others who push the protection of US laws beyond the country's borders. So too are the rising stars of the foreign service, the men and women working on reconstruction, stabilization, and development in Iraq, Afghanistan, and other risky regions; organizing the rapid and relatively mishap-free evacuation of Americans from Lebanon in 2006 or the massive civil-military relief effort after the earthquake in Haiti in 2010; and running foreign assistance programs to combat poverty, disease, and lawlessness around the world.

Operations are the new growth area of American diplomacy. Until quite recently, the phrase *threat to American security* implied a military or political challenge to American interests or an economic development that posed a risk to American prosperity. Such threats were and still are met with traditional diplomacy, a mix of inducement and menace conveyed through official representations and designed to change state behaviors. Now the definition has been expanded to include epidemic diseases, environmental depredations, and other natural phenomena that traditional diplomacy, traditionally exercised, cannot easily address. The events of September 11, 2001, revealed the dangers that arise when states fail and governments no longer inhibit the most reckless, barbaric expressions of human hatred. Here too traditional diplomacy, conducted between states, has no effect. Diplomats with the skills and languages to take money and programs into the field and bring about societal changes are likely to be a rising proportion of the foreign service over the next ten or fifteen years, and as long as they are in short supply they are likely to progress faster than their colleagues.

Policy

In the diplomatic history of the United States, with its strong democratic traditions, professional diplomats have rarely achieved the influence over policy that they have done in other nations. Historian Dexter Perkins has written, "In a sense that is true in no such degree in other nations, American diplomatic action has been determined by the people." As a result, "the professional diplomat has always played a subordinate role" to "men with substantial political experience" who "pay heed to the voice of the great body of citizens" and "shape their decisions with that voice in mind."[32]

For the foreign service, policy involves advising the officials who define national interests and decide what resources should be deployed to secure them. Professional diplomats carry out policies. They try to manipulate events to produce the outcomes policymakers desire; at times, they serve as policymakers. Diplomats in a position to advise on policy must know how to bring their knowledge of foreign cultures, languages, institutions, leaders, aspirations, capabilities, and intents to bear constructively on the questions confronting the policymakers. That requires an understanding of how American foreign policy is made and an awareness of the forces, including the domestic political forces, that are at work on any issue. The value that the foreign service brings to the development of foreign policy is its knowledge of the motivations and levers of power in foreign countries, its sense of the range of possibilities in a negotiation, its ability to predict foreign reactions to a given set of circumstances, and its skill, based in language, personal contact, and a record of honest dealing, at communication without misunderstanding.

Experienced FSOs are uniquely qualified to advise policymakers on what is required—in human, financial, and physical resources; in time; and in political will—to carry their ideas into effect. Such advice is not always well received. Ron Neumann, American ambassador in Afghanistan in 2005–7, who devoted many hours and much energy to laying out the resource requirements for success to the Department of State, the National Security Council, and members of Congress, sounds almost plaintive about the difficulties he confronted: "Searching for a new strategy seems to be policymakers' default reaction to problems. Instead of asking whether the problem lies in some mix of funding, procedures, and troops—all of which would require additional money and people—to implement the strategy already decided, the search is launched for a new idea. Certainly ideas are come by more easily than money and soldiers."[33]

Diplomatic Practice

The three areas of diplomatic practice—representation, operations, and policy—are bounded by the blurriest of lines. An FSO over the course of a career can expect to train and perform in all three areas.

No foreign service job is confined to one area of practice. A consular officer, faced with the repetitive challenge of applying US law to an endless line of visa applicants, represents the United States on a powerful, personal level to scores of families each day. An AID chief of party (as project managers are called) is thoroughly operational, but he or she is also shaping public opinion and, through control of the disbursement of substantial US resources, shaping US policy as well. A commercial officer who represents US export interests is a source of advice for Washington on US commercial policy and strategy for trade negotiations. The most successful diplomatic professionals work in representation, operations, and policy simultaneously.

Carlucci in Portugal

Frank Carlucci, a career FSO who later served as national security adviser and secretary of defense, came to Portugal as ambassador in January 1975, eight months after a revolution by military officers who were fed up with colonial wars in Africa had toppled a rightist authoritarian government. In the political vacuum that followed, the country had a series of weak governments (six in two years) that moved successively to the left. Washington felt a rising level of concern that Portugal might become the first NATO country to fall under communist control.

Most concerned was Secretary of State Henry Kissinger, who told a conference of American ambassadors in Europe that "the dominance of Communist parties in the West is unacceptable. . . . It is hard to imagine that, if one or the other of these parties takes control of a Western government, it will permit the democratic process to operate and thereby face the possibility that it may itself be removed from office. . . . We must do our utmost to assure [*sic*] the survival of democratic processes and to preserve the Western political orientation of western European countries."[34]

Many at the State Department felt that "it was probably best to write Lisbon off and teach them a lesson" that would dissuade voters in other European countries, especially France and Italy, from following the Portuguese example. Carlucci and his embassy, however, argued for vigorous US support of the country's democratic parties, including in particular the socialists, in the belief that "the electoral process could serve to undermine communist control of the country." This conclusion was not based on faith; Carlucci had personal knowledge of Portuguese politics. "I would make it a goal of meeting at least two or three political figures a day," he told an interviewer in 1999. "I spent many, many hours in long debates and discussions with the prime minister," as well as with the foreign minister and the president. "I would go over and talk to the archbishop quietly, have lunch with him and find out what his views were. . . . I became fairly close to some of the original coup plotters [and] spent a lot of time with them."[35]

He fought for his position against bureaucratic opposition in Washington. He went to Brussels: "I went up to [the US mission to NATO] and participated in the drafting of a cable . . . recommending a military aid package for Portugal, and then went back to Portugal and wrote an endorsement of the USNATO cable." When the State Department said there were no funds, he went back to Washington, to the Office of Management and Budget (OMB), where he had been a deputy director. There he was told he needed congressional support. So he went to members who had Portuguese constituents and secured their backing. "It was unique," Carlucci said, "an ambassador pushing through his own aid program."[36]

Carlucci had experience with aid programs. In 1972 President Nixon had detailed him to supervise relief efforts after a hurricane had caused extensive flooding along the Susquehanna River. While still an FSO, Carlucci had served in the White House in the now defunct Office of Economic Opportunity (OEO), in the OMB, and as an undersecretary in the Department of Health, Education, and Welfare. He knew President Ford and his chief of staff Donald Rumsfeld, who had been his direct boss at OEO.

In June 1976, Carlucci used his political connections to arrange a meeting with the president. He then met with Secretary Kissinger, who in Carlucci's account "said something to the effect that the President has asked to see me. . . . At that meeting Henry did say that he would give my policy option a chance, he would back me. So, I told him there was no reason for me to go to the White House. Henry couldn't have been more supportive from that day on."[37]

These extraordinary efforts paid extraordinary dividends. France, Germany, and Britain joined the United States in a program of covert support for the democratic opposition. As Carlucci had predicted, the electoral process worked, a left-wing rebellion in the armed forces failed, and a socialist government took power with a decidedly Western orientation. The Portuguese example had a powerful effect in Spain, where, after the death of Europe's last fascist dictator, Francisco Franco, in November 1975, the transition to democracy was peaceful and the communists were marginalized. Spain joined the North Atlantic alliance in 1982, and no Communist Party members entered the government of any NATO country until well after the collapse of the Soviet Union and the end of the communist military threat.

Could an amateur have done what Carlucci did in Portugal? Not likely. Carlucci's immediate predecessor in Lisbon was an amateur and left behind what the undersecretary of state for management called "the worst embassy in the world."[38] Carlucci spoke Portuguese, which he had learned as an FSO in Brazil in the early 1960s, and had a grasp of the political dynamics in Lisbon. He was a visible, voluble spokesman for the US point of view, and he followed through on programs that established his credibility with key groups. He could navigate around the State Department, Congress, the White House, and NATO. In other words, he had mastered the skills of the profession, and when given the opportunity to perform at a high level, he justified his country's trust.

Happiness Is Multiple Pipelines

The combination Ambassador Carlucci displayed—policy insight with influence on one's own government and successful advocacy overseas—is the trifecta of high-level diplomacy. But diplomacy must adapt to circumstances. The public diplomacy Carlucci practiced relied on media access that is not always available. Despite the recent emphasis on operations that transform foreign societies from the bottom, diplomacy that relies almost wholly on official contacts has lost none of its importance. Foreign service reporting and analysis are still the US government's single most important source of intelligence. Government-to-government negotiations and face-to-face encounters with foreign leaders are still the most important tools in foreign relations. They are the tools that the foreign service applied to one of the most fascinating and important geopolitical puzzles of our time.

What may be the world's largest undeveloped reserves of oil and natural gas lie beneath the soil and inland seas of Central Asia and the Caucasus, in eight new countries that for most of the twentieth century were part of the Soviet Union. These countries are poor and erratically governed, with democratic institutions in their infancy or yet to be born. They face pressure from the north from a Russia that seeks to restore its influence, and from the south from an Islamist movement that finds supporters among tribes and clans with little sense of nationhood.

After the Soviet breakup, American policymakers, urged on by the new US embassies in places such as Baku, Tbilisi, Almaty, and Ashgabat, saw an opportunity. A commitment by the United States and the West to develop these oil reserves and bring them to market could increase and diversify global supplies; promote economic development and political stability across a volatile, strategically important region; forestall the expansion of Russian and Iranian influence; reduce the political space for violent Islamist extremism; and land some business for US companies. One stone, five birds.

Western energy companies had a strong interest in the region, but even companies accustomed to working in the world's least stable environments had doubts about investing in the Caucasus or Central Asia. Banks were doubly nervous about project finance. For their part, the new governments and state-owned oil companies in the region lacked experience in international negotiations and faced heavy pressure from Russia, which controlled all existing pipelines, to continue to market through Russian facilities exclusively.

The challenge for the United States was to build private-sector confidence in the possibility of success and persuade governments in the region that fair dealing with Western partners would produce results and revenues that Russian partners could not. Also important was to maintain good relations with Russia throughout the process. Many agencies of the US government were involved in the effort, but the foreign service led the way.

"The foreign service has unique strengths in energy affairs," said Steve Gallogly, director of the Office of International Energy and Commodity Policy in the State Department's Bureau of Economic and Business Affairs:

First is information. We are in touch with governments and US energy companies all over the world, all the time. We know the latest decree from the government of Peru, the latest projection of refining capacity in Venezuela, the latest estimate of gas reserves in Algeria. Second is access. Governments are mixed up in energy every step of the way, in exploration, development, extraction, production, transport, distribution. Foreign service people, including foreign service nationals, have access to policy people and especially leverage with them that US companies don't have. So US energy companies need to stay close to us. That gives the foreign service an ability to understand and influence how the energy companies behave.[39]

Transportation is the key to developing the resources of Central Asia and the Caucasus. One FSO working on the problem put a bumper sticker on his car: "Happiness is multiple pipelines." But in the end the main US effort aimed at developing an east-west pipeline route from Baku, the capital of Azerbaijan on the Caspian Sea, through Tbilisi in central Georgia and

Erzurum in western Turkey, to Ceyhan, a Turkish port on the Mediterranean. The United States launched an initiative that involved diplomatic efforts in half a dozen countries, as well as constant contact with energy, pipeline, and oilfield service companies; their bankers; and various international organizations. Controlling the initiative presented a managerial challenge that in fact is not unusual in the foreign service.

Because so many countries and agencies were involved, the US government named a special envoy, a senior official outside the usual bureaucratic structure with responsibility for a specific and limited issue. Special envoys don't always succeed. An envoy charged with accomplishing just one goal may easily end up in conflict with those who have other missions and other priorities. But because the Caspian Basin energy project served so many purposes, and because the special envoy was a foreign service professional familiar with the range of issues that the pipeline project would affect, internal conflicts were generally avoided.

The United States between 1996 and 2005 had four special envoys who traveled constantly throughout the region. They came to know the heads of state, the energy ministers, the oil company executives, the engineers, and the financiers. They built confidence through personal commitment and personal trustworthiness, and through an unyielding insistence on transparency.[40] They worked closely with US embassies in the region and enjoyed strong support from the intelligence community.

"The foreign service really is a team," said Ambassador Steven Mann, special envoy from 2001 to 2005. "The embassies welcomed someone who was following the issue in minute detail. And it didn't hurt that we all knew each other. The ambassadors in that part of the world were all veterans of work on Soviet affairs. We had all been junior officers together. That made our cooperation frictionless."[41]

The work was diplomacy of a high order, practiced at the ministerial and presidential levels. "For the countries involved we were the reality check," Ambassador Mann continued. "They would look at the documents and ask us, 'What's the meaning of this provision? What do you think of the environmental arrangements, the security provisions?' And we would tell them."

Over a decade, the US special envoys created the political infrastructure that supported the physical and financial infrastructure of the pipeline itself. In the end, eleven oil companies from eight countries joined the pipeline consortium, and nine oil companies from five countries joined the oilfield operating consortium. Even though US companies have only a 13 percent equity share in the new pipeline, "the United States is strongly identified with the project," Mann explained. "Our name is on it." The Baku-Tbilisi-Ceyhan pipeline, 1,100 miles long, opened May 25, 2005, and began moving 150,000 barrels per day to market. Five years later, the line was carrying up to 1.2 million barrels a day, close to 6 percent of US consumption and 1 percent of world demand.

With the opening of the pipeline, the work of the special envoy for Caspian Basin energy affairs was complete, but Steve Mann's expertise and unique knowledge of the region did not go to waste. He next moved on to become the State Department's special adviser on Europe's frozen conflicts—four unresolved ethnic and secessionist disputes in the former Soviet Union (Nagorno-Karabakh between Armenia and Azerbaijan, South Ossetia and Abkhazia on the borders of Georgia, and Moldova's eastern region of Transdniestria). In that capacity he traveled to many of the same capitals and dealt with many of the same people that he had come to know through his work on the pipeline. He built on the trust he enjoyed throughout the region to mediate these disputes, which threaten peace and stability in a volatile and strategic part of the world. "My job gives me the opportunity to work in policy and to execute," Mann said. "I have a free hand to travel to the countries, I decide on the tactics. I have great support from the rest of the State Department, from the Pentagon, and from the intelligence community. It's the best job in the foreign service."

Transformational Diplomacy to Smart Power

American diplomatic practice began to change after the attacks of September 11, 2001. The administration of George W. Bush, especially in its second term, introduced new methods and reordered the relative importance assigned to different types of diplomatic work. The administration of President Obama altered the terminology but carried forward, and often accelerated, most of the changes launched in the Bush administration. From Secretary Rice to Secretary Clinton, even where foreign policies and diplomatic strategies have shifted, the diplomatic tactics employed have not.

After the attacks of September 11, 2001, the Bush administration made the political transformation of other societies an explicit goal of American diplomacy. A White House paper, published in September 2002, put it this way: "The US national security strategy will be based on a distinctly American internationalism that reflects the union of our values and our national interests. The aim of this strategy is to help make the world not just safer but better."[42] A second *National Security Strategy*, published in April 2006, was even clearer: "The goal of our statecraft is to help create a world of democratic, well-governed states that can meet the needs of their citizens and conduct themselves responsibly in the international system. This is the best way to provide enduring security for the American people."[43]

The administration drew on and appealed to a long American tradition. The convictions that governments that respond to their people are less threatening than those that don't and that democratic reform abroad improves security at home are deeply rooted in American political thought and experience. So is the belief that American foreign policy should promote democracy in foreign lands. The United States from its founding embraced certain human rights as God-given and universal, and from the early days of the country's twentieth-century emergence as a global power, it sought "a world made safe for democracy."[44] Ambassador Carlucci's active intervention in Portuguese politics certainly favored democratic outcomes, but the language of the Bush administration (and in particular of Secretary Rice), which described the impulse to change foreign societies as transformational diplomacy, used universal, moral terms that Ambassador Carlucci, Secretary Kissinger, and President Nixon did not employ.

Traditional diplomacy aims to influence how states relate to other states. "Governments," wrote Henry Adams, "were meant to deal with governments, not with private individuals or the opinions of foreign society."[45] Transformational diplomacy aims also—even primarily—to influence how states behave inside their own borders.

This shift of emphasis implied a change in American diplomatic practice and in the demands placed on the foreign service. Rice told an audience at Georgetown University's School of Foreign Service that the nature of risk in the postcommunist world required a new diplomatic mission: "The greatest threats now emerge more within states than between them. The fundamental character of regimes now matters more than the international distribution of power.... We seek to use America's diplomatic power to help foreign citizens to better their own lives and to build their own nations and to transform their own futures."[46] In seeking resources for the Department of State, she told the Congress much the same: "This time of global transformation calls for transformational diplomacy. More than ever, America's diplomats will need to be active in spreading democracy, reducing poverty, fighting terror, and doing our part to protect our homeland."[47]

The first reaction of most members of the professional foreign service was applause, mixed with a sense that appreciation of their work was overdue. "United States foreign policy has been encouraging democracy for a hundred years," said retired Ambassador Tom Boyatt. "And you know what? It's been a huge success."[48] "I think it's what we've been doing all along," Ambassador Rea Brazeal observed. "The Georgetown speech reminded me of the Home Depot slogan: 'You can do it but we'll be there to help.'" Another ambassador with long service in Africa said, "I think we started about fifteen years ago to do what Secretary Rice calls transformational diplomacy." A public diplomacy officer with twenty years of service remarked, "I've been doing transformational diplomacy since the beginning of my career."[49]

Some saw the risks. What if a host government did not wish to see its country transformed? Would it consider transformational diplomacy subversive agitation and interference in internal affairs, another example of US imperial arrogance? Some scoffed. A retired ambassador called "this transformational diplomacy nonsense" a fad or a mistake that would end when Rice and the administration left office.

The retired ambassador was half right. Although the Obama administration killed the name—transformational diplomacy was out, "smart power" was in—it kept much of the practice. "The ideas behind it made sense," said Harry Thomas, head of State Department human resources during the transition.[50] The Obama administration also dropped its predecessor's idealistic rhetoric, which paradoxically had drawn inspiration from Democratic forebears, especially Woodrow Wilson and Jimmy Carter. The Obama administration's approach drew more on Republican realists like Theodore Roosevelt and Richard Nixon.

Harvard professor Joseph Nye had coined the term *soft power* to refer to the diplomatic power of attraction, which he defined as inducing others to do what you want without coercion or bribery. He later used the term *smart power* to refer to the ability to make soft and hard (coercive) power work together. Secretary Clinton described smart power as "central to our thinking and our decision-making." She defined it as "the intelligent use of all means at our disposal ... a blend of principle and pragmatism." And she popularized smart power with phrases borrowed from her predecessor, linking diplomacy, defense, and development—called the three D's or Diplomacy 3.0—as the three equal pillars of American foreign policy and stressing the importance of interagency coordination in a whole-of-government approach to policy execution. For those parts of a whole-of-government approach over which the secretary of state had greatest control, diplomacy, and development, Secretary Clinton added one more phrase to the lexicon: civilian power.[51]

Transformational diplomacy, smart power, and civilian power had similar implications for American diplomatic practice and for career diplomacy. Members of the foreign service saw staff at embassies in western and eastern Europe cut back and shifted, along with other resources, to China, India, central and near eastern Asia, and to regions where governments were unstable or dangerously weak. They saw a shift toward operations and away from reporting and analysis; toward spending more time in civil (or in some countries, clerical) society and less with foreign government officials; toward a higher premium on speaking foreign languages well, especially the languages of the Middle East and the developing world, and a lesser premium on writing in English. The Department of State placed greater stress on public diplomacy and on integrating foreign assistance with other elements of foreign policy. In conflict and postconflict regions, foreign service personnel would work literally side by side with US and allied military forces to build up friendly local authorities, establish local institutions to provide basic public services, and promote short- and long-term economic development. Skills in planning and managing complex operations, which neither the foreign service nor the civil service in the Department of State had ever really cultivated, became highly prized. FSOs and specialists whose careers were already focused in these areas saw opportunities for more rapid advancement, and those with less experience in the developing or unstable countries became concerned that their work might be undervalued.

Inside the Department of State and AID, discussion of ways in which the foreign service would adapt to the new diplomatic strategy and tactics eclipsed debate about the strategy itself or the policies it supports. Building a service with a different mix of skills required changes in recruitment, hiring, retention, training, assignments, and promotions. Such changes, discussed in part III of this book, will show their full effect only after some years, as they work their way through the corps. Overseas, diplomats adopted new practices on the fly, with varying degrees of success.

Fighting AIDS

Diplomacy that promotes security through social change in foreign countries is not confined to counterinsurgency. The President's Emergency Program for AIDS Relief (PEPFAR), launched in 2003, is the exercise of smart, civilian, and soft power, at its most successful. The program began with the recognition that AIDS, beyond the threat it poses to public health and economic development in countries where it is prevalent, is also a matter of national security to the United States. The program's objectives are to prevent the spread of the disease and to improve the treatment and care of those infected or affected, with a focus on the fifteen countries, twelve in Africa, where more than half of the world's HIV-infected population lives.[52] Achieving these objectives, or just moving toward them, requires changing the behavior of individuals, social groups, and governments. In smart-power terms, PEPFAR links US medical knowledge to US persuasive power, brings multiple actors to bear on the problem, and backs the enterprise with plenty of money—$18 billion in the first five years and more than $5 billion a year thereafter.

The year 2004, when the first PEPFAR funds were appropriated, was a time of White House and congressional dissatisfaction with the status quo in foreign aid. New approaches were the order of the day. The year before, Congress deliberately placed the new Millennium Challenge Corporation outside of USAID and the Department of State and chartered it to promote economic growth in poor countries. Later that year, with administration support, Congress put the US military in the foreign aid business with section 1206 of the Defense Authorization Act, enacted in October 2004. In the same spirit, Randall Tobias, the administration's choice for global AIDS coordinator and first director of PEPFAR, promised "a new way of doing business." Tobias, who had just retired as chief executive of the pharmaceutical company Eli Lilly, wanted to put his own PEPFAR people overseas, to make sure the program would be run as he wanted.

That did not happen. Ambassador Jimmy Kolker, deputy global AIDS coordinator, told the story this way:

> The day after taking office, Tobias left to attend the annual conference of US ambassadors serving in Africa. His deputy, John Lange—my predecessor—went with him. Like me, John was a career FSO, a former ambassador to Botswana. He urged Tobias to hold off on his plans. "You already have a staff in the field," John told him. Tobias spent an entire morning with the US ambassadors in the designated focus countries—I was ambassador in Uganda then—and each one of us gave a briefing on AIDS, not just the numbers and ongoing programs, but the different political and cultural factors that affected possibilities for care, treatment, and prevention.

Tobias was impressed. Ambassadors wanted responsibility, authority, and resources to tackle the problem. We were ready to move. The idea of bringing on a new staff just fell away. PEPFAR went in just the other direction, decentralizing decisions and minimizing staff.

The State Department office that manages PEPFAR, the Office of the Global AIDS Coordinator, has just seventy people, running a budget of $15 billion over five years. The bulk of the work is done in the field, by country teams of PEPFAR agencies headed by the ambassador. The main agencies are State, USAID, and the Centers for Disease Control.

The teams write the COPs, I mean the country operating plans, and ambassadors sign off on them. These are detailed plans, sometimes several hundred pages, that set out HIV/AIDS targets and plans to meet them, linked to partners and resource levels. The partners are the local organizations, public and private, that do the work. The COPs have to be integrated with each country's national HIV/AIDS strategy. All the programs are flexible. We share best practices, but we adapt everything to local circumstances.

This is where the foreign service shines. Our local knowledge of partners, of who's reliable, of what works in the local environment has been tested again and again, and we've passed gloriously. We know the local conditions, constraints, and capabilities. We've been able to make the connection between the scientific and economic data—we've got lots of data—and the public policies that can set priorities and put the data to work.

We give the COPs a technical review and a policy review, but we don't micromanage. We might spend many hours on a review, but the review is also the clearance for the agencies in the program. We give the posts what they determine will achieve best results, within the guidelines that Congress and the administration establish and the limits of the total budget. In my thirty years of experience in the foreign service, what we see in PEPFAR is an unprecedented level of trust in our ambassadors and embassies.[53]

The program has had considerable success. By fiscal year 2010, PEPFAR had reached more than 3.2 million patients with antiretroviral treatment and had brought care to another 11 million people infected or affected by the disease.[54] A May 2009 study found that mortality from the human immunodeficiency virus (HIV) dropped by 10.5 percent in the twelve PEPFAR focus countries, which suggested that the program over five years averted 1.2 million deaths. Congress has given strong and bipartisan support, appropriating $6.5 billion for PEPFAR for fiscal year 2009 alone. The program is losing its emergency character and is focusing more on building capacity in host governments to manage and operate their health systems. But PEPFAR'S approach to management has not changed: "Decisions on country-level activities are made by the USG country teams," said Jimmy Kolker; "a whole-of-government model," said the QDDR.[55]

"I have no training in public health," said Ambassador Kolker, "but foreign service skills and foreign service experience give me the perspective I need, and I can learn the rest. I love this work. Maybe I was born for this job." Ambassador Kolker retired from the foreign service in 2007. He is now chief of the HIV/AIDS section at the United Nations International Children's Emergency Fund (UNICEF).

Smart Power on the Northwest Frontier

Steve Mann's success showed the value of persistence and steadiness. But when the situation is precarious, steadiness is hard to achieve.

Few situations outside of combat zones are as precarious as that of Pakistan's Northwest Frontier Province, the rugged and breathtakingly beautiful region that lies east and south of Afghanistan, north and west of Kashmir, and north of Pakistan's federally administered tribal areas. It was here in 1897 that twenty-three-year-old Brigade Major Winston Churchill was decorated for bravery in battle with "fierce wild warlike Afghan tribes," where, he said, "civilisation is face to face with militant Mohammedanism."[56]

For more than fifty years, the United States has maintained a diplomatic presence, a consulate, in Peshawar, the capital of the province.[57] The consulate is the focal point for US efforts to understand the politics of this strategically vital region and to win understanding and support for the US struggle against its enemies in Afghanistan and on the Pakistani side of the border.

Lynne Tracy was the top US official, the principal officer, at the Peshawar consulate from 2006 to 2009. It was not her first tour there, she explained.

> I joined the foreign service in 1994 as a political officer with a degree in Russian studies and a law degree. I wanted a post that would fit my background, but there was nothing available in the former Soviet Union when I was ready for assignment. But Peshawar was open. I thought about the Soviet failure in Afghanistan, and I went to Peshawar as an Afghanistan watcher in 1995, when we had no embassy in Kabul. I had the most amazing first tour. It was the time of the rise of the Taliban, but a time when

foreigners could still travel freely, and mostly safely. I probably visited every major Afghan city except Kandahar.[58]

Tracy left Peshawar in 1997 to do consular work (and refurbish her Russian) in Bishkek, Kyrgyzstan, and she followed that tour with work in Washington on the former Soviet Union. Then came the attacks of September 11, 2001. "In 2002, they began sending people to Kabul on one-year assignments, and I went out. We had freedom of movement in Kabul, but I saw more of Afghanistan when I was posted to Peshawar than to Kabul. When I left Kabul in September 2003, the indicators of trouble were on the rise. An ISAF [International Security Assistance Force] bus was attacked in Kabul, a Red Cross expat worker was murdered near Kandahar—we were in a deteriorating security situation."

Tracy worked for the next three years on Kazakhstan, a year in Washington, and two as the principal officer at the embassy's branch office in the country's capital-under-construction, Astana.

When a posting to Peshawar opened up, I wanted to go back. I'd had a wonderful time there, and I thought I could contribute. When I got back to Peshawar, the post had grown, from ten Americans in the 1990s, maybe five State and five DEA [Drug Enforcement Agency], to about forty in 2006. By the time I left in 2009, we were up to about eighty Americans. But we had lost ground politically since my first tour. In the 1990s, as part of USIA budget exercise, we shut the American center in Peshawar and lost a huge resource.[59]

We made the most of our opportunities. The public diplomacy section had very strong relationships with the university—it was a godsend to have those contacts. We were able to host events at the university, my predecessor opened a Lincoln corner [a multimedia library about the United States] there in the spring of 2006, we had students in. We had good cooperation. The students gave us lots of criticism, but there were healthy exchanges.

We couldn't do enough political work. The appetite for information, in Washington and in the embassy in Islamabad, was insatiable. When I arrived Ambassador [Ryan] Crocker had been two years in country and had absorbed quite a bit, but he supported the need to provide Washington a lot of basic information—how the judicial system functions, how government services are delivered, the history of governance. Information had to be constantly refreshed, updated or recapitulated, as Washington staff turned over. We sent in a lot of primers. We saw that how things functioned in the tribal areas was different than in settled areas. We explored the differences between the Northwest Frontier Province and other areas, differences in ethnicity, economics, et cetera. The political section was very engaged.

Demonstrating US steadiness and willingness to persist to a skeptical Pakistani audience tested Tracy's managerial skills, and eventually her nerve. Management in this case had two sides, managing resources and managing policy:

> I did a lot of political work, I was the public face of the consulate, and I had a huge job running operations. USAID opened an office, and OTI [AID's Office of Transition Initiatives] came in. We added a couple of military liaison officers. Special Forces people came in to provide training to the Pakistani Frontier Corps. Those additions were a big part of the increase from forty to eighty Americans. Peshawar was not Iraq, and State really had the lead, the job of reconciling the work and the missions of the various agencies, making sure they all meshed and reinforced each other.

The growing number of USAID officers in the consulate was a fraction of the growing number of USAID contractors in the field. Most USAID projects are aimed at economic development or humanitarian relief. OTI bridges the gap between the two. "Small infrastructure," Tracy explained, "a lot of it having to do with water—digging wells, irrigation, building retaining walls. Refurbishing schools." The contractors hired local staff whenever possible, to build goodwill, ensure language skills at the job site, and reduce reliance on Americans who needed extra security and permission from the Pakistani government to travel in the tribal areas.

The Pakistani government at all levels was concerned about USAID and its contractors operating without regard to the government's interest or desires. "I called on contractors in the field, met with their staffs, and regularly asked local government officials and host community contacts for feedback on how they were doing," said Tracy. "Over time we moved from skepticism on the part of the government to a very appreciative attitude, and high regard for the model that AID developed. But as security deteriorated, keeping in touch with provincial-level officials, especially those outside the city of Peshawar, became a growing problem." Tracy sees persistence as a key to success:

Why was I effective in Peshawar, to the extent that I was, despite the security situation? Part of it is just continuity, being there three years, and on a second tour. Continuity gives us credibility with our local partners. I stuck around long enough, I was able to build a good relationship with provincial officials and local Pakistani military officers. Internally, I went through three cycles [of people on one-year tours] and became the continuity not just for State but even for other agencies. I knew how AID and the US military worked at the post. We have a decent level of institutional memory through our local staff, but we need American institutional memory too, and we don't have enough of it. It's a tough problem to solve, but we will continue to be handicapped in what we're trying to do if we cycle people out of there after only one year.[60]

On August 26, 2008, as she rode from her home to work, Tracy's vehicle was attacked by gunmen in an SUV, who shot out the front tires and riddled the car with bullets. She survived, thanks to the car's armor and protective action by her bodyguard and driver, who also came through. Tracy had already extended her two-year assignment for a third year. Despite the attack, she went to the office the same day to reassure staff and remained at her post to the end of her tour. Secretary Clinton later presented her with the State Department's award for heroism:

For the next year, Lynne continued serving as a public face of our mission in Pakistan, hosting several iftaars for members of the Pakistani community just weeks after the attack, even hosting some of the Consulate's official visitors in her home when it was too dangerous for them to stay in hotels. By working with the local population—even as the militants' presence grew stronger and the threats on the Consulate became more frequent—Lynne helped strengthen the Pakistani people's trust and confidence in the United States and in our efforts to help bring stability to that country.[61]

Staying on after an attack was the strongest possible representation of US will to persist. USAID and its contractors stayed on too, even after a contractor, Stephen Vance, was murdered in a similar attack three months later. The attacks brought new security restrictions on movement and led to the transfer of some staff to the more secure embassy in Islamabad, but they did not stop the consulate's work. After the attack, said Tracy, "I had a lot of access. I realized talking to Pakistani friends that staying on was an important signal. What I went through was not so different from what many Pakistanis were experiencing. I'm not saying you should want something like this to happen so you can form a bond, but it certainly strengthened my credibility and that of the United States. It said, we're not going anywhere, we're going to stick it out."[62]

5

The Foreign Service at War

The work that Carlucci, Mann, Kolker, and Tracy did was what American diplomats have been doing for many years, at least since the 1960s. Their purpose was to enhance American security and prosperity by achieving objectives that were primarily political (Carlucci), politico-military (Tracy), economic (Mann), or humanitarian (Kolker). Although none of them would have used terms like *transformational diplomacy* or *smart power*, their diplomacy was intended to change behavior within states as much as between them, and it used the influence and resources of many agencies of government.

Diplomacy in a combat zone, or in a fragile, militarized environment that is short of combat, is different. There is little tradition or history of diplomatic practice to draw on. In the conventional wars of the past, diplomats were pushed to the side. In December 1941, immediately after the declaration of war, American diplomats in Germany and Japan, and German and Japanese diplomats in the United States, were arrested, interned, treated fairly well, and exchanged within months for their counterparts.[1] The conditions of war and a political objective of unconditional surrender left little room for diplomacy between belligerents until the shooting stopped.

The war in Vietnam, which combined elements of conventional warfare with counterinsurgency operations, marked a departure from past practice. Under the CORDS program, FSOs from State and USAID were deployed in civilian-military teams in large numbers in South Vietnam, in relatively peaceful areas, to conduct political-economic programs intended, in the phrase of the time, to win the hearts and minds of the population. And, of course, the American Embassy in Saigon, which managed the difficult and dangerous relationship with the government of South Vietnam and ran the pacification program of which CORDS was a part, was by far the largest US mission at the time. "Military proficiency," wrote General Wesley Clark, who, as a young major, was wounded in combat in Vietnam, is "just one component of any larger national security operation. Many of us thought we'd learned this already, in Vietnam." But Iraq and Afghanistan, he said, showed the need to learn again how to mount an effort "whose requirements extend beyond the traditional air, land, sea, and space forces of the organized military to encompass integrated diplomacy, political and economic development, and intelligence operations."[2]

Not only Vietnam was forgotten. Ambassador James Dobbins has pointed out that, at the time of the invasion of Iraq in March 2003, the United States had recent experience in liberating and helping to rebuild six other societies—Kuwait, Somalia, Haiti, Bosnia, Kosovo, and Afghanistan—of which all but Haiti were predominantly Muslim. But, as Dobbins wrote, "neither the American military nor any of the relevant civilian agencies had regarded post-conflict stabilization and reconstruction as a core function," and if lessons were learned in these struggles, they were ignored.[3]

The United States invaded Iraq with little attention to planning for the aftermath of the quick battlefield victory that transpired. National Security Presidential Directive 24, issued in January 2003, only two months before the invasion of Iraq and three months before the fall of Saddam Hussein and his regime, gave the Pentagon lead responsibility for postwar Iraq. The Defense Department hurriedly established an Office of Reconstruction and Humanitarian Affairs and brought Army Lieutenant General Jay Garner out of retirement to head it. Ambassador Barbara Bodine was in Kuwait and Baghdad in March–April 2003 as the senior State Department member of that office. "There was," she wrote, "no staff, no structure, no recruiting process, and no resources."[4]

The Office of Reconstruction and Humanitarian Affairs gave way to a new Coalition Provisional Authority (CPA) established in Baghdad in May 2003 and headed by retired career FSO L. Paul (Jerry) Bremer, who reported to the secretary of defense and to the president.[5] Bremer left Iraq and the CPA dissolved on June 28, 2004, following the election of an Iraqi government and the arrival of a US ambassador, career FSO John Negroponte. In late 2005, with levels of violence in Iraq rising toward civil war, the president issued National Security Presidential Directive 44, which assigned the Department of State to lead in the political stabilization and economic reconstruction of countries and regions "at risk of, in, or in transition from conflict or civil strife."[6] The department and the ambassador, however, had no authority over the 135,000 American armed forces in the country.

It should come as no surprise, then, that American diplomats in Iraq and Afghanistan struggled to define and fulfill their roles. The diplomatic effort was unprecedented in scale and ambition. By 2009 the Baghdad embassy was the world's largest, with a budget of around $1.6 billion and a staff of more than 1,800 employees and 13,000 contract personnel. The embassy in Kabul was a close second, with a staff of more than 1,200 employees and plans for rapid expansion.[7] In both countries, the task of the embassy, including personnel working in the field, was to create the political and economic environment for defeating insurgencies, to build functioning democracies from the bottom up. In both countries, the United States had anticipated a quick military victory and had not planned on confronting a subsequent insurgency. The counterinsurgency effort, of which the embassy was the civilian side, was late and initially haphazard.

In Iraq the work of the foreign service in the immediate wake of the invasion was unstructured and improvisational. As security deteriorated it became progressively more constrained, with objectives more narrowly defined but no less difficult to accomplish. Security did not improve until 2008, when the United States increased its troop levels and modified its political strategy. In Afghanistan security deteriorated from 2005 until well into 2009. Secretary Clinton testified in April 2009 that "in Afghanistan, the casualty rate for USAID employees, contract employees, locally engaged employees, and other international aid workers, is, one in ten have been killed in the last eight years. Our comparable percentage for military casualties in Afghanistan is one in fifty-seven."[8]

The mission of stabilization and reconstruction was a test of the idea, the soundness of which many doubted, that diplomats can do this work. The enormity of the challenges in Iraq and Afghanistan forced the foreign service, an institution famously slow to change, into new thinking and new behaviors that continue to shape the service and will do so for years to come.

Provincial Reconstruction Teams

The term *provincial reconstruction team* (PRT) was first adopted in Afghanistan, where American and allied forces began stability operations soon after the fall of Kabul in November 2001.

In Afghanistan

According to Ambassador Bob Perito of the US Institute of Peace, the PRTs began as " 'Coalition Humanitarian Liaison Cells' that the US military forces

... established in early 2002." By the end of 2002, the first PRT, adding a few US civilian officials and a force protection component to a military outpost, opened in the province of Gardez. Other PRTs quickly followed. The US embassy in Kabul defined the PRT mission in early 2003: extend the authority of the Afghan central government, improve security, and promote reconstruction.[9] That definition remained valid in 2010. Although the PRTs were a US creation, many of the countries participating in the NATO-led International Security Assistance Force (ISAF) established PRTs or took over PRT locations from US forces. By early 2010, the US military operated nine PRTs in Afghanistan, and other ISAF countries led another fourteen.

The foreign service had little to do with the PRTs in Afghanistan at the outset. The teams were almost entirely military, and as late as 2009, a typical team in a US-led PRT had 80 to 250 members but only three or four civilians, one each from USAID, the Department of State, the Department of Agriculture, and the Afghan ministry of the interior.[10] The military predominance was true in all US locations, even in regions that were relatively secure. The civilian role, though small, was vital, and often poorly managed. The foreign service agencies were unable to meet the demands placed on them in Afghanistan. They had neither the people nor the skills nor the money required.

Even though the State Department had ordinarily to provide only one FSO to a PRT, gaps and vacancies were frequent enough and long enough to provoke a complaint in May 2006 from the CENTCOM commander General John Abizaid to the American ambassador in Kabul, Ronald Neumann. The ambassador explained to the general that they "had created new PRTs and political officer positions with the regional commands at the military's request, but the personnel system could not find and forward new officers to keep up with even the handful of additional new positions. . . . John wrote back . . . 'My concern is that the Government of the United States needs to be in the field to its full capacity everywhere if we expect to win this war. That we have fallen short for nearly five years is a disgrace.'" As Neumann noted later, "The problem was not just the State Department but the lack of civilians from the Departments of Justice, Agriculture, and others. . . . The administration needed to put the country on a war footing, not only by ordering other cabinet departments to participate but by finding the funding for them to do so. That was not happening."[11]

Panjshir

The PRT in the Panjshir valley is a case in point. The valley, northeast of Kabul, was the stronghold of Ahmad Shah Massoud, the Tajik leader of the Northern Alliance who was assassinated two days before September 11, 2001. The Northern Alliance, supported by US special forces, led the march into Kabul two months later. "The Panjshiris," wrote Ambassador Neumann, "were solidly anti-Taliban and well able to control who entered the valley."[12] As a result, members of the PRT moved about relatively freely, at least until a suicide bomber killed four team members in an attack on a PRT convoy in May 2009.[13]

Civilian staff were hard to find and skills were sketchy. Amy Frumin, an AID FSO, wrote that when she arrived in Panjshir in July 2006 to take the position of USAID representative on the PRT, the position had been vacant for nine months.[14] USAID, Ambassador Neumann wrote, did not have the personnel to implement technical projects. The agency relied on contractors, as it does in most of the world, but in Afghanistan it did not have the personnel to oversee the contracts. USAID in 2006–7 had one American FSO and two Afghan foreign service nationals at the Panjshir PRT, managing two PRT contracts with three-year budgets of about $120 million and several other USAID contracts. In Washington, at the end of 2008, USAID had seven people working on the Afghanistan country desk—one FSO and six contractors.[15]

Frumin faced bureaucratic rigidities that had a Joseph Heller quality. Team members held meetings with village elders and district leaders to discuss what projects would best meet local needs. By May 2006, USAID had promised to build women's health facilities in each district. But money could not be obligated until project proposals had been prepared and sent up the bureaucratic chain for approval. The military commander of the PRT offered to help prepare the documents that USAID required, but AID officials in Kabul, fearful that the military would end up implementing an AID project that should belong to the consulting company that was AID's implementing partner in Panjshir, said no. By the time the project proposals were complete in good form, money that had been available—about $1.5 million—had been swallowed up by the consulting company's overruns elsewhere. New money came through in April 2007, but only $600,000—enough for equipment but not construction. The equipment was purchased and given to Afghan midwives, but instead of earning goodwill for American generosity, the project was remembered as a serious disappointment—remembered at least by the Afghans.[16] With a year's delay between the meetings with the elders and the funding of the projects, the Americans who had promised the buildings had all finished their tours of duty and were gone before their promises were broken.

Long-term projects fared better. Between 2004 and 2006, USAID built a paved road into the valley that linked farms to markets and improved the reach of the central government by halving travel time to Kabul.[17] Indeed, once policymakers in Washington came to accept that the United States would need to remain in the country for the long haul, road building, with projects planned jointly by USAID and the Army Corps of Engineers, became the centerpiece of US assistance for Afghanistan's infrastructure.[18]

The road projects and other long-term projects at which AID excelled were managed out of Kabul and Washington, not out of the PRTs. The civilian side of the PRTs in Afghanistan were not designed, staffed, or funded to manage long-term projects. Yet as Amy Frumin learned, they had neither the resources nor the bureaucratic agility to manage short-term projects either. They could determine the needs of the local population, but they had to rely on others, often the military, for funding and support.

Failed Project Cycle

That reliance often led to conflicts between the civilians and the military, conflicts rooted in the different missions and cultures of the two organizations. Frumin wrote that in Panjshir, where livestock were essential to the well-being of the population, the military and the civilians in the PRT agreed on the desirability of improving veterinary medicine. USAID set up a project to equip and train Afghan veterinary field units, but the military brought in American veterinarians who provided free veterinary services. The military program undercut the initiative. USAID wanted to build a self-sustaining Afghan capacity, but the military, said Frumin, wanted to win friends and push into areas they had not yet reached.[19]

Similar tensions developed in Iraq. The military favored programs like garbage collection that would immediately employ large numbers of youth, even at US expense, and get them off the streets, but the State Department looked for ways to develop long-term economic activities that Iraqis would own and operate. David Satterfield, senior adviser to the secretary of state on Iraq and former deputy chief of mission in Baghdad, spoke about an anonymous army officer quoted in an army manual on lessons learned in the PRTs: "The State Department wants to build Iraqi capacity. We need to get shit done." Satterfield commented, "One of our gifted PRT leaders has a great cycle called the Failed Project Cycle, pointing out how 'getting shit done' actually makes things worse a lot of times. If it's not incorporated into the Iraqi budget cycle, and we build it for them, then they don't maintain it, they don't staff it, they expect us to, we're mad at them because they didn't do it, they're mad at us because we didn't do it.... That's a bad cycle. We would argue that getting stuff done is actually not the top priority."[20]

In Iraq

In the months after coalition forces invaded Iraq, diplomats joined with military officers in what were initially called governorate coordination teams, small civilian-led groups whose mission was to strengthen local governments and make them responsive and accountable to the local population. The teams in Iraq were largely improvisational; they relied on insight, quick-wittedness, luck, and a monopoly of military power. When any of these were lacking, the teams lost their influence over events. "Improvisation," Ambassador Robert Perito pointed out, "is not a concept of operations."[21]

The teams were disbanded in 2004, then reconstituted as PRTs in 2005, and greatly expanded in 2007. Many of the PRTs wound down their work in 2010 as US armed forces began their withdrawal. The teams initially relied heavily on Defense Department funds in the Commanders Emergency Response Program (CERP), whose expenditure could be authorized on the spot by military commanders at the brigade level. Later, additional US money became available through various civilian foreign assistance appropriations, chiefly economic support funds (ESF) and a small quick response fund (QRF), a civilian counterpart of the CERP. But the PRTs were relatively small spenders. Once an Iraqi government was in place in Baghdad in June 2004, PRT efforts turned to helping local authorities identify projects to be funded from Iraqi, not US, sources.

The PRTs in Iraq differed from their namesakes in Afghanistan in structure and mission. In Afghanistan, a "model PRT," as designed by the US Combined Forces Command in 2006, numbered eighty-three military and four civilian personnel—but only sixteen people, including the civilians, had duties that took them outside the wire to interact with the local population. The commander was a military officer with the rank of lieutenant colonel.[22] A typical PRT in Iraq was larger, more diverse, and led by an FSO from the

Department of State. In some Iraq PRTs, the Department of State hired contractors to provide security, which did not happen in Afghanistan. Beginning in 2007, some Iraq PRTs were embedded in combat brigades in the most dangerous parts of the country—but even there, the civilian and military components were on a roughly equal footing. The PRTs in Afghanistan, as the name implies, worked at the provincial level. In Iraq, a PRT was not necessarily provincial, and its focus was likely to be less on reconstruction (the Iraq PRTs had no funds for infrastructure) than on long-term political and economic development.

Major General Rick Olson, who commanded all the PRTs in Afghanistan in 2004–5 and oversaw PRT operations in Iraq in 2006–7, contrasted the missions in the two countries: The PRTs in Afghanistan, he said, were "more intimately involved with the counterinsurgency effort, they were more interested in short-term effects . . . to convince the population that the coalition and the Afghan government had a more attractive alternative to offer than did the Taliban." In Iraq, however, "the primary mission was what we called capacity development," a long-term endeavor to build "a capability in governing bodies to deliver to the people" what governments are supposed to provide.[23]

Despite false starts and a mixed record, the still-evolving PRTs are a model for future cooperation between the foreign service and the military in troubled regions—not necessarily war zones—that present an actual or potential threat to the national security of the United States. The stories that follow are ground-level, first-person accounts told during or soon after the events they describe. They show, without benefit of hindsight, the range of challenges that confronted the PRTs and their personnel, and they show how foreign service work in Iraq changed over the grim course of the war.

"Get the Diplomat in Here!"—Provincial Reconstruction, 2003

Toby Bradley, a five-year veteran of the foreign service, arrived in Nasiriyah in September 2003, six months after US and allied forces crossed the border into Iraq. The Coalition Provisional Authority in Baghdad had charged him with setting up a civilian presence in Dhi Qar province that could organize economic reconstruction and turn power over to Iraqi authorities who were yet to be chosen. Bradley recalls the experience:

> I was the political adviser on what was called a governorate coordination team, headed by a British FSO, John Bourne. An Italian force provided

security, and some Romanian troops were there as well. There were five officers in the team when I arrived, and more than a hundred when I left [eight months later]. There were similar teams in seventeen of the eighteen provinces, most of them staffed by military civil-affairs personnel. The idea was that we were the CPA presence, able to nationalize CPA policies and identify problems that needed CPA attention. We were to report on what was happening, build up the infrastructure needed for reconstruction, and solve problems or flag them for Baghdad.[24]

The team in Nasiriyah operated pretty much on its own. "We didn't really have communications," Bradley said.

We had no reliable phone system. We had satellite phones, but we had to be outside to use them, and that raised security issues. So we stayed in touch with Hotmail and Yahoo mail accounts.

I was assigned as the political adviser, but my work was much broader. We'd roll into a town and ask to see the city council. I never knew if two, ten, or a hundred people would show up. I asked them what they wanted to do, how we could help, and get them to set some priorities in the process. It was difficult to get the idea across. They had grown accustomed to receiving whatever policies Baghdad handed down. They had never articulated their needs before. At night I'd report what I'd learned to John Bourne, and he would get the different ministries to work on the issues. There were twenty cities in the province, so I was on the road most of the time.

Bradley and other members of the team organized council elections around Dhi Qar province. "I had no training for this," he recounted, "other than my experience growing up in a democratic society. And I had some Arabic from a six-month State Department course and a tour doing visa and political work in Amman, Jordan." The first election efforts were rocky:

In the town of Ad Dawwayah, Sheikh Saoud, a tribal leader, had taken control, and a cleric who opposed him headed the committee to prepare for elections. The sheik complained to me that the cleric wanted him out—he was right about that—and argued that elections would be unfair and unnecessary. I was completely uncomfortable with the cleric in charge, but told the sheik that I would be there to make sure the vote was honest. I also told him that he had until the day before the voting to decide whether to run.

The day of the election we drove out to the town. An Italian civil affairs military unit had set up a perimeter around the school, with the townspeople inside. No one could leave until they had voted. It was a mess. I literally kept my hand over the ballot box to make sure no one could stuff it.

Then the Italians came to me and said, "There's a sheik outside that wants to speak to you." I entrusted the ballot box to a colleague and walked outside, scared to death. I'm twenty-nine years old, I don't know what I'm doing, my Arabic is limited, and I'm going to confront a sheik and a mob. There were twenty or thirty men, no doubt armed, with banners saying "No to Elections" and "Down with America," all led by Sheikh Saoud. He warned there would be violence if the elections were not stopped. I took a deep breath and decided on my course of action. I shouted to Sheikh Saoud so bystanders could hear: "You had a chance to run in this election, and you chose not to run. Today everyone here with a ration card is equal, everyone with a ration card has the right to vote. Today you have a choice, you can take your right to vote like everyone else, if you have a ration card, or you can go home. And if there is violence, all will know who started it, and who could have prevented it. Any injuries will be on your head."

Sheikh Saoud stood down, and the day passed quietly. We counted votes until one or two in the morning. The ballots weren't printed, each voter had to write in the names of the candidates. A vote for Mohammad would have to be thrown out—was it Mohammad Hassan or Mohammad Ismail? My reading got a lot better that day.

Bradley went on to organize "fourteen or fifteen" elections, learning from mistakes:

In every town we met with all elements of society, former Baathists, clerics, teachers, illiterate people. Even though Dhi Qar is 99 percent Shi'a, there were vast differences of opinion. Through elections and a change in the local authorities law, we were able to curb the power of mayors, who tended to become strongmen, and shift power to elected city councils, which then chose the mayor. That system brought decisions closer to the people. It introduced checks and balances. It was exciting work. I could see the results of my efforts every day.

The foreign service can do this kind of work. I had no special training, but I learned that the foreign service selection process had identified the skills I needed, the ability to work with foreign cultures. In Iraq, people kept

saying, "Get the diplomat in here," because I had a knack for getting local people to solve their problems. I found I could get the Iraqis to tell me what they wanted and then work with them and with the bureaucracy, the CPA in Baghdad, to get things done.

Not enough people are doing this kind of work. A lot of what the foreign service does is answering the mail. Too often going out to talk to people is the extra thing we do, not the central thing. But that mentality is changing. Foreign service officers, especially the new ones coming in, definitely have the skills. Now we need to build on those skills and move them to the heart of our profession.

"The Meetings Were Fairly Hostile"—Political Work, 2005

Toby Bradley and all of the governorate coordination teams left Iraq by June 28, 2004, when the Coalition Provisional Authority (CPA) closed down and turned power over to an Iraqi-led government intended to lead the country's transition to democracy. But the electoral techniques developed and tested in Dhi Qar province—with the support of the embassy in Baghdad and regional embassy offices (REOs) in Mosul, Kirkuk, Hillah, and Basra—took hold nationally.[25] The year 2005 was the year of the ballot, with the election of a Transitional National Assembly in January, a constitutional referendum in October, and parliamentary elections in December.

FSO Vincent Campos arrived in Iraq in January 2005 to work on the elections. Campos, a former coast guard officer, came to the embassy in Baghdad's Green Zone on his first tour, four months after his swearing in, as the policy that designated Iraq assignments for more experienced officers began to erode. He had no language training—in fact, he knew no more than a few Arabic phrases—and only a brief introduction to Iraqi culture. He joined a political section of about seventeen officers. Campos said the section head—the political counselor—and his first deputy spoke Arabic (the first deputy spoke it quite well), and the second deputy "had a grasp of the language." Later, "another entry-level officer" came on board with fluent Arabic, but "only a few of the rest had any Arabic at all."[26]

My portfolio included the elections of January 2005, constitution development during 2005, the referendum of October 2005, and the national elections of December 2005 based on the new constitution. I worked on Sunni outreach programs, and I was the point of contact for several nongovernmental and international organizations and liaison with USAID. I worked about fourteen or fifteen hours a day, usually from about eight in the morning to ten or eleven at night. We had a half day off a week, like a Saturday or Friday afternoon off.

We lived inside the Green Zone. That's a very large area, about four square miles. The embassy complex, with its own security, is in the former Republican Guard palace that was also the primary location for the multinational force working with the embassy. We had our dining, laundry, living facilities inside the perimeter. The living conditions were tolerable—no, better than that. I had no complaints. We lived in what some called dog boxes, essentially small trailers just big enough for two single beds, a closet to hang clothing, and a very small chest of drawers. There was not really as much room as aboard some Coast Guard cutters. They were small, but even so they were adequate. We really just slept there. The quality of life in general, except for the occasional rain of mortars and bombs, was pretty high, actually.

A lot of our work was inside the Zone. Parliament and a lot of government offices, including the president and the prime minister, were there, along with a few ministries. But work on the elections, and outreach to the Sunnis, took me out of the Zone and out of Baghdad.

I made trips to Kurdistan, Fallujah, Ramadi, Anbar province, Baqubah, some other areas as well. We brought Iraqi election commissioners out from Baghdad to Sunni communities to meet with Sunnis who absolutely distrusted the commissioners and felt the elections were skewed against them.

A typical meeting involved a lot of planning and coordination. Even before a trip, we had to sell the commissioners on making the dangerous trips out and working with the Sunnis. That was my job. Another junior officer from the political section was the primary contact with the Sunni community. A third junior officer was embedded with the US military unit that would work with us in the field.

Once we had a meeting and a date, I had to make it happen from Baghdad. I arranged the schedule, transportation—helos, Suburbans, security, all that. Then we had to make sure that the election commissioners were delivering the right message (their message was consistent with ours), that Sunni votes would count and that they should get involved. At that point, we withdrew and disappeared so that it would in fact be a purely Iraqi event. As the meeting wound down, or if a threat appeared, we got them back to Baghdad.

Those trips were sometimes pretty harrowing. Going to Baqubah our helicopters were shot at and we got hit by an IED [improvised explosive device, or roadside bomb]. We were rained on by mortars in Ramadi, and there were television reports that we'd been taken hostage. That shows how difficult it is to get accurate reporting from the middle of a war zone.

The meetings were typically fairly hostile at the beginning, and sometimes at the end. The Sunnis were not enamored of the Shi'a and felt they were being marginalized. If they were going to get involved, they wanted guarantees. Despite all the voices raised and all the arguments the commissioners generally kept their cool, kept working with Sunni leadership, tribal or political or just as civil society, and in the end they could talk on decent terms with each other. But there were always problems of promises made and not kept, especially in places like Anbar, which was a very difficult environment in which to work. But in the end both sides typically remained very respectful of one another.

In the end we had a huge impact on the elections by making changes in procedures that allowed the Sunnis to participate more fully, which they did. It was a great credit to the foreign service officers in the field and to our military, which was with us every step of the way.

"In Spite of All the Violence"—PRTs, 2006–7

In late 2005 the regional embassy offices, except in Basra, gave way to PRTs, which looked more like Toby Bradley's governorate reconstruction team than the typical consulate office on which the REOs had been modeled. The PRTs had mixed civilian-military staffs, with an FSO in charge. Civilians included personnel from State, USAID, Justice, and Agriculture, outside contractors, and Iraqi employees, joined by a military civil-affairs unit and other military personnel.[27]

Even as the security situation deteriorated, the number of PRTs grew and their mission expanded. By August 2007 there were twenty-five PRTs, ten paired with US military units and others relying for security on non-US coalition forces or civilian contractors, or both. The PRT team leader and the brigade commander shared responsibility: The brigade commander reported to the commanding general, exercised tactical control, and was able to veto any planned movement; the PRT team leader reported to the US ambassador and was in charge of political and economic matters.[28]

The PRT mission, originally limited to fostering economic development and building Iraqi capacity to manage and govern at the municipal and provincial levels, expanded to include additional political objectives: to bolster moderate political forces, promote reconciliation, and strengthen counterinsurgency efforts. PRTs were called the key to the build element in the clear-secure-build strategy for Iraq.[29] Dan Speckhard, the deputy chief of mission at the Baghdad embassy, said the PRTs promote "self-reliance. This is really about transitioning, to Iraqis being able to successfully do the governance and economic work that they need to do in their own provinces."[30] Steven Buckler, a PRT leader, said, "We are working very hard to convince [the Iraqis] to basically change their relationships with one another."[31] Barbara Stephenson, who backstopped the PRTs from her position as deputy coordinator for Iraq in the Department of State, said the teams' first goal is political change—to make the environment more hospitable for moderates, less comfortable for extremists. Then more technical specialists can come in to help with reconstruction, working largely with funding and direction from the Iraqi government.[32]

To call these goals ambitious is an understatement. The grandeur of the mission seemed at odds with the modesty of the effort. Total civilian staffing at the peak was just more than six hundred. Total funding for the Iraq PRTs in the fiscal year (FY) 2008 Iraq supplemental budget request was $679.2 million.[33] But, as one PRT team leader noted, "We don't reconstruct anything. The money flowing from the government of Iraq now dwarfs anything coming through the coalition forces. The coalition funding is less than 10 percent of what goes in."[34]

FSO Kiki Munshi came out of retirement in 2006 to head up a PRT in Baqubah, Diyala province. She told reporters, "I felt a sense of moral obligation to try to help rebuild Iraq." Security problems made things difficult. The PRT, at Army Forward Operating Base Warhorse, had been hit by a car bomb in 2005. Private contractor Blackwater handled security until the Department of State decided the expense was more than the budget could handle and worked out an arrangement with the army. "Life is much easier" with army security, Munshi said, because Blackwater allowed the team only three trips a week off the base. In Muqdadiyah, where a Sunni Muslim cleric had been murdered at a mosque in November 2004, and where US forces arrested twenty people in two bomb-making cells in March 2005, the PRT helped bring local leaders together to sign an agreement to end kidnappings and killings. The agreement collapsed ten days later in a wave of hostage-taking and murder. By February 2007, after a year at Baqubah, Munshi was disheartened enough to quit. A Reuters story quoted her: "In spite of the magnificent and often heroic work being done out there by a lot of truly wonderful people, the PRTs themselves aren't succeeding. The obstacles are too great."[35]

Her successor, John Melvin Jones, disagreed.

We have had a great success with the opening of our radio and television station . . . a major step in the direction of getting the warring parties to at least sit down and listen to radio stations that broadcast a message of reconciliation. We have five young people who have spent their time at the station, of course guarded by US troops, but they've been able to put together a program that's on the air twenty-three hours per day. . . . We have had success in getting money from the central bank . . . up to Baqubah so that salaries could be paid to public servants. We've already set in place a process by which we can get fuel oil into the province. And we are working on a procedure to get food into the province. So this is an attempt by the PRT and our support brigade to assist the people of Diyala province in spite of all the violence.[36]

In Hillah, in agricultural Babil province, a forty-five-person PRT, about half civilian and half military, replaced a regional embassy office in November 2005. By January 2007, team leader Chuck Hunter, a midlevel FSO fluent in Arabic, was able to reassure reporters:

The local leaders are engaging with the idea of democracy. . . . We've now got a local council that has a radio call-in show and puts out its ideas through a newspaper. . . . In terms of provision of basic services, we've been able to do sector studies . . . to give [local officials] a base for their analyses to decide how to prioritize resources now that there's increasingly Iraqi government money that is coming their way. . . . My local staff also comes to work day in and day out, even though, for some of them, that presents a very real risk. One of my colleagues unfortunately had a close relative kidnapped and killed just a couple of weeks ago, and he feels that he's under observation. And yet they believe in this mission too.[37]

The PRT in Saddam Hussein's native town of Tikrit, in Salah ad Din province, opened in May 2006, just north of the city on an old Iraqi air force base that became Camp Speicher, headquarters for the 101st Airborne Division. The first team leader, Stephanie Miley, was an FSO who did not speak

Arabic. She headed a group of about forty, including civilians from the departments of State, Agriculture, and Justice; USAID officials and contractors; and military personnel, mostly reservists, with a range of civil-affairs and technical specialties. Miley told reporters in January 2007 that the PRT had persuaded the local provincial council to publish minutes and bring media into their meetings; improved fiscal management by showing officials how to use "simple but usable" Excel spreadsheets and graphs to track the flow of resources; and strengthened the rule of law by hosting meetings that led to Iraqi decisions to have investigative judges teach police officers about preserving evidence and building a case.

Security problems limited travel off-base by team members to five or six trips a week, for fairly short meetings with local officials. Miley's successor, FSO and Arabic speaker Steven Buckler, called the security requirements "extremely inconvenient" and said, "we are always keenly aware that we're putting the young soldiers at risk who are operating the convoys that transport us in and out of the city. [Even so,] I've worked in embassies for several decades now and I have never seen an embassy as actively engaged on a daily basis in a personal way as I have our office in Tikrit. The military unit that helps us with security is very, very, responsive."[38] Buckler's brigade combat team commander, Colonel Michael McBride, pointed out that "the most effective work happens in places that are the least secure." The State, USAID, and other civilian members of the PRT, he said, "have never backed down from going into some of the most tenuous places that we have in this province, because that is where the most good is going to be done."[39]

All Generals and Ambassadors—Baghdad, 2007–8
Assessments of the provincial reconstruction teams began almost as soon as the teams were organized. The Department of State, USAID, the military command, the congressional oversight committees, and various nongovernmental organizations sought to understand how the teams functioned, what they did well or poorly, and how they could be improved.[40] At the same time the teams themselves and their various masters in Baghdad and Washington had constantly to adapt to the rapidly changing situation in Iraq and in each province and district.

Management of the PRTs became an issue early in their activity. In Afghanistan, where the teams were led by military officers and included only a few civilians, the chain of command was generally clear. For foreign service offices on the PRTs, however, compliance with direction not only from the team leader but also from the embassy and AID mission in Kabul and policymakers and overseers in Washington could be a struggle.

Management was more muddled in Iraq. The embassy established a national coordination team (NCT) in 2005 to provide guidance and direction to the PRTs, and then replaced the NCT, headed by a major general, with an office of provincial affairs (OPA), headed by an FSO, in 2007. The first OPA director was Ambassador Henry Clarke, a retired FSO who had experience in stabilization and reconstruction work as supervisor in Bosnia's Brčko District for the Office of the High Representative. Clarke was in charge of twenty-four PRTs, including ten teams embedded in brigade or regimental combat units (ePRTs), and three teams run by coalition partners. He saw two management problems right away: conflicts between military and civilian leaders and conflicts between the field and the center. "It was all generals and ex-ambassadors over there," he said. "All the ills of the Pentagon and Foggy Bottom put together. We had to decentralize," he said. "There's no way you can manage twenty-four teams from Baghdad. Team leaders have to do it."[41]

Clarke, an army veteran and an army brat, saw the differences between the civilian and military approaches as a function of different missions and time horizons more than as a product of different institutional cultures. "The mindset of some generals was that Baghdad had to tell everybody what to do, and then it was up to the brigade commanders to do it. DOD wanted the embedded teams to report to the brigade commander, while the State Department wanted a civilian chain of command." The departments of State and Defense had to negotiate a lengthy, formal, and elaborate agreement, signed by their deputy secretaries on February 22, 2007. Under the agreement, the chief of mission (the US ambassador to Iraq), through the OPA, would give PRTs and embedded PRTs political and economic direction, while the battalion or regimental commander "will exercise his authority over security and movement of personnel for PRTs embedded in military units based on security concerns but will not direct members of the PRT as to who they should see, nor deny the members of the PRT the ability to make the contact with certain interlocutors, based on a judgment of priorities other than security."[42]

But the State-Defense agreement had not focused on what happened when the brigade rotated out. "When the brigade left," said Clarke, "it was the whole brigade, and a new brigade would come. But the PRTs would be replaced one person at a time. They didn't move with the brigade. Their focus was on their Iraqi counterparts." Despite friction with the military that sometimes rose to high levels, Clarke worked to ensure that rotation in the PRT, including replacement of military reservists, did not rupture continuity of contact.

Like many others involved with the PRTs in Afghanistan and Iraq, Clarke recognized that the military mission called for solving problems right away and provided the necessary resources. The FSOs from State and AID, however, wanted their Iraqi counterparts to identify and solve their problems using mostly Iraqi resources. "Our job," said Clarke, "was to get out there and work with the counterparts and show results. The military had a different approach. The brigade would come in, see a problem, throw some money at it, fix it, and leave. The new brigade would come in, maybe do the same thing over again." Like David Satterfield, Clarke talked trash: "I don't know how many times they paid people to pick up the garbage in Baghdad," when what the city needed was an Iraqi-run, Iraqi-funded public sanitation system.

The conflicts between the center—the embassy in Baghdad and the agencies in Washington—and the field could be at least as damaging. The center wanted metrics—easy-to-grasp and preferably quantitative goals whose achievement would indicate success and ease the chore of relating program costs and benefits. But in Clarke's view, metrics like "dollars spent, hours of training, numbers of Iraqis trained, meetings or conferences held, and so forth . . . measure effort, not success, and the outcomes can still be failures. . . . [F]alse indicators quickly become the objectives because they were so much easier to fulfill than the real goals of qualitative political and economic change in the provinces."[43]

Ambassador Ron Neumann in Afghanistan had faced similar problems. "Washington staff had multiplied procedures, metrics, tables, and instructions. The work at post had gone up by hundreds of hours. . . . Metrics—collecting statistics to measure how programs are performing—often actually retard real work. . . . I cannot recall an instance in which the data reported [in a massive data-collection exercise] told us of a problem of which we were unaware by other means. . . . What was far more important was to insist on honest reporting from every level of our staff and the military commands and to transmit our evaluations of what we learned to Washington in clear language."[44]

Clarke disagreed with the judgment of a congressional study that argued that "until PRTs receive consistent and clear direction from higher headquarters, they will not be able to maximize their efforts or success."[45] Clarke said, "This is precisely the *wrong* 'bottom line.' More lives, time, and billions of dollars have been squandered in Iraq due to poor planning and decision making in Washington, US Central Command, and Baghdad than by anyone dealing with provincial Iraqi counterparts on a daily basis."[46] Clarke acknowledged the mistakes that many PRTs made, through poor (and sleep-deprived) leadership, inadequate training, lack of planning, lack of resources, and lack of guidance, but he said that mistakes are less calamitous and easier to repair when they are confined to individual PRTs, not generalized throughout the country through top-down micromanagement.

Avoidance of micromanagement should not be an excuse for absence of strategy or lack of leadership. The president's 2005 directive that placed the Department of State in charge of stabilization and reconstruction efforts has so far failed to resolve conflicts among the many agencies necessarily involved in the effort. The Special Inspector General for Iraq Reconstruction, whose report *Hard Lessons: The Iraq Reconstruction Experience* may be the most thorough examination of PRTs and related efforts, argues for establishing a single point of authority, responsibility, and accountability. "The lack of unity of command in Iraq," the report read, "meant that unity of effort was seldom achieved."[47]

Whether the Department of State and the foreign service can carry out the mandate of the president's directive is very much open to question. The record to 2010 is mixed at best. As this book is being written, the PRTs are entering a new phase. The budget for FY 2011 calls for closing down most of PRTs in Iraq as troops withdraw. Some, including Basra and Irbil, should be transformed into freestanding diplomatic posts, either consulates or embassy branch offices or some other designation, but most will close. During the transition, the PRTs and their foreign service leaders will have to adapt to circumstances that are likely to change more rapidly than policy or management guidance from Washington. The efforts of the department, and of the foreign service, to acquire the resources and skills they will need are discussed in chapter 10.

Unprepared

For the foreign service, the experience in Iraq and Afghanistan has been traumatic and revelatory. The service was willing, but neither ready nor able, to meet the demands placed upon it. Readiness, in terms of professional preparation and training, was inadequate. Shortcomings in language skills were glaring and easy to measure. Arabic speakers were and still are in notoriously short supply. Among the more than one thousand US government employees at the Baghdad embassy in 2009 were more than three hundred members of the foreign service, of whom fewer than twenty spoke Arabic at a level of professional utility (the S-3 level). In the political section, with twenty-five officers, there were no more than three or four Arabic speakers available.[48] In 2007, in the service as a whole, only 1 percent of all officers (112 of 11,467) had working proficiency in spoken Arabic.[49] In Afghanistan in 2009, of forty-five FSOs serving in positions that required proficiency in Pashto or Dari, only twelve met the standard.[50]

Iraq is not the only place where diplomacy requires fluency in Arabic. In mid-2007, 219 positions around the world, according to the Department of State, required staffing with FSOs who speak Arabic (some of those positions are designated at the S-2 level). If every FSO qualified in Arabic were to spend 40 percent of his or her career in Arabic language-designated positions, the service would need 547 Arabic speakers to keep 219 positions staffed. Training from scratch to professional utility in Arabic normally takes two years of full-time study, time away from other duties that need to be performed.[51] In 2007, four years after the start of the war, the department announced that it would immediately break any assignment to redirect into Arabic language training any FSO or specialist who volunteered for it, regardless of the staffing gaps that might result.[52] That was a policy decision that may have sound priorities, but it also certainly showed a poor sense of planning.

Lack of readiness extended beyond language. In February 2007, the Department of State had to turn to the Department of Defense to fill 129 civilian positions in Iraq because State had neither the personnel nor the wherewithal to hire or contract the personnel with the necessary skills in areas like civil engineering, veterinary medicine, and public sanitation. Secretary of Defense Gates, testifying before the Senate Armed Services Committee, was publicly irritated with the request, and he was not alone.[53] Foreign service personnel assigned to Iraq or Afghanistan typically received no more than two weeks of training to cover language, civil affairs and reconstruction, and how to conduct oneself as an unarmed civilian working in a combat zone. Forty years ago, FSOs assigned to Vietnam routinely received four months or more of training, and many spent twenty-two weeks in full-time Vietnamese language study.

If the service had not prepared its members for Iraq, neither was it able, just in terms of numbers, to fill the positions required. The replenishment of the ranks under the Diplomatic Readiness Initiative of 2001 through 2004 proved inadequate. Even before the expansion of PRTs in 2007, Iraq and Afghanistan had absorbed all of the float—personnel available for training or in transit—that the DRI had constructed.

The service took a number of steps to stretch its resources. It moved three hundred positions from low-priority areas, chiefly in Europe, to high-priority regions in the Middle East, China, India, and Africa. By sacrificing the important to the urgent, it curtailed long-term training, defined as training lasting four months or more. It banned extensions of tours in nonhardship posts, making personnel in those positions available for assignment to less comfortable places and making their positions available to people coming out of places like Iraq. It determined to make assignments in a particular order: Positions in Iraq, Afghanistan, and other posts where minor dependents were not allowed were filled first, followed by other high-hardship and high-danger posts, posts with critical needs, and posts that historically have been hard to staff (see chapter 9 for more information on how assignments are made).[54]

Even so, unplanned gaps and vacancies began to appear in posts around the world as personnel departed with no replacement in sight. The Government Accountability Office reported in May 2006 that 15 percent of State's worldwide public diplomacy positions were vacant. A year later, despite the high visibility and high priority assigned to public diplomacy, that number rose to 22 percent.[55] Other areas were similarly shortchanged. In November 2007, 21 percent of foreign service positions, overseas and in the State Department, had no one in them.[56]

In December 2007, the service finally admitted the obvious, that it could not fill its own positions. The admission allowed vacancies to be planned instead of occurring randomly. Director General Harry Thomas ordered each regional bureau to identify the least critical 10 percent of positions—consular positions excepted—which would stay empty at least in 2008.[57] Vacancies above the 10 percent rate remained haphazard. Despite the effort to plan the gaps, posts of greatest hardship had a vacancy rate of 17 percent in September 2008, and many positions had to be filled by relatively inexperienced officers.[58]

The difficulty in staffing positions called into question the performance and willingness of the foreign service and the State Department in Iraq and Afghanistan. The increase in staffing demanded by the expansion of the PRTs in 2007 and the practice of one-year rotations meant that about 250 foreign service positions would have to be filled in Iraq in 2008. By October

2007, the service had identified only two hundred volunteers. Director General Harry Thomas announced that the department was prepared to order people to go. Reuters quoted Thomas: "If someone decides they do not want to go, then we would then consider appropriate action. We have many options, including dismissal from the foreign service."[59]

Thomas held an open meeting on the new policy on October 31, 2007. The event was a public relations debacle during which one officer reportedly called assignment to Iraq "a potential death sentence." John Naland, president of the American Foreign Service Association (AFSA), reportedly said that there were "only about thirty spaces left" on the plaque in the State Department lobby that honors members of the service who died on duty (see chapter 3). Less melodramatically, others at the meeting chastised the department for its failure to provide treatment for employees affected by post-traumatic stress disorders.[60]

Critics for months had accused the foreign service and the State Department of weakness, particularly in Iraq—and especially in contrast to the military. Ralph Peters of the *New York Post* in December 2006 had attacked "our self-adoring diplomats" and identified State as the source of "the worst failure" in Iraq: "State couldn't get enough volunteers even for its 90-day stints in Iraq—*every* major program that it insisted on running failed."[61] Two months later, Admiral Edmund Giambastiani, vice chairman of the joint chiefs of staff, contrasted the foreign service and the military: "We send out orders, we execute orders, we deploy our military, and guess what happens? They turn up and do their job."[62]

The shortage of volunteers and the tone of the October open meeting reinforced that line of thinking. Max Boot of the Council on Foreign Relations suggested that "diplomats aren't pulling their weight in Iraq and Afghanistan"[63] The State Department's newly launched blog, DipNote, posted some two hundred messages on the topic, many of them easily located with an internet search linking the terms "diplomat" and "weenie."[64]

Less attention was paid to the outcome of the affair. Perhaps in reaction to the media coverage, the department redoubled its efforts to find volunteers, and members of the service came forward. Assignments were completed for all Iraq vacancies in January 2008, without the need to order unwilling diplomats to go.

The willingness of the foreign service, despite its lack of readiness and the shortage of personnel, was the untold story. By the spring of 2007, 22 percent of foreign service personnel had already served in postinvasion Iraq or Afghanistan on permanent assignment or temporary duty of ninety days or more.[65] All of these volunteered for their assignments.[66] In the 2008 assignment cycle, about 7 percent of all postings (252 of 3,577) were in Iraq, and all were filled by volunteers.

To encourage volunteers, the department offered incentives, including hardship pay, unenforceable promises of rapid promotion, and opportunity to choose future assignments. (Government-backed life insurance, however, remained a benefit available to the military only.) Some of the most effective incentives involved nothing more than administrative flexibility. One especially welcome innovation allowed the dependents of an officer or specialist transferred from an overseas post to Iraq to remain at their overseas post, rather than be shipped back to Washington with the prospect of moving again in a year's time.

But most foreign service volunteers in Iraq were surely not there for the money. Andy Passen, a fifty-year-old senior FSO who headed a PRT in Baghdad, described his motivation:

> Like many of us, I questioned, back in 2003, whether it was the right decision for our country to go to war. But it's no longer March 2003; it's late in 2007, and our involvement in Iraq is unquestionably the single most important foreign policy issue of our generation. . . . Now, as a senior officer, I can make a contribution to this new foreign policy priority. I can respond to our secretary's call for volunteers, and use my talents and skills to engage with Iraqi leaders, to build capacity in provincial governance, to help Iraqis to rebuild and reconstruct their country and their government. There is no doubt that service on a PRT is among the most dangerous assignments in the Foreign Service. But I look at the thousands of young soldiers patrolling Baghdad's streets—some of them on their second deployment—every day serving as some of our most effective street-level diplomats, and I am honored to put on my body armor and move out beside them.[67]

Iraq and Afghanistan made plain the need for a larger foreign service. The most eloquent argument for this proposition came from an unexpected source, the secretary of defense. "My message," he said, "is not about the defense budget or the military power. My message is that if we are to meet the myriad challenges around the world in the coming decades, the country must strengthen other important elements of national power both institutionally and financially," and he called for "a dramatic increase in spending on the civilian instruments of national security—diplomacy, strategic communications, foreign assistance, civic action, economic reconstruction and development." He lamented the loss of USIA and the depletion of USAID but called for "new institutions." He contrasted the Defense Department's $500 billion budget (not counting operations in Iraq and Afghanistan) with the Department of State's $36 billion. "Despite new hires," he said, "there are only about 6,600 professional Foreign Service officers—less than the manning for one aircraft carrier strike group."[68]

Gates did not comment on the State Department's timid budget request for fiscal year 2008, which asked for 254 new positions to support transformational diplomacy, including 104 positions for training enhancement.[69] At the time, the administration planned three annual increases that, if approved, would increase the authorized size of the foreign service by about 550, or 5 percent. The last of the actual bodies would presumably be on board only in 2011.

The modesty of the request stood in contrast to the grandeur of the mission. The chairman of the Senate Appropriations Subcommittee with jurisdiction over the State-AID budget chided Secretary Rice, " 'Transformational diplomacy' is a lofty slogan for what amounts to adding new positions at posts that have been understaffed for years. I welcome it. But beyond that, your 2008 budget offers little confidence that this Administration is prepared to devote the resources necessary to successfully exert America's influence in such a complex and dangerous world."[70] Former House Speaker Newt Gingrich, a harsh and frequent critic of the Department of State and the foreign service, argued that the service needs another four thousand members—"a Foreign Service that is at least 40 percent larger"—to do its job.[71]

The department did instruct promotion boards to give more weight to performance in Iraq, Afghanistan, and other posts where service entails hardship and danger and where the job calls for leadership, imagination, and diplomatic skill. Even this step to reshape the service on the cheap drew complaints from some FSOs. An anonymous officer told the *Foreign Service Journal*, "The general perception is that service in Iraq equates to instant promotions and/or preferred onward assignments. Those of us serving elsewhere often feel that no matter how hard we work or how deserving [we are], we'll be overlooked for someone who has 'done time' in Iraq."[72]

The military and, it is said, Secretary Rice, had little patience with this kind of whining. One navy veteran, a senior officer in personnel, put it this way: "We call what we do 'orders.' When volunteers are insufficient, we direct.... The key, in the long term, is to ensure that when the system requires hard service, those who perform it will find career reward. Sooner or later it will dawn on folks that the way to success is to serve. State may be coming around to that."[73]

Whatever its reasons were—the staffing shortages, the public criticism, the impending end of its term—the administration changed course and in its final budget, submitted in February 2008, asked Congress to fund more than one thousand additional foreign service positions in FY 2010, roughly triple what it had contemplated before. The administration knew, of course, that its budget had no realistic chance of enactment during the months remaining in its term, but the figure set a starting point for the successor team taking office in January 2009.

The aggressive budget reached Congress as the presidential candidates, in a rare election with no incumbent standing, began to debate the need for more robust American diplomacy, to provide an alternative to military action. Perhaps paradoxically, the shortcomings revealed by the pressures of Iraq and Afghanistan set the stage for a golden moment for the foreign service, when the outgoing and incoming administrations, a solid majority in the Congress, and much of the public seemed determined to rebuild the service and instill it with the skills and character required for demanding work in anarchic environments. The progress and future of that effort are the subject of chapter 10.

If the department's leadership is right about the kind of diplomacy the world demands of us now, then FSOs and specialists who can perform with distinction under the most stressful and dangerous conditions will be the elite of the service in the years ahead.

6

Politics and Professionalism

Tension between the professional foreign service and its political masters is inevitable. It can be invigorating or corrosive. The professionals are proud of their knowledge, skill, and experience, but it's the elected officials and those they appoint who set the policies and vote the taxes and budgets to carry them out. Foreign service professionals must give effect to the policies of the administration and the laws of the land, even as the policies change and the laws are revised. To maintain the flexibility they need, many professionals try to hold themselves above politics. If they succeed, they succeed just barely, for try as they may they are in politics up to their eyeballs.

There is no way around it. As members of the foreign service advance in their careers, they take on jobs of increasing responsibility and public presence. Whatever their position in closed-door debates, when ambassadors, their deputies, their press officers, and their senior aides deal with foreign officials or the public, they have to follow the official line and defend it vigorously. So do assistant secretaries, their deputies, and their office directors. All foreign service officers (FSOs) are commissioned by the president and, at least notionally, serve at his pleasure. They speak not only for their country but also for their government, which means for the administration in power.

Once upon a time, the adage goes, politics stopped at the water's edge. The adage belongs to Senator Arthur Vandenberg, the Republican chairman of the Foreign Relations Committee who abandoned isolationism to support the Marshall Plan and the United Nations during Truman's presidency. But bipartisanship in foreign policy was a bit of a myth even during Senator Vandenberg's ascendancy (he died in 1951), and in recent years it has been rare and fleeting.

One reason surely is that foreign policy is no longer foreign. Ambassador L. Craig Johnstone wrote in 1997, "Almost every international issue has a domestic consequent, more visible and direct than ever before. Almost every major domestic issue has an international component. The distinctions between domestic and foreign are gone."[1]

The past decade has proven him right. How we respond to international terrorism affects our civil liberties, and how we define our liberties affects our response to terrorism. Taxing and spending decisions made in the US Congress affect the value of the trillion dollars of US bonds held by the Bank of China, and what China does with its holdings affects US economic welfare. How we deal with global warming affects spending by domestic business, and vice versa. Political differences over privacy, health care, bank regulation, or almost any other domestic issue have powerful implications for our foreign relations as well.

Political clashes over foreign policy pose two questions for the foreign service: First, how does the foreign service remain professional while carrying out policies that may change radically with each election? Second, how can each new political leadership comfortably entrust its policies to a foreign service that had worked hard and effectively for the policies of its predecessor?

Staying Professional

The first question is less difficult than it seems. Diplomats represent their governments the way lawyers represent their clients. They do not speak for themselves. The placard on the green baize table says "United States," not "Ambassador Patterson" or "Ms. Woods." An FSO conducting official business always says "my government believes" or "the position of my government is." An officer's personal views are of no consequence and should never enter an official discussion.

The result of this self-effacement is that when policies change, the foreign service—both as a whole and as individuals—can remain zealous advocates. It is still "my government believes" and "the position of my government is." An FSO below the rank of ambassador or assistant secretary who becomes personally identified with a policy has probably let ego interfere with professional detachment.

Sudden or radical changes in foreign policy may pose problems for the country's international credibility and influence, but foreign service personnel have to cope as best they can. Henry Kissinger wrote that "frequent gyrations in our national direction demoralize the Foreign Service, as they do foreign nations."[2] But Tony Motley, a political ambassador and assistant secretary of state in the Reagan administration, says partisan struggles over foreign policy should not be an issue for the foreign service: "It's not the job of foreign service officers to figure out what America really thinks. Their job is to defend the policy, and they shouldn't complain when a policy is unpopular at home or under attack in Washington."

How the Secretary Sees the Service

The second question, how to create trust between the political leadership and the foreign service professionals, is more problematic. How bad can things get? Former House Speaker Newt Gingrich in 2003 called the State Department "ineffective and incoherent," engaged in "a deliberate and systematic effort to undermine the President's policies."[3] When such attitudes prevail, they ensure that the White House and the National Security Council staff will keep the State Department and the foreign service in the dark and on the margins—a recipe for a diplomacy that is ineffective and incoherent after all.

As Henry Kissinger observed, the foreign service has little influence through any formal role; its ability to shape policy depends on an "intangible bond" between the secretary of state and the president.[4] When that bond is lacking—as was arguably the case between President Nixon and his first secretary of state, William P. Rogers; between President Carter and Cyrus Vance; between President Clinton and Warren Christopher; or between President George W. Bush and Colin Powell—the foreign service will be generally ignored in policymaking and often left uninformed about decisions and actions taken.

Even a secretary of state who is close to the president may not fully trust the professional foreign service. Dean Acheson was infuriated by FSOs who believed the career service should control the formation of foreign policy.[5] James P. Baker III, secretary of state from 1989 to 1992 under President George H. W. Bush, deliberately put the professionals on the sidelines:

> I thought the institutional rigidity of the Foreign Service, with its separate rules, mores, and bureaucratic hierarchy, precluded a reliance solely on it in order to meet the challenges at hand. Most FSOs are talented and loyal public servants, and any Secretary would be foolish not to harness their strengths. I did so, and was served very ably by many of them. But as with any large group, some of them tend to avoid risk taking or creative

thinking. . . . Primarily for these reasons, I preferred to centralize policy authority in a small team of talented, loyal aides, and build outward from them. This approach has been a hallmark of my government career.[6]

Baker is not alone in finding the foreign service bureaucratic and excessively cautious. Alexander Haig, Ronald Reagan's first secretary of state (1981–82), and Henry Kissinger both thought the service had been traumatized by past attacks. Haig said that "the recriminations of the McCarthy era" led to "intellectual timidity" and "professional diffidence" and taught the service that "it is prudent to equivocate."[7] Henry Kissinger wrote that "the permanent career service has endured so much abuse that its sense of beleaguerment is accompanied by an acute consciousness of bureaucratic prerogative." The appointment of amateurs to top policy jobs compounds the problem: "Leadership clearly incapable of grasping the complexity of the office or in constant need of briefing on the most elementary issues elicits the most self-willed assertions of Foreign Service parochialism."[8]

Haig and Kissinger both fretted about how difficult it is to harness the talents of the service. Their accounts hold lessons for the foreign service and for its leadership today. Kissinger argued that the secretary needs to ride close herd on the service, lest the service follow its own lead instead of the secretary of state's:

> On one level, gaining control of the machinery of the Department of State is relatively easy. The Secretary's unambiguous orders are scrupulously carried out, at least at the outset, because the Foreign Service begins with the presumption that the Secretary deserves its support—until it has tested the limits of his tolerance. . . . In the hands of a determined Secretary, the Foreign Service can be a splendid instrument, staffed by knowledgeable, discreet, and energetic individuals. They do require constant vigilance lest the convictions that led them into a penurious career tempt them to preempt decision-making.[9]

Haig called the foreign service "a remarkable group of men and women, scholarly and sober and versed in foreign languages and the nuances of foreign culture and politics." He wanted "a strong ring of professionals" around him: "I needed their experience and their competence. The Foreign Service . . . helps to preserve political appointees who temporarily reign over the department from error." Like Kissinger, though, he found the service difficult to manage: "It is like an asteroid, spinning in an eccentric orbit, captured by the gravity of its procedures and its self-interest, deeply suspicious of politicians who threaten its stability by changing its work habits." Haig also remarked on the special difficulty of getting the foreign service to sign on to the policies of a Republican administration: "The Foreign Service . . . is not infected by Republican sentiment."[10]

To strengthen political control over this unruly bureaucracy, the department during Haig's tenure instituted the practice of assigning every assistant secretary of state in charge of a bureau at least one deputy who was a political appointee. In subsequent administrations, some especially sensitive bureaus also acquired special advisers—that is, political appointees named under Schedule C of the civil service rules.[11] With few exceptions, these practices have continued to the present day.

Despite their doubts, Kissinger and Haig became strong supporters of the foreign service, and the service became a strong source of support for their stewardships of the Department of State. Kissinger issued a warning to those who think America's diplomats should be sacked or relegated to menial chores:

> In American folklore, our professional diplomats tend to be maligned as
> a collection of striped-pants fuddy-duddies, excessively internationalist
> in outlook, soft in defense of the national interest, as often a contributory
> cause of our difficulties abroad as agents of their resolution. The need to
> "clean out" the State Department has become a staple of our political ora-
> tory. Several Secretaries have begun their tours of office with that expressed
> determination. I know of none that has left office without having come
> to admire the dedicated men and women who supply the continuity and
> expertise of our foreign policy. I entered the State Department a skeptic, I
> left a convert.[12]

Dissent

Dedication and loyalty do not imply servility. On the contrary, members of the foreign service owe their political superiors their honest opinions and their best judgments even, or especially, when these conflict with the current line of policy. Sometimes, though, conflicts between the policies adopted by the administration and those favored by the individual member of the foreign service are more than differences of opinion. They may be differences of values or of conscience.

How do members of the foreign service remain true to their profession, their country, and their consciences when each may pull in a different direction? What military historian S. L. A. Marshall wrote of the military officer applies to the FSO and specialist as well: "His ultimate commanding loyalty at all times is to his country, and not to his service or his superior. He owes it to his country to speak the truth as he sees it. This implies a steadying judgment as to when it should be spoken, and to whom it should be addressed."[13] Marshall's answer starts with clarity but ends in ambiguity. No better answer is likely to be found.

Tony Motley, who taught a State Department seminar for new ambassadors from 1986 to 2001, has straightforward advice for dissenters: "When you don't like a policy, admit it." A professional member of the foreign service should be enough of a diplomat to figure out how to tell his boss what he thinks without committing sabotage, and how to be loyal without pandering. "It's more art than science," says Motley. "Some people are just better at it than others."[14]

Of course, supervisors, whether political or professional, need to be able to tell the difference between frank advice on the one hand and disloyalty or flattery on the other. Ambassador Chas Freeman wrote, "Governments that condone candor will get it; those that don't, won't. . . . The candor of diplomatic reporting depends on the integrity of the reporting diplomat, which in turn reflects the degree of official tolerance for the confidential expression of unconventional, nonconforming, or dissenting views."[15]

Many FSOs—no telling how many, but more than a few—believe that the top levels of the Department of State have a low tolerance for candor, even privately expressed. "This [George W. Bush] administration poses every question in terms of loyalty," said a political officer with twenty years of service. "In the past, professionals were chosen for senior positions so that policymakers could draw on their knowledge and experience. Now they're yes-men. You don't have people who will stand up and say, 'Madam Secretary, what you propose won't work in my region of the world, which I know intimately.' There is no discussion of policy or policy implementation, at least none that involves the foreign service."[16] Another officer, quoted in the *Washington Post*, said, "I've heard about low morale and a number of people seeking to leave because they don't find the atmosphere so rewarding as it had been when it was not so politicized."[17]

Ambassador Craig Kelly, a career officer who served as executive assistant to Secretary of State Colin Powell, said, "Powell and his top aides— Deputy Secretary Armitage and Undersecretary for Political Affairs Marc

Grossman—were always willing to listen to people who walked into their offices with divergent views. They often pushed back, but their minds were open. Meetings on policy issues were free-wheeling, with no punishment for contrary views."[18] FSOs did not seem to have the same feelings about Secretary Rice.

No one should doubt that an officer who delivers unwelcome news or takes an unwelcome stand also takes a chance. What Secretary of Defense Robert Gates told midshipmen at the US Naval Academy applies as well to FSOs: "The time will come for each one of you when you must stand alone in making an unpopular difficult decision; when you must challenge the opinion of superiors or tell them that you can't get the job done with the time and resources available; or when you will know that what superiors are telling the press or the Congress or the American people is inaccurate. These will be moments when your entire career is at risk."[19]

For FSOs, the risk of retribution comes not only from the political levels of the State Department or the White House but also from members of the Senate and their senior staff, many of whom are in a position to delay or block confirmation of an officer nominated to be a chief of mission or assistant secretary of state. At times of great political controversy, when stakes are high, senior officers may be trapped between the administration's official position, their own understanding of the situation, and the position of a senator or committee in opposition to the president. Character and integrity are tested at such times. An officer should be willing to accept that being true to one's duty may mean forgoing an opportunity for advancement and fulfillment of ambition.

The State Department's leadership recognized years ago that employees who are afraid to say what they think may become unhappy and unproductive, but the results of the department's efforts to protect the expression of views that challenge the official line have been mixed. In 1971, during the Vietnam War, the department created a dissent channel to allow foreign service personnel to express their opinions on important policy issues in writing directly and confidentially to the department's most senior officials. But use of the channel has declined to fewer than ten messages a year.[20] The American Foreign Service Association (AFSA) presents annual awards for constructive dissent. In recent years, most of the honored dissents dealt with management issues or the policy process, not with the substance of policy.[21]

Fear of retribution is not the only reason why dissent is rare. Would-be dissenters may also stay silent because their messages almost never carry the day. Dissenters are often speaking for the losing side of a policy debate that has already taken place. The arguments they raise may have been considered and rejected or discounted before the decision was taken.

What should members of the foreign service do when they disagree with a policy or course of conduct that as a matter of professional duty they must publicly support? The Department of State puts this answer on its website: "As public servants, Foreign Service [specialists and officers] must publicly defend US government policy, despite personal reservations. There is an internal channel through which an employee may present dissenting views on specific foreign policy issues. If a [specialist or officer] cannot publicly defend official US policy, he or she has the option to resign."[22]

Are the choices really so stark? One senior officer laid it out this way: "In the beginning we were told that if you didn't agree with a policy you could, one—shut up; two—move and work on something else; or—three—tackle the issue and seek to change it. I think I have done all three." But, she added, "In some cases I argued for change, sometimes successfully, sometimes not, with no consequences to my career."[23] Another said, "For the most part we manage to put our views and our politics aside. There are times when that's hard to do, but I've usually found that there are at least some rational policy grounds on the other side of the argument, so I can say there are good reasons behind this, and I can live with that."[24]

Most members of the foreign service have had serious reservations about some US policy at some point in their careers, but in fact very few people resign over policy. Attrition rates in general are low compared to the private sector, or indeed to the rest of the government, and they have not changed significantly in more than twenty years, despite policy shifts and ups and downs in the general morale of the service.[25] However disgruntled some members of the service may be, they are rarely unhappy enough to quit, and it's news when they do. In recent years, three FSOs have resigned over Balkan policy, three over Iraq, and one over Afghanistan.[26]

Family obligations are one reason why dissenters stay on the job. One unhappy officer said, "It's hard to quit your job when your skills are esoteric, your kids are growing up, and your benefits, including your pension, are not portable."[27] Some dissenters may be too cynical, or too timid, to take an action based on principle. A more important reason, though, may be that most members of the foreign service, especially those who have spent long years abroad, are deeply if quietly patriotic and passionate about their work. They believe that what they do over time will make America a better, safer country, and even if they believe current policies are profoundly wrong, they will not abandon their profession.

Congress

Congress looks to members of the foreign service, and to civil servants in the foreign affairs agencies, to provide prompt, accurate information untainted by partisanship. At the same time, Congress and the administration expect members of the service to transmit and defend the administration's views. Performing at a high level in both capacities requires skill, practice, time, and effort. Abroad or at home, professional diplomats should be able to carry a politically colored message without discarding their professional status.

The executive branch has the lead in foreign policy. As many presidents have learned, however, Congress has the tools to block almost any presidential initiative. Keeping key members of Congress informed of the administration's strategy, plans, and activities does not prevent clashes between the executive and the legislature. However, it does reduce their number and make debate more constructive. Members of congress challenge the administration every day over foreign policy, often in dramatic ways, but for every headline about clashes, there are literally thousands of cooperative transactions.

In Washington, the foreign service deals with Congress in four areas: policy, oversight, personnel, and resources. A glance at the list of testimony given before Congress shows that policy presentations to the House Foreign Affairs Committee and the Senate Committee on Foreign Relations receive the most attention, closely followed by budget presentations to the appropriations committees.[28]

Most personnel matters are internal to the foreign service agencies, but because FSOs—whether at State, USAID, Commerce, or Agriculture—are commissioned, their inductions and promotions, like those of the armed services, must be approved by the Senate. Promotion lists are almost always approved without controversy and by voice vote or unanimous consent, but almost always is not always. Ambassadors and policy-level officials (roughly assistant secretary and above) also require Senate confirmation.[29] AFSA, the collective bargaining agent for foreign service members in all four foreign service agencies, maintains active contact with congressional staff and key members of the foreign affairs committees on issues of pay and working conditions.

Congress also exercises oversight responsibilities, reviewing the way in which the executive branch carries out the laws that Congress has enacted. For the foreign service, oversight is especially intense where the service bears direct responsibility for execution of the law, for example in issuing visas pursuant to the Immigration and Nationality Act or licensing weapons sales under the Arms Export Control Act. Oversight hearings are generally conducted by the committees with primary jurisdiction over the legislation, but other committees with an interest may also become involved.

Foreign policy is not a congressional preoccupation. The House Foreign Affairs Committee, said a member, "is not an 'A' committee. It's not linked to any interest groups" that are willing and able to finance campaigns.[30] A serious interest in foreign relations can be an electoral millstone for a representative or senator, taking time away from matters of greater or more immediate interest to important constituents. "If it doesn't benefit a member's short-term political considerations," said a staffer, "he loses interest."[31] Under these circumstances, it is remarkable how many members have taken risks to perform great service in foreign affairs, through legislation and sometimes through direct diplomacy. The list is long, distinguished, and bipartisan.

Much of the work of liaison with Congress falls to the State Department's Bureau of Legislative Affairs, called H for [Capitol] Hill, and to USAID's Bureau of Legislative and Public Affairs. There is no lack of contact: The H bureau says on its website that each year it handles 1,500 pieces of legislation, 8,000 pieces of correspondence, 8,000 congressional inquiries, and 300 hearings and that it sends the Hill more than 500 mandated reports and notifications.[32] The website doesn't count them, but the bureau also arranges scores of briefings for staff and members.

The department has struggled, though, to make its liaison effective, and congressional staffers often feel frustration at the tight control they believe the H bureau tries to exercise over the flow of information. A 2002 study prepared for the Una Chapman Cox Foundation documented some serious problems. One Senate aide said this: "We have a devil of a time just getting State Department folks to come up and talk off the record. And then when we do get them, we have this legislative shop person in the middle, making sure they don't say anything out of the box." A House staffer said of H, "I swear, if they could, they would come up to the Hill with their foreign service officers with ankle shocks and a remote control to make them shut up and say what they want." The usual view from the Hill is that FSOs are intelligent, dedicated to public service, professional, and nonpartisan, but also aloof and cautious to a fault.[33]

An aide to a member of the Senate Foreign Relations Committee had some advice:

> When you say "career diplomat," my member says, "career bureaucrat, career talker, stuffed shirt, someone who's not going to give me a straight answer." I sympathize with the diplomats—it's not like everyone up here is looking out for them, and certain diplomats have been burned for telling certain things to certain people. But what State needs to send up here are people with big egos, people who can make a convincing case and win our trust. If you come up here and whine, say about earmarks, then we say, "you're weak, you suck, we're going to write some earmarks now."[34]

Jennifer Butte-Dahl, a civil servant who handled Near East Asian affairs in the H bureau, is now an adviser to the deputy secretary of state for management and resources and doesn't dispute that a little ego can be helpful, but most important is making the case. "We have to see the whole picture, just the way the appropriators do," she said. "We have to explain how our resources—our programs and our people—are supporting our foreign policy goals." Congressional hostility is overplayed, and congressional liaison is undervalued. "Day to day," she said, "you have good relations with people on the Hill. Relations are better than people think.... There's a sense inside the State Department that H doesn't really help. If they realized the ability H has, based on access to information and personal relationships, to change the course of events on the Hill—for example, to tweak bill language, kill a damaging amendment, or negotiate budget allocations—they'd be a lot more appreciative."

And on rare occasions everything falls into place. Butte-Dahl explained,

> In 2008 we did a claims agreement with Libya that was a model of bipartisan, legislative-executive cooperation. Bilateral relations with Libya had been improving since 2003, when Libya publicly renounced its support for terrorism and voluntarily gave up its WMD programs. As time passed, outstanding unresolved claims by victims of previous Libyan terrorism, including the bombing of Pan Am 103 and the LaBelle discotheque, were becoming an increasingly problematic element in the relationship. The Executive and Congress both had an avid interest in resolving these claims,

and when the Libyans approached us quietly with a plan for resolution, we went immediately to the Hill to consult with members on our next steps. This is what Congress always tells us they want us to do: consult it early and often. We engaged leadership, the committees of jurisdiction, and members of both chambers who had constituent interests. Engaging early was a critical element of our success. It was a highly contentious issue and we knew resolution would be most successful with supportive legislation. Every stakeholder needed to be informed, engaged, and ready to act.

NEA [the Bureau of Near East Asian Affairs] and the legal adviser's office led the negotiations. I handed off the rest of my portfolio so I could deal exclusively with the congressional component of the Libya talks.

It was a complicated mechanism we had to negotiate with the Libyans and the Hill. The Libyans needed confidence that if they resolved the pending claims they would not face additional lawsuits, and that legal restrictions would be lifted and not reimposed. That required congressional action, yet Congress did not want to act until the Libyans had provided adequate compensation for their constituents. The Libyan Claims Resolution Act provided certain immunity for Libya upon receipt by the Executive of adequate funds. The Secretary of State was given the authority to certify to Congress that the funds received were adequate to appropriately compensate victims in the outstanding claims.

The Congress was Democratic, and the administration was Republican, but the work was bipartisan. We did the bulk of the negotiating quickly and quietly in about six weeks. The bipartisan bill passed unanimously through the Congress on the last day of July 2008, in just thirty hours from the time it was introduced in the Senate to final passage in the House. The president signed the bill into law three days later.[35]

Personal relationships are the heart of congressional relations, but not many FSOs have the prolonged exposure to the Hill that builds mutual trust and respect. The H bureau is off the beaten career track for most FSOs. Unlike most of the State Department, where foreign service and civil service personnel work under a fairly thin layer of political leadership, the H bureau is about evenly divided among the three groups, one-third foreign service, one-third civil service, and one-third political appointees. In the regional bureaus, FSOs come and go, but when they go, they often go to jobs in the region and remain closely connected to the bureau in Washington. In H, when FSOs go, they don't go to the Hill, they just move on.

Civil service personnel provide more continuity, but even though many have been in the bureau for ten years or more, they cannot match the longevity of members and staff on Capitol Hill. In 2010, on the Senate side, the chairman and ranking member (the senior member from the minority party) of the Foreign Relations Committee had twenty-five and thirty-five years of seniority, the chairman and ranking member of the Appropriations Committee had forty-seven and thirty-one years of seniority, and the chair and ranking member of the appropriations subcommittee on State, foreign operations, and related programs had thirty-five and seventeen years. On the House side, the figures for the equivalent positions were twenty-seven, twenty-five, forty, thirty-one, twenty-one, and thirteen years.

Overseas, members of the foreign service work with senators, representatives, and staff traveling on official congressional delegations, or codels, of which in 2005 there were about 650 involving more than 2,000 travelers. Codels are not the only congressional travel: State Department lingo includes staffdels (congressional staff traveling on official business but without members) and nodels (members of Congress traveling unofficially). Some codels are ugly junkets, but most are serious business. Embassies take all of them seriously.

Codels give embassies a chance to take policy out of the briefing paper and put it on the street. They are a chance to show, not just tell, the legislative branch how resources are being used and what is being accomplished. To host-government officials, members of Congress are outside voices that can reinforce, or undercut, the US government's message.

Of course, codels can also be used to make a political point. In 2007 several leading congressional Democrats, including the then new House Speaker Nancy Pelosi, traveled to Damascus in defiance of the administration's long-standing policy of refusing to engage the government of Syria in high-level meetings. That kind of travel placed the ambassador and the embassy in a difficult position, one that called for—what else—some delicate diplomacy.

Embassies catch the brunt of congressional travel. The H bureau has a travel unit to handle codel logistics, and the regional bureaus handle substantive issues, but the main effort takes place overseas. Although many elements of an embassy, and large numbers of hours, are involved in even a small codel, the ambassador or his deputy usually assigns one person, called the control officer, to take responsibility for all administrative elements of the visit: arrival and clearance through customs and immigration;

accommodations; all ground transportation; and substantive, social, and recreational schedules for all members of the party. Control officers, often junior or midlevel officers, are thrown into close contact with staff and members of Congress, under circumstances that are often less than ideal on both sides—lost luggage, failed appointments, missed flights, sudden illness, bad food, bad press.

"In Moscow," said a midlevel officer, "the foreign service nationals in the embassy's visitor's unit knew the routine, and we would have everything lined up when the delegation arrived. Then something would happen, the plans go out the window, and you have to react to the situation. It was hard to get high-level meetings. President Putin would only meet with the president or secretary of state. Some staff understood and were gracious, but others said, 'What good are you?' Being control officer is what you call a learning experience."[36]

Members of the foreign service who deal with the Congress need to understand the institution and the motivations of its members as well as or better than they do foreign governments and parliaments. Fortunately, foreign service work offers opportunities beyond codels for members of the service to develop personal relationships with members of Congress and congressional staff. Unfortunately, neither State nor USAID seems to know how to build on those relationships as part of career development. For example, seven or eight FSOs are assigned each year to a one-year tour on detail to a congressional office under a program started by Senator James B. Pearson of Kansas in the 1970s.[37] "We have a Pearson fellow on our staff every year," said a Senate staffer. "They should double or triple the number. It's a way to build relationships, build understanding. We reach back constantly to former Pearson fellows who've gone back to State or AID or overseas."[38]

Budgets

The relationship between Congress and the foreign service faces a test each year at budget time, though the budget yields only a murky picture of congressional satisfaction with the service's past performance or its expectations for the future. That is because in the vast federal budget, there is no line or box marked foreign service. The funds for America's diplomats are dispersed and hard to find. Foreign service people watching the progress of the budget through the Congress are often confused or disheartened, because the process is confusing and often discouraging.

One source of confusion is the difference between legislation that authorizes programs and legislation that appropriates funds. Authorizing laws establish or modify federal programs but do not necessarily provide the money to run them.[39] Authorizing legislation often indicates a dollar amount for a program, but authorizers cannot bind appropriators to provide it. Appropriators can effectively kill an authorized program by failing to fund it, although, because by law the State Department cannot spend money on an unauthorized activity, they cannot effectively fund a program without support from the authorizers.[40]

The authorizing committees for most international activities are the Foreign Affairs Committee in the House and the Foreign Relations Committee in the Senate. The law requires the State Department to keep these committees "fully and currently informed with respect to all activities and responsibilities" within their jurisdiction.[41] The committees are responsible for oversight, for making sure that the executive branch is faithfully carrying out congressional intent. A strong committee or subcommittee chairman can use oversight hearings to influence policy, but to their deep frustration and occasional anger, the budgetary dominance of the appropriations committees often leaves the authorizers unable to work their will.

A second source of confusion is the calendar. Budgeteers juggle three or four or more budgets at once. Phil Lussier, director of the Office of Resource Management and Organizational Analysis, explained,

> Right now [December 2009], we're on a continuing resolution from the old administration which will carry us to March 2010. But we also have bridge funding to hire an additional hundred positions. An appropriations bill in March 2009 gave us some two-year money, and later in the spring we got a supplemental appropriation. We hope to have an FY 2010 appropriation this week, because the continuing resolution expires December 18. OMB passed back our FY 2011 budget request last week—that will go to the Congress in February. We're beginning this week to work on the budget for FY 2012. So right now we're tracking the 2009 continuing resolution, the 2010 budget, the 2011 budget heading to Congress, and the 2012 budget in the early stages. And the supplementals.[42]

Supplemental budgets related to funding of the wars in Iraq and Afghanistan were part of funding for State and USAID in each fiscal year from 2003 through 2010, and the administration added a second supplemental for Haiti in 2010.

Money available for an activity or program in one period may not be available in another. Nor is money appropriated for one activity available to be spent on another, though sometimes adjustments can be made with notification to Congress. Students in Economics 101 learn that money is fungible; students in Budgets 101 learn that it isn't.

The meat and potatoes for the foreign service—salaries, allowances, positions, and so forth—are in the State Department's budget for administration of foreign affairs and AID's budget for operating expenses. Beginning with the 110th Congress (2007) and with the budget for FY 2008, State and AID received their funds in the same appropriations bill, handled in the appropriations committees of both the House and the Senate by subcommittees on state, foreign operations, and related programs.[43] The US Commercial Service is in the Commerce Department's budget, under the jurisdiction of the House and Senate subcommittees on commerce, justice, science, and related agencies. Funds for the Foreign Agricultural Service are bundled in the Agriculture, Rural Development, Food and Drug Administration, and Related Agencies Appropriations Act, which covers nearly all of the Department of Agriculture and comes under the jurisdiction of the subcommittees of the same name in the House and Senate.

The budgets that directly affect the foreign service are small portions of the bills in which they appear. In the FY 2011 budget request, the operating expenses for State, AID, the FCS, and the FAS were around 11 percent, 2 percent, 0.4 percent, and less than 0.1 percent of the total appropriations in the bills in which those funds were included. "That can be a problem," said Jim Morhard, former staff director of the Senate Appropriations Committee. "It's hard to hold members' attention on budget issues that don't have much impact on the bottom line."[44]

It's not just the Congress that sees the budget with a short attention span. FSOs also tend to neglect the budget, for several reasons. The budget is Washington work, which most foreign service people find less appealing than work overseas. It's numbers, which many foreign service people regard with fear and boredom. And it can be astonishingly complex. Foreign service people, with their three-year rotations, barely have the time to learn the intricacies of the budget process and to build necessary negotiating relationships before they are off to another assignment. They are at a disadvantage.

But Steve Dietz, a member of the civil service who handles State's budget in the department's Bureau of Resource Management, wants to attract more FSOs and specialists to the Office of State Programs, Operations, and

Budget. "They understand the real impact of funding reductions on posts overseas. And when they finish a tour here, they go back to the field and educate others about the budget process and budget pressures. That leads to stronger input from the posts and bureaus and makes the justifications that we send to Congress more informative and persuasive."[45]

Long before the budget gets to the Congress, it is thrashed out inside the administration. The first step is presidential guidance on fiscal policy, which depends in part on forecasts of how the country's economy will perform two and three years in the future. With that guidance in hand, OMB sends its initial targets to the agencies funded by the budget, usually in the spring, at least eighteen months before the fiscal year begins. (The government's fiscal year begins October 1 and ends September 30. OMB sent agencies guidance for fiscal year 2012, beginning October 1, 2001, in March 2010.) This is the point at which budget officers all over Washington know whether they are facing a lean year or a fat year. Agencies have about six months to put their detailed budget requests together and get them to OMB in the fall, a year before the start of the fiscal year. Negotiations inside the administration last another six months or so, but by law and custom, the president must send his budget proposal to the Congress on the first Monday in February, eight months before the fiscal year begins.

The budgets that State and USAID send to OMB don't look like the budgets that will go to Congress. Congress carves the pie of federal spending into thirteen appropriations bills, but OMB slices the same pastry into nineteen areas or functions of government (agriculture, defense, income security, etc.). Each function is typically carried out in more than one agency, and each agency is typically engaged in more than one function. For the foreign service, the key budget is Function 150, international affairs. A summary of the president's budget request for Function 150 for FY 2011 (the year that ends on September 30, 2011) appears in table 6.1.[46]

The Department of State and USAID receive nearly all their appropriated funds through the 150 account, as do more than a dozen other government agencies and a few nongovernmental organizations that depend on government funds. Bits of the 150 account also go to agencies principally funded elsewhere. The State Department assembles the Function 150 request and leads the negotiations with OMB, which effectively decides who gets what in the president's budget.[47]

This is where the embassies weigh in. In every post overseas, and in every bureau, State and AID submit a joint budget request called a strategic plan. Plans from overseas missions go up through the regional bureaus. Mission strategic plans (MSPs) and bureau strategic plans (BSPs) identify the objectives they are supposed to achieve and connect them with the resources— not just money, but people, counted as full-time and part-time positions or contract employees—they need to achieve them. The objectives often come from the top, from the president and the secretary of state, but bureaus and missions have latitude to devise the programs and estimate the resources needed to accomplish the objectives in the local arena.

The final products are a State/USAID joint strategic plan and a budget request jointly submitted to Congress, but in two parts to distinguish which agency requests, and will be accountable, for what. Many in USAID are uncomfortable with State's growing involvement, and the degree of jointness can be questioned. In a sentence which must have been dragged kicking and screaming into the light of day, the QDDR says, "The Deputy Secretary of State for Management and Resources and a strong USAID Administrator each separately, but also working closely together, play a key role in managing foreign assistance funding and programs."[48]

Ambassador Craig Johnstone led resource planning in the State Department for Secretaries Christopher and Albright. "The biggest problem State has," Johnstone explained, "is aligning resources and objectives. If you have a clear objective and a clear strategy, and you have a plausible argument and avoid political minefields, you have a good chance in the Congress. For State and AID, the performance plans define what it is you're trying to get done in the country. They affect thinking in the regional bureaus. Only State and AID do this kind of regional planning."[49]

Steve Dietz explained in 2007 how the FY 2009 budget request would come together:

> We start with the current level of services. How much will it cost in 2009 to do what we are doing in 2008? We have to make assumptions here about inflation and exchange rates. Then we take out expenditures for what we did in 2008 that we won't do or don't plan to do in 2009. Then we add what we have to do in 2009 that we didn't do in 2008—mandatory pay raises go here, for example. Finally we add what we want to do in 2009 that we are not doing in 2008, discretionary spending. The MSPs and BSPs are essential to this process.[50]

The budget process is competitive, especially in the lean years, when resources are static or shrinking. Posts compete within a mission. In South Africa, the US consulates in Johannesburg, Cape Town, and Durban compete with each other and with the embassy in Pretoria to press their claims, and the ambassador resolves disputes. Within a bureau, the missions compete. More money for South Africa may mean less for Nigeria; adding an HIV/AIDS officer in Botswana could mean cutting a press officer in Nairobi. At the next level up, the bureaus compete: Africa against the Western Hemisphere against East Asia, refugee affairs against counterterrorism against public diplomacy. The agencies and programs funded in Function 150 compete: USAID against State, bilateral assistance against money for international organizations. In OMB, Function 150, international affairs, competes with the other eighteen functions in the federal budget. The ultimate arbiter is the US Congress.

FSOs, especially those in the field, see themselves as budget takers, not budget makers. For the most part they are right. They are too distant from budget decisions, in time and place, to have much impact on them. They are poorly placed to weigh competing claims for scarce resources. But FSOs, and especially ambassadors, should not underestimate the importance of the mission and bureau strategic plans, which build toward the State-AID joint

Table 6.1

International Affairs (Function 150) Budgets (Billions of US dollars)

Department	Actual FY 2009	Enacted FY 2010	Requested FY 2011
State Department			
Administration of Foreign Affairs, subtotal	10.9	11.0	12.4
Highlights			
Diplomatic and consular programs	7.2	8.2	9.5
Capital investment fund	0.3	0.1	0.1
Embassy security, construction, and maintenance	2.7	1.7	1.7
Foreign service retirement (net)	(0.2)	(0.2)	(0.2)
International Organizations, subtotal	4.0	3.8	3.8
Highlights			
Contributions to international organizations	1.6	1.7	1.6
Contributions to international peacekeeping	2.4	2.1	2.1
International commissions, subtotal	0.3	0.1	0.1
International broadcasting, subtotal	0.7	0.7	0.8
Related appropriations, subtotal	0.2	0.2	0.2
State/Broadcasting/Related agencies, Total	16.2	15.9	17.2

Table 6.1 (*continued*)

Department	Actual FY 2009	Enacted FY 2010	Requested FY 2011
USAID			
USAID administration, subtotal	1.3	1.7	1.7
Highlights			
USAID operating expenses	1.1	1.4	1.5
USAID capital investment fund	0.1	0.2	0.2
Bilateral Economic Assistance, Subtotal	21.5	21.9	24.6
Highlights			
Global health and child survival (State and USAID)	7.3	7.8	8.5
Development assistance	2.0	2.5	3.0
International disaster and famine assistance	0.8	0.8	0.9
Economic support fund	7.1	6.3	7.8
Assistance for Europe, Eurasia, and Central Asia (AEECA)	0.9	0.7	0.7
Democracy fund	0.1	0.1	—
Migration and refugee assistance	1.7	1.7	1.6
Independent agencies, subtotal	1.3	1.6	1.8
Peace Corps	0.3	0.4	0.4
Millennium Challenge Corporation	0.9	1.1	1.3
Department of Treasury	0.1	0.1	0.1
Military/Security Assistance, subtotal	10.1	7.0	10.0
Highlights			
International narcotics control and law enforcement	1.9	1.6	2.1
Nonproliferation, antiterrorism, demining	0.6	0.8	0.8
International military education and training (IMET)	0.1	0.1	0.1
Foreign military financing (FMF)	6.2	4.2	5.5
Peacekeeping operations	0.5	0.3	0.3
Pakistan counterinsurgency fund	0.7	—	1.2
Multilateral Assistance, subtotal	1.8	2.4	3.3
Department of Agriculture, Total	2.4	1.9	1.9
Food for Peace	2.4	1.7	1.7
McGovern-Dole International Food for Education	0.1	0.2	0.2
Foreign Operations, Total	34.3	32.8	39.4
State/Broadcasting/Related agencies, Total	16.2	15.9	17.2
State-Foreign Operations, Total	50.5	48.8	56.6
Function 150, Total	52.6	50.6	58.5

Sources: Author's compilation based on US Department of State, *Congressional Budget Justification, FY 2011*; White House, Office of Management and Budget, *President's Budget for Fiscal Year 2011*; Lawson, Epstein, and Nakamura, *State, Foreign Operations, and Related Programs*.

Note: Numbers do not include FY 2010 Afghanistan/Pakistan/Iraq supplemental or FY 2010 Haiti supplemental.

strategic plan that goes to Congress with the budget. A US ambassador in Africa remarked, "Initially I thought the mission plan a waste was of time, but over ten years it's evolved into a useful tool. You have control over your priorities, and to some extent over your budget."[51]

Interagency Conflict and Coordination

The competition for budgetary resources—money and people—is part of a broader contest over who shapes policy and controls its execution. Most of these struggles take place in Washington, not overseas. The foreign service as an institution rarely takes part in these struggles, because the service itself rarely has reason to favor any particular policy. But, as the Washington adage puts it, "Where you stand is where you sit." The positions advanced by individual members of the service depend on where they are in the foreign affairs bureaucracy. In Washington, members of the foreign service, like their civil service colleagues, spend many hours in inter- and intra-agency wrangles, advancing the point of view of the bureaucratic unit to which they are assigned. For nine out of ten members of the foreign service, that unit is somewhere in the Department of State.

Thrashing out positions within and between government agencies is time-consuming and often frustrating. George Shultz, who may have headed more large bureaucracies than anyone in American government, wrote that "in government, if [a] decision is going to stick, the divergent and divisive constituencies with a stake in the decision have to be persuaded—or if not fully persuaded, at least consulted—so they feel that their views were considered. Even then," he added, "they can give you plenty of grief."[52] Business executives and others from outside government who take on cabinet and subcabinet positions are almost always astonished by the amount of effort and the degree of compromise required to move a proposal or project through the system. "Don't we all work for the same president?" they lament. "Aren't we all on the same team?"

In fact, the team must be built anew for each issue. No agency has a full grasp of all the considerations that bear on a negotiation. Finding an efficient way to tap the government's expertise across agencies is a central task of management—and one not always carried out successfully. In foreign affairs, interagency coordination aims first of all at developing positions that fairly reflect the full range of US interests, and second at maintaining discipline in negotiations and in the execution of policy. The formal mechanisms for accomplishing these aims are, for the first, the interagency group and, for the second, the widely hated clearance process. But the informal machinery of government, the networks of professionals who know and respect each other, is at least as important.

Interagency groups have been around since George Washington's cabinet met in Philadelphia, but in the areas of security and foreign affairs the current system begins with the 1947 National Security Act, which established the National Security Council (NSC). The NSC today includes the president, the vice president, the secretaries of state, defense, energy, treasury, and homeland security, the attorney general, the ambassador to the United Nations, the president's chief of staff, and the assistant to the president for national security affairs (the national security adviser, who heads the NSC staff). The chairman of the joint chiefs of staff, the director of national intelligence, the White House counsel, and the deputy national security adviser attend every meeting, and other officials are included as appropriate. An NSC principals committee (cabinet level) and an NSC deputies committee (subcabinet level) oversee the work of dozens of policy coordination committees and working groups, including committees organized along regional lines that mirror the regional bureaus of the Department of State. The NSC staff, part of the executive office of the president, provides executive secretaries for each of these committees and manages their work.[53] In areas outside of national security, similar pyramids of interagency committees and working groups derive their authority from other statutes or from executive orders.

Positions are debated through the hierarchy of groups and committees, usually from the bottom up. This interagency process, and the groups and committees themselves, are often called simply "the interagency." Differences that cannot be resolved among office directors move up to deputy assistant secretaries, and then to assistant secretaries, undersecretaries, and heads of department. When disagreements persist, events may overtake the debate. The pressure of time, as well as the desire for unconstrained action, often leads one agency or another to ignore the process, which it can do so long as it retains the president's confidence. No amount of fiddling with organizational structures can force consensus.

Clearance

No bureaucratic battle is ever really over. A policy once decided must still be carried out. Any instruction to an overseas post requires approval from all the offices and agencies involved with the issue, and losers in the policy debate may use this clearance process to win back ground. The clearance system, intended to maintain discipline, often serves only to push instructions for action to a lowest common denominator, or to delay action until, again, events make the matter moot. Small wonder that the system often breaks down and back channels—unofficial communications—proliferate.

Aggressive embassies can use these Washington logjams to make policy by default. When instructions are late or inadequate, an ambassador can write his own, telling Washington (usually, the State Department officer in charge of the issue) that "unless otherwise directed, I intend to carry out the following actions," setting a short deadline for response. This device—known as *you know, dear,* for UNless Otherwise DIRected—is bureaucratic jiujitsu that flips the inertia of the clearance process around, making action as difficult to stop as it had been to initiate. Slightly less confrontational is using e-mail to achieve the same purpose.

Foreign service officers (FSOs) assigned to Washington quickly become familiar with interagency work, and they learn to recognize the downside of agency or ambassadorial freelancing. The State Department is a relatively small agency with a relatively small budget. It cannot carry out its mission without the political support and often the resources of other agencies. Other agencies, of course, have international interests but not the mandate or, in most cases, the global reach of State. Without coordination, either nothing gets done, or what does get done is done badly.

Coordination is a constant challenge often poorly met. For many foreign service officers in USAID as well as State, other agencies, which have their own priorities to address and their own constituencies to serve, are decidedly unwelcome participants in the complex business of foreign affairs. (The mistrust is mutual—other agencies often fear the State Department will sacrifice or sabotage their objectives in the name of foreign policy.) The QDDR recognized the need for change. The Department of State and USAID, it said, "must adopt new attitudes and new ways of doing business. We must actively engage other agencies in strategy development and planning, in addition to policy implementation. We must recognize other agencies' expertise and welcome their ability to build relationships with their foreign counterparts. And we must improve our own strategy, planning, and evaluation processes."[54]

Ambassador Owens-Kirkpatrick, recalling her time as the State Department's officer overseeing US representation at NATO, said,

I can't emphasize enough the importance of understanding interagency coordination. You have to learn how to be a constructive player. Collegial relationships with people in the Department of Defense, the White House, and other agencies, are critical to success. You need to deal, to negotiate, to horse trade. It's a lot of fun and you can become very good at it. Sometimes the need to coordinate would hold up instructions until the early morning hours, which is frustrating, but in the end you reach a higher quality outcome.[55]

The presence of active and former FSOs in agencies outside State can make coordination a bit easier. The trust and confidence needed for effective cooperation are more quickly established between people who know each other, or at least share common experiences, than between strangers. FSOs, especially those in midcareer, can benefit from the new perspective that an out-of-agency tour provides.

Numbers vary widely from year to year, but there are often as many as fifteen or twenty FSOs serving temporarily in White House agencies, mainly the NSC staff and the US Trade Representative's office. These assignments can be heady stuff. Ambassador Hugo Llorens was director of Andean affairs on the NSC staff when Lucio Gutierrez won election as Ecuador's president in 2002:

At seven thirty in the morning I got the call to brief the president for a nine o'clock congratulatory call. I got six or seven minutes to be alone with and brief the president, then I had the opportunity to listen in on the call. . . . But you do have to be careful. I always knew that I had to go back to the Department of State. Sometimes I had to pass a message, to tell a more senior State Department official, "Look, that's not the way the White House wants it done." I wasn't the FSO at the NSC, I was part of the NSC team.[56]

On the Southern Border

Coordination is especially challenging where relations are deep as well as broad, and US government agencies communicate easily and frequently with their foreign counterparts—places like Mexico, and especially the Mexican border. In the range of cross-border issues—trade, crime, pollution, transportation—the most sensitive and important is immigration.

Travel across the border is vital to commerce and family life. Legal border crossings number more than one million a day, and daily trade is worth about $1 billion. The US embassy in Mexico City calculates that twelve million people live in the counties and municipios adjacent to the border. The Mexican-born population of the United States numbers well over ten million, and one million US citizens live in Mexico. The United States struggles to control the transit of people and goods along the two-thousand-mile border, but these efforts, though they certainly affect US relations with Mexico, are not really part of American foreign policy.

Ambassador James Derham, a career FSO who was the US ambassador's deputy in Mexico from 1998 to 2002, explains, "Humane, orderly, legal immigration. That's the goal and the policy as they come down to us from Congress and the White House, and we reinforce that message with Mexico at every opportunity. But immigration is essentially a US domestic issue. Mexico has a role, of course, and the Mexicans can be helpful or harmful by their actions, but immigration policy is not like trade policy. There are no international negotiations."[57]

So what is the role of the foreign service? Derham explains it this way:

The foreign service has no direct role in setting immigration policy, but we do want to make sure that the domestic debate is an informed debate, that the realities from the Mexican side are understood. It's important that we understand how Mexico thinks about immigration and that we explain to Washington what effect it has on other areas of our relationship. It's our job, the job of the foreign service, to place enforcement work, including our own visa work, in the context of all US interests in Mexico, and to maintain consistency between our policies and our actions.

Consistency is hard to achieve. Most of the federal, state, and local agencies involved in border control see their work in purely domestic terms. Three bureaus of the Department of Homeland Security—Citizenship and Immigration Services, Immigration and Customs Enforcement, and Customs and Border Protection (including the Border Patrol)—strike a balance as best they can between maintaining security and promoting commerce. The Department of Justice is also heavily involved along the border, through the Bureau of Alcohol, Tobacco, Firearms, and Explosives; the US Marshals Service; the Federal Bureau of Investigation; and the Drug Enforcement Administration.

They don't always cooperate. "All these agencies have their jobs to do," said Derham. "They don't spend a lot of time thinking broadly about Mexico or even about each other, but they understand precisely what they're doing."[58] A former US consul at a border post added, "Law enforcement agencies don't do foreign policy, they do law enforcement. They don't like to share information, even with each other. We talk about 'humane, orderly, legal,' immigration but there's a gap between policy and what happens on the border. And the border region has its own culture. Local officials on both sides have a big say in everything that happens, including law enforcement, and they don't necessarily respond to their capitals. People along the border like to do things their own way."[59]

Working on or with the border means constant negotiation, not all of it with Mexico. The State Department calls its officer in charge of border affairs a coordinator, not a director, and for good reason. "Before we can deal with the Mexicans," said John Ritchie, who held that job, "we have to negotiate among ourselves. For example, if someone wants to open or close or modify a border crossing, we issue the licenses for construction. At a minimum we have to clear our decisions with twelve federal agencies, plus the affected states. We're long on responsibility but short on resources. We have to be very good at dealing with people in our own society and government."[60] Without that coordination, US-Mexican relations would deteriorate, and cooperation on the border would break down.

In many ways, the breakdown has already occurred. "The flow across the border, legal or illegal, is so massive," John Ritchie said, "a million legal crossings every day, maybe half a million or a million illegal crossings every year.[61] In the past few years Mexican migration has spread way beyond the border states. It's transforming the United States."[62]

"The border is a great example of 'you can't fix just one thing,'" said Jim Derham. "You need a coherent approach, one that looks at the incentives and disincentives, the economic differentials, the lack of employer sanctions, enforcement at the border, and everything else that's going on. If you focus just on one part of the problem, you will have consequences throughout the system that you failed to predict, with results that may not be at all what you wanted."[63]

No policy, however, has any meaning unless it is enforced. The Department of Homeland Security establishes visa policy and frames its regulations and enforces policy on the US side of the border. The foreign service, through its consuls and vice consuls, carries out US immigration policy on the Mexican side of the border.

The Mexican border is where many new members of the foreign service start their careers. Entrants typically spend at least a portion of their first overseas tours in consular work, and especially in visas. The United States issues visas and similar official travel documents at ten posts in Mexico, including seven along the border.

Visa work is hard, tedious, and challenging. It entails long hours in front of a line of nervous applicants, trying to separate legitimate travelers from potential illegal immigrants and security threats in interviews that last little more than a minute. A new officer may conduct one hundred interviews in a day, an experienced officer may conduct two hundred or more each day, one thousand in a week. There is no time for a lot of analysis. An experienced visa officer comes to rely on visual clues, an applicant's manner and air of confidence, as much as on answers to questions: "A good consular officer can make good decisions about 90 percent of the time as the applicant walks up to the window."[64]

A year on the visa line, one former visa officer said, "is absolutely the best way to learn about a society—what people do, how much they earn, how they live and how they would like to live, how their families are put together, how they relate to the United States."[65] Visa work tests stamina, language skills, and the willingness to say "no" to people who are desperate for "yes." It is daily instruction in making quick decisions, and daily proof that sensitivity to a foreign culture does not mean softness.

Role of the Ambassador and the Country Team

Interagency conflicts are more acute in Washington than in posts overseas. The opportunity for conflict certainly exists—some fifty US agencies are represented abroad, and in the typical embassy less than one-third of the American staff gets its paycheck from the Department of State. But the opportunity for strife is rarely seized. There are many reasons why this is so. Here are a few of them:

1. Embassies are policy takers, not policymakers. There are fewer fights because there is less to fight about.
2. Small is beautiful. In all but the largest posts, everyone knows everyone else. Relationships are more personal, less bureaucratic. There are few or no layers of staff. Decisions can be quickly and cleanly taken.
3. We're in this together. In a foreign clime and culture, agency identification fades and national identity takes over. And the more

difficult the circumstances, the closer the embassy staff becomes. Morale tends to be high in hardship posts.

4. The boss is nigh. In Washington the president is distant, his wishes made known through surrogates and artifacts—an initial on a memo, an ambiguous speech. Like Russian peasants thinking of the tsar, even high-level officials may believe against the evidence that the president really sides with them. But overseas, the president's representative, the ambassador, is right there, face to face. There should be no doubt about what the boss thinks or what the boss wants.

The idea that the ambassador is fully in charge of the embassy and all subordinate posts in the country seems an ancient notion, dating to the Greeks perhaps. But in US practice it dates to the postwar period, and particularly to the administration of John F. Kennedy and the idea of the country team. Since 1961 the president has provided each chief of mission with a letter that charges him or her with responsibility for the conduct of foreign affairs in his or her country of assignment, and gives him or her authority over all executive branch personnel in the country, except those under the command of a US area military commander, those seconded to an international organization, or those serving under another chief of mission. For example, the US ambassador to Belgium has no authority over the US missions to the European Union or to NATO, which are also in Brussels. Ambassadorial responsibility was placed in law in the Foreign Service Act of 1980, but ambassadorial authority needs to be perennially refreshed.[66] "Chiefs of mission must be empowered and accountable as CEOs of multiagency missions," says the QDDR, suggesting that their present authorities could use a booster shot.[67]

The terms *chief of mission* and *ambassador* are often used interchangeably, but chiefs of mission are not always ambassadors, and vice versa. A chief of mission (COM) is the principal officer in charge of a diplomatic mission of the United States. A COM is usually an ambassador—indeed, an ambassador extraordinary and plenipotentiary, or AEP—but may be a chargé d'affaires. The COM usually heads an embassy, which may have subordinate posts, typically consulates and consulates general. The heads of subordinate posts are also called principal officers, but they are not chiefs of mission.

Some ambassadors are not chiefs of mission. Ambassadors at large, such as the ambassador at large for war crimes issues or the ambassador at large for international religious freedom, both established by acts of Congress, have no missions, and others, such as the US global AIDS coordinator, are confirmed by the Senate with the personal rank of ambassador. A few individuals, appointed by the president for no more than six months, may be given the title of ambassador without Senate confirmation. By custom, once an ambassador, always an ambassador: If you ever hold the title, you may use it for the rest of your life.

An area commander does not command all forces in the area. Excluded are service attachés, military advisory groups or liaison offices, marine security guards, or other military elements that are part of the diplomatic mission and are under the COM's authority.

The chief of mission carries out his responsibility through the country team, which is made up of members of his staff he chooses to advise him and on whom he relies to see that policy is carried out. The chief of mission has a free hand in choosing the country team. Some ambassadors prefer a large group, with representatives of every element in the embassy. Others want a smaller group, focused on the most important areas of the ambassador's concern. A typical country team is shown in figure 6.1.

An ambassador's responsibilities have grown over the years. The State Department's *Foreign Affairs Manual* lists them in nineteen numbered paragraphs: opening markets for US exports, halting arms proliferation, preventing conflict, countering terrorism, upholding human rights, promoting international cooperation on environmental issues, suppressing narcotics, and assisting refugees—and these are just in paragraph one. Eighteen others follow.[68] Every ambassador has to be concerned about whether his authority, which depends largely on his leadership and support in Washington, is commensurate with these responsibilities.

A chief of mission has several tools he can use to maintain his mission as an integrated structure. One is *country clearance.* Any government employee not already stationed in the country must have the approval of the chief of mission before entering the country on official business. Is a delegation from the Department of Energy about to visit to promote an exchange of research and development with an institute that, according to intelligence sources, is mixed up in illegal transfers of nuclear technology? The chief of mission can just say no. Is an FBI team coming to investigate a kidnapping, just as negotiations on a bilateral agreement regarding child custody cases approach a conclusion? The chief of mission can put the FBI on hold. An ambassador may refuse clearance, or place restrictions or conditions on official travelers, as he or she considers necessary.[69]

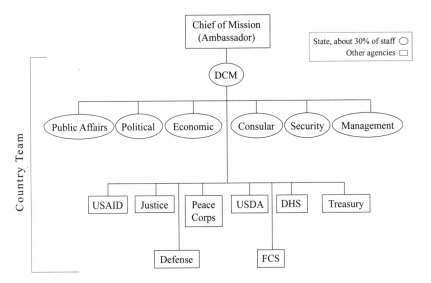

Figure 6.1
Organization of a Typical Mission

A chief of mission also has limited control over the structure and staffing of the embassy and its subordinate posts. The COM cannot increase staff without Washington's approval, including budgetary authority, but he can often block attempts by Washington agencies to send staff he does not want—at least if the Department of State backs him up.[70] The ambassador is, by law, accountable for the security of his mission and all US government personnel and their dependents in the country. If AID wants to put additional personnel in the field, but the COM sees an unacceptable security risk, the COM will likely prevail. He can reorganize State Department staff (combine the political and economic sections, for example, or establish separate sections for immigrant and nonimmigrant visas), but he cannot do much with the staff of other agencies without their approval.[71] He can, however, terminate the assignment and send home anyone under his authority whose behavior or performance is seriously unsatisfactory.

Of course, the wise ambassador picks no unnecessary fights and keeps Washington well informed of his thinking. All foreign service personnel should remember this: If you want the State Department to watch your back, make sure they know which way you're facing.

The State Department helps the ambassador out by negotiating some of the toughest interagency issues—who provides security, who controls communications, who pays for what, whose writ runs how far—in memoranda of understanding (MOUs) signed in Washington, not at post. Some MOUs have been contentious (State has negotiated at least four with the FBI), but all of them tend to reinforce the ambassador's authority in the embassy and across the host country. Agreements between the chief of mission and the local agency, or—most important—between the chief of mission and the area combatant commander, can supplement agency-to-agency understandings.

Nearly every embassy has a military component. The highest-ranking military officer inside a US embassy is ordinarily the defense attaché, a member of the worldwide defense attaché system run by the Defense Intelligence Agency (DIA). The defense attaché, typically an O-6 (full colonel or navy captain), may be from any of the services, and DIA often rotates the assignment from service to service. The defense attaché is principal military adviser to the ambassador and operates under the ambassador's authority. He is a member of the country team. His office carries out traditional responsibilities: liaison with the forces of the host country, including sharing of intelligence; weapons sales programs like foreign military sales (FMS) and foreign military financing (FMF); military-to-military exchanges, like International Military Education and Training (IMET, which brings foreign forces to the United States); and management of programs like the Global Peace Operations Initiative (GPOI, which provides US training and equipment for host-government forces engaged in international peacekeeping). GPOI and the FMS, FMF, and IMET programs are all funded through the Department of State.

In some embassies, a separate security assistance component, which may be called military liaison office, military group, office of defense cooperation, or any similar name that is acceptable to the host government, handles weapons sales. The officer in charge of this unit may outrank the defense attaché, but even if he does not, his chain of command runs to the Pentagon, not to the defense attaché. He is, however, subject to the authority of the ambassador. Most ambassadors will include the head of security assistance in the country team, along with the defense attaché.

Much of the military's growing nontraditional engagement abroad is in the area combatant commands, which lie outside ambassadorial authority. Area combatant commanders have funds available to them that allow them to deploy civil affairs teams to carry out humanitarian and reconstruction projects in countries where the US conducts military operations.[72] Also outside ambassadorial authority are the area commands' public-diplomacy efforts—every command engages in strategic communications and information operations that that may or may not run parallel with the efforts of the embassy or the Department of State, and may be better funded.[73] And in a gray area between the area combatant commands and the defense personnel subject to ambassadorial authority are military personnel under the Special Operations Command (SOCOM), which provided military-to-military counterterrorism training.

The Senate Foreign Relations Committee staff found in 2006 that "the number of military personnel and Defense Department activities in non-combat countries is increasing significantly" and warned that "the increases of funding streams, self-assigned missions, and realigned authorities for the Secretary of Defense and the combatant commanders are placing new stresses on inter-agency coordination in the field."[74] The trends noted in 2006 have not abated.

An ambassador needs to develop and maintain solid working relationships with the area combatant command and with other relevant military centers, whose activities may have as much or greater effect on local perceptions and bilateral relations as anything the embassy itself may be doing. Coordination can be tricky. "We had six hundred or eight hundred military personnel, mostly air force and army, on a base in Honduras, by agreement with the Honduran military," said Frank Almaguer, who was ambassador to that country from 1999 to 2002:

> Its primary mission was training, for the Corps of Engineers and others. Honduras was a beneficiary of various projects. The Illinois National Guard might come in, go to a village and in three weeks build a health-care center. But it was training [for the Guard], not foreign assistance. The location wasn't based on Honduran needs or wants, it was based on training priorities—a mountain, a jungle. Maintenance wasn't part of the deal. There was tension between USAID and the military, and sometimes with the local ministries. As ambassador I had mixed feelings. The public relations side was great, but for development purposes it was not always the best investment of American dollars.[75]

An embassy of any size is always at risk of breaking down into a collection of agency staffs, each pursuing its own goals. Ambassadorial authority is not enough to hold things together—that takes ambassadorial leadership. The ambassador who understands his mission's mission, who articulates an integrated set of objectives for the people and resources under his control, will find a strong and positive response. Foreign service, civil service, armed service—everyone who is part of the mission wants to feel the pride of working together for the good of the country. The ambassador who provides that feeling will be rewarded with effort, loyalty, and success.

The Foreign Service and the Military

FSOs like to refer to themselves as "the first line of defense."[76] The phrase is a cliché worn thin with time, but it has never resonated with the general public because the image does not ring true. Diplomats are not soldiers. Even when matters of life and death are at issue, riding in a sedan to the foreign ministry is not like riding in a Humvee on patrol. Confronting a hostile audience is not like confronting an armed enemy, and running an embassy's political section is not like commanding a brigade. But the relationship between the foreign service and the military deserves special attention. It is close and essential yet filled with tension, like the relationship between diplomacy and force.

Since World War II, three military men have led the Department of State (General Marshall from 1947 to 1949, General Haig from 1981 to 1982, and General Powell from 2001 to 2005), and one FSO has headed the Department of Defense (Frank Carlucci, from 1987 to 1989). The two departments, however, are as much competitors as collaborators. They are inevitably involved in each other's business.

The military's growing involvement in what had been civilian diplomatic activities is clear. Between 1990 and 2000, as the international affairs budgets were shrinking and the foreign service was growing smaller by the year, the budgets of the military regional commands grew rapidly. Each of the then five area combat commands—Northern (NORTHCOM), Southern (SOUTHCOM), European (EUCOM), Central (CENTCOM), and Pacific (PACOM)—saw increases of at least 35 percent.[77] The commands, headed by the area military commanders, who are exempt from ambassadorial authority, put those resources to work in nontraditional ways, expanding their role in peacekeeping, civil reconstruction, suppression of narcotics trafficking, de-mining, and disaster relief. Their purpose was and is to forestall the anarchy that provides cover for terrorism and transnational crime by creating or shoring up governments that function with the consent of the governed. Now, with the new emphasis on integrating diplomacy, defense, and development, the foreign service is devoting more attention to similar assignments. This kind of work, which used to be called nation-building, is not new to either the foreign service or the military, but neither is entirely comfortable with its current role.

A growing share of the foreign assistance budget goes to security assistance, where military involvement is, of course, greatest. Amy Frumin calculated that "between 1999 and 2005 the share of [US] official development funds channeled through the Department of Defense increased from 3.5 percent to 21.7 percent."[78] The trend has slowed, but the role of the Pentagon and the armed services continues to grow. Tensions with the Department of State and USAID have grown as well. When Senator Lugar, then chairman of the Senate Foreign Relations Committee, asked Secretary Rice about a new provision of law that placed some foreign aid programs directly under the Department of Defense, she replied with a fine example of testy gobbledygook:

> Select new DOD authorities offer an essential means of addressing rapidly evolving security challenges posed by, among other things, the GWOT [global war on terrorism]. . . . I support such authorities in many cases, contingent upon the explicit preservation of my aforementioned statutory role with respect to foreign assistance, through their exercise "with the concurrence of the Secretary of State," and in some cases through joint development procedures.[79]

Military attitudes toward these nontraditional missions are decidedly mixed. At the level of doctrine, the military would just as soon get out of the nation-building business. *Counterinsurgency*, an army and marine corps field manual published in 2006, states that "in COIN [counterinsurgency] it is always preferred for civilians to perform civilian tasks." But what is preferred isn't always possible: "The more violent the insurgency, the more unrealistic is this division of labor."[80] The manual quotes counterinsurgency expert David Galula: "To confine soldiers to purely military functions while urgent and vital tasks have to be done, and nobody else is available to undertake them, would be senseless. The soldier must then be prepared to become . . . a social worker, a civil engineer, a schoolteacher, a nurse, a boy scout. But only so long as he cannot be replaced, for it is always better to entrust civilian tasks to civilians."[81]

The decision to give the Department of Defense, and especially the armed services, broader responsibilities in foreign relations is in part a natural consequence of wartime. But it also flows from the great respect that policymakers have for the military's competence and energy. There is a sentiment, not always unspoken, that associates the US military with decisiveness, a grasp of core issues, and a single-minded focus on US interests, and associates US diplomacy with hesitation, infatuation with complexity, and a too-tender regard for the opinion of foreigners.

A report by the RAND Corporation identified three main obstacles to cooperation in the field between the military and civilian agencies, principally the army (which paid for the report) on the one hand, and the foreign services of State and USAID on the other. First, said the report, State and AID simply do not have much money—especially in comparison to the army—and Congress has constrained the way they can use the money they have. State and AID are also few in number and lack the capacity to mount a civilian surge. Finally, the civilian agencies have an entirely different approach to planning, and AID in particular has "an organizational distrust . . . of thinking jointly of US security policy and developmental goals."[82] Working through these differences, the report argues, will be difficult but not impossible.

Barry Blechman, who was a member of both the Defense Policy Board and the secretary of state's Advisory Committee on Transformational Diplomacy, believes that even in times of armed conflict diplomats should be heeded. "If you look back historically, the most successful American interventions have been those where there was a real partnership between the military commander and the diplomats on the scene." Blechman recognizes, though, that FSOs and military officers approach problems in different ways, often leaving the diplomats at a disadvantage. People in the military, he says, "are trained to take a problem, break it down into subparts, think about the solution to each subpart, organize it into specific tasks, and get each task done." At the same time, most FSOs are "oriented to be observers, analysts, reporters. Naturally they are not so operational."[83]

Military officers also gain command responsibility at a much earlier stage in their careers. "As a twenty-four-year-old army lieutenant I was responsible for thirty men," said Richard Miles, who joined the foreign service in 1993 after four years in uniform. "The foreign service can't offer that. I probably won't have that level of responsibility until I make deputy chief of mission," after about twenty years of service. Miles also sees the foreign service as a bit loose in discipline. "If the division or brigade commander says, 'This is going to happen,' and it doesn't happen, someone pays a price. But if the ambassador says, 'This is going to happen,' and it doesn't happen, there may be no consequences."[84]

The flip side of having fewer troops to command is having fewer chiefs to report to. "It's amazing how close you are to the top," said Steve Dietz, a State Department civil servant and naval academy graduate who spent twenty years as a submarine officer. "I talk to assistant secretaries every day. I brief the deputy secretary. That never happened in DOD."[85] Another State Department officer who served as an adviser to a military unit in the Middle East said that hierarchy is more rigid in the military than at State. "I was a civilian, a young woman, serving above my pay grade. The hardest thing was to break through the colonels into the inner circle around the commanding general."[86]

The differences between military and FSOs in background, training, mission, resources, and responsibilities almost guarantee tension and misunderstanding when the two work closely together. Each group has its own stereotype of the other. To the military, FSOs are smart but indecisive and can't get things done; to FSOs, military officers get things done but leave a huge political mess behind them (and spend more money before breakfast than the whole foreign service does in a year).

During his time in Iraq in 2005 and 2006, FSO Vincent Campos saw "a lot of discomfort" among FSOs who lacked a military background. "People seemed to have the notion that if the military would just leave economic and political affairs alone everyone would be better off," he said. Working together under pressure, though, changed attitudes. "Across the board where I worked, and talking with foreign service people embedded with military units, we had excellent working relationships—people became friends, socialized. We absolutely depended on each other."[87]

The military in the field sees events from a unique perspective. But the military in the Pentagon, and its civilian leadership as well, are also deeply engaged in the nation's foreign policy. On the civilian side, the office of undersecretary of defense for policy [OUSD(P)] includes assistant secretaries, deputy assistant secretaries, and office directors with geographic responsibilities like those of the regional bureaus of the Department of State. On the military side, in the office of the joint chiefs of staff, the figure most directly engaged in politico-military affairs, international negotiations, and interagency coordination is the director of strategic plans and policy (J5), a three-star general with a two-star vice director and five one-star deputies.[88]

Cross-training and exchanges of personnel are one way to bridge the gap between military and diplomatic officers. Virtually every class of the new FSOs and specialists includes former members of the armed forces, who are joining the foreign service in rising numbers. FSOs and State Department civil servants serve in the office of the secretary of defense, mainly in OUSD(P), under a State-Defense officer exchange program. Military officers on loan to the State Department serve throughout the building, but especially in the office of the secretary and her undersecretaries and in the bureau of politico-military affairs. Each year about eighty-five mid-level FSOs (classes FS-03, FS-02, and FS-01) attend the National Defense University at Fort McNair in Washington (where a senior FSO serves as vice president) or one of the other educational institutions attached to the Department of Defense—the Army War College in Carlisle, Pennsylvania; the Air Force War College at the Maxwell Air Force Base in Alabama; the Naval War College in Newport, Rhode Island; the Naval Postgraduate School in Monterey, California; the Joint Forces Staff College in Norfolk, Virginia; and the Army Command and General Staff College at Fort Leavenworth, Kansas. Military officers study at the Foreign Service Institute in Arlington, Virginia, on the campus and through distance learning. About 90 senior FSOs serve as policy advisers—POLADs—to general officers at regional and joint commands, and both State and USAID plan to expand the program.[89]

Ambassador Robert Loftis, a retired career FSO deeply involved in political-military affairs, is a strong proponent of the POLAD system. Loftis discussed the POLAD program in 2006, when the numbers were much smaller. "We're trying to expand our political-advisor program," he said.

> Traditionally, State has supplied a senior foreign service officer—a flag-rank officer—to work as political advisor to a four-star at a regional or joint command. Now we're trying to push that idea down to more subordinate commands and midgrade officers. For example, we're assigning a POLAD, a specialist in the region, to train and deploy with the First Infantry Division in Iraq, an eighteen-month tour. We've got a foreign service POLAD at the air base in Baghram, Afghanistan. The POLAD provides political advice and is a link back to the State Department—sort of a mirror image of what a defense attaché does in an embassy. We're working on a virtual POLAD, who would sit in Washington and be available to his or her military unit for role-playing and informal advice, with travel as necessary.[90]

The military also places a high value on the POLADS, not for their analytic abilities, but for their operational impact. When the Defense Department established AFRICOM, the area combatant command for Africa, in 2008, it wanted more than an adviser and created the position of deputy to the commander for civil-military activities (DCMA), filled by a senior foreign service officer. The DCMA is responsible for the planning and oversight of the majority of AFRICOM's security assistance work and is equal in rank to the deputy to commander for military operations (DCMO), a position filled at this writing by a vice admiral.

The military's counterinsurgency field manual says that the position of political adviser "is not suitable for intelligence professionals" because "their task is to understand the environment," whereas the "political advisor's job is to help shape the environment." The manual notes that "the current force structure gives corps and division commanders a political advisor" and says that "a force optimized for COIN operations would have political and cultural advisors at company level."[91] A company has one hundred to two hundred soldiers.

Exchanges notwithstanding, Loftis was concerned about the expansion of the military's mission. "There's an unfortunate tendency in the United States right now to idealize the military uncritically," he said.

> Anyone who says anything about the military has to preface it by saying, "We have the best armed forces in the world," which is true of course, but the military doesn't have a monopoly on wisdom. The military has a great can-do culture, but that doesn't mean it can or should do it all. There's a certain contradiction when a lieutenant colonel is trying to set up, for example, a microcredit facility somewhere in the field. And most military officers see the contradiction and are unhappy with it.
>
> The stereotype—see Robert Kaplan's *Imperial Grunts*—of the soldier in the field who knows what's really going on, while the diplomat is clueless and isolated in the capital, is false. Many soldiers in the field, smart as they are, are in one place for only a few weeks. They talk only to a small group of people. They don't have the same depth that someone a long time in the country can acquire. The idea that the military is always right, while the State Department only cares what foreigners think, is powerful, but it's just not true.[92]

Loftis, who negotiated agreements on military bases and the status of US forces all over the world, is an exemplar of diplomatic-military integration. His negotiating team typically included the desk officer and a civilian lawyer from the Office of the Secretary of Defense, the desk officer and a military lawyer from the Joint Chiefs of Staff, and relevant experts from the regional command. His chief legal adviser in the State Department was a navy judge advocate general (JAG) on loan to the State Department, and his deputy was an air force colonel. But Loftis said that personnel exchanges, training, and the growing number of former military like Richard Miles coming into the foreign service will not end tensions between the foreign service and the military, or between State and Defense.

"Tension starts at the top and flows down," Loftis explained. "If there's a fundamental disagreement at the top, you can mitigate it with personal relations, but in the end you can't work around it. You have to resolve it."

The Foreign Service and the Intelligence Community

For a brief period after World War II, the Department of State was the center of US intelligence. In 1945, President Truman disbanded the Office of Strategic Services (OSS) and transferred many of its personnel and functions to the Department. Truman was unhappy with the often conflicting reports he received each day from army intelligence, navy intelligence, the State Department, and other sources. He asked the secretary of state to "take the lead in developing a comprehensive and coordinated foreign intelligence program for all Federal agencies concerned with that type of activity."[93]

But senior officials of the department, including the distinguished career diplomat Loy Henderson, decried intelligence as a mere duplication of foreign service reporting. One assistant secretary, showing that reckless accusations of disloyalty were not limited to the department's enemies, denounced OSS personnel transferred to State as "collectivists and 'do-gooders.'" The secretary of state, James F. Byrnes, ignored the president's instructions and allowed the intelligence function to languish. In the end, Truman created the Central Intelligence Agency (CIA) in 1947 as his second-choice solution. Dean Acheson, then State's undersecretary, later wrote that the department lost control of the intelligence function through "gross stupidity" and an abdication of leadership.[94]

Sixty years later, however, relations between the foreign service and the intelligence community are generally good, and less contentious than the service's relations with the military. Foreign service work, practice, and culture are far closer to intelligence work than to military activity. FSOs are producers, analysts, and informed consumers of intelligence, and often very skilled at their work. The first director of national intelligence (DNI) was a career FSO, Ambassador John Negroponte, later named deputy secretary of state.

Overseas, it's an open secret that officers of the CIA work in many US embassies under diplomatic cover. In most cases the intelligence affiliation of these officers is declared to the intelligence service of the host government, with which they exchange information. Military attachés, who work in the open, are also engaged in intelligence, as are legal attachés (who are agents of the FBI), officers of the DEA, and to some extent Treasury attachés. FSOs and specialists generally work comfortably with these colleagues, all of whom are under the authority of the chief of mission. Deputy chiefs of mission (DCM), who are career FSOs, may prepare personnel evaluations on the senior officers at post from each of these agencies, and ambassadors review them. How heavily a DCM's opinion weighs in the promotion process at the FBI, the DEA, or any other agency is a separate question.

The opportunities for conflict that arise between personnel under the authority of the ambassador and personnel under the authority of an area military commander do not arise, or are much reduced, when everyone works within the same mission, under the same chief. Jim Pavitt, a former deputy director for operations (head of the clandestine service) at the CIA, explained it this way: "The ambassador is the president's representative. Period, end of discussion. Any intelligence personnel abroad are the representatives of their organizations. They are members of the country team. The only time there are major problems is when someone thinks he's smarter than the system, and you have an intelligence operation that bypasses the ambassador, or an ambassador who compromises an intelligence operation by talking about it. Successful foreign service officers and successful intelligence officers have good, productive exchanges."[95]

Their work overlaps. Intelligence officers conduct diplomacy as well as espionage. "At the height of the cold war, intelligence officers were talking to the KGB," Pavitt said. "And at the height of the coldest war, we were talking to the Chinese. These were exchanges that diplomats could not have. A diplomat's ability to maneuver is encumbered by considerations that don't weigh on an intelligence officer. The main difference is secrecy."

Diplomats do not conduct covert operations, but they do collect and analyze intelligence. Foreign service reporting is one of several streams of information, along with signals intelligence, imaging, and reporting from clandestine sources, that flow into Washington's pool of analysts and policymakers. "Intelligence is about informing," said Pavitt, "and how intelligence is collected is less important than whether it informs accurately and effectively."

FSOs rely on what people freely tell them, and on their own observations. "They are not stealing information," Pavitt continued. What FSOs hear, whether from official or unofficial sources, is information that is often passed to them for a reason. "You have to recognize that ministry officials sometimes say what they do because they are acting in their interest, not ours. That's when you want a clandestine source, who can steal the briefing book, the talking points."[96] Of course, the motives of a clandestine source— which may be money, ideology, revenge, or some other human impulse— are often more obscure than those of a government official.

David Newsom, a retired three-time ambassador and former undersecretary of state, observed some years ago that "some officials in Washington, particularly in the higher echelons, place a special value on clandestine reporting, believing that it may give a more accurate picture. . . than the more overt reporting of the regular embassy personnel."[97] That prejudice still exists. "What's unknown, what's secret, what's black, is sort of sexy," Pavitt acknowledged. "In the minds of the uninformed consumer, something marked 'secret' has to be more important." The sense among FSOs that reporting by the spooks (which few FSOs in an embassy ever see) may cause readers in Washington to disregard their own analyses can be a galling source of friction. But knowing whether the source of information was overt or covert by itself says nothing about the information's value and validity. Collectors of overt and covert intelligence form judgments about the reliability of their sources, but sorting fact from fiction, integrating the data, and making forecasts with varying levels of confidence in the end is the analyst's job.

In Washington the State Department participates in the intelligence community through its Bureau of Intelligence and Research (INR). *Intelligence community* is a defined term, identifying a group of seventeen government agencies:[98]

- the office of the Director of National Intelligence
- the Central Intelligence Agency
- the Defense Intelligence Agency
- the National Security Agency, the National Reconnaissance Office,

and the National Geospatial-Intelligence Agency, all part of the Department of Defense

- Army, Navy, Air Force, and Marine Intelligence
- the Department of Homeland Security, through its Information Analysis and Infrastructure Protection Directorate
- the Coast Guard, which is part of DHS
- the FBI
- units within four more agencies, the Department of State (Bureau of Intelligence and Research), the Treasury Department (financial intelligence), the Department of Energy (for nuclear matters), and the Drug Enforcement Administration

About 80 percent of the intelligence budget flows through the Department of Defense.

After events in Iraq proved that many of the judgments of the intelligence community were wrong, and sometimes disastrously so, some in the bureau and in the department argued that INR, which had been generally more cautious and skeptical than other agencies about weapons of mass destruction and chances for a quick transition to democratic rule, should have equal status with them. State's INR bureau is small, numbering only about 170 analysts. The CIA has between two thousand and three thousand analysts, and DIA has perhaps six thousand. "These agencies cannot, should not, be equal," said Pavitt. "They have different structures and different missions. If they have the same mission, that's a mistake."[99] A senior INR official agreed. "INR's mission is to supply all-source intelligence to the secretary, her staff, and to posts abroad. We serve the secretary and the director of national intelligence, but if their priorities conflict, the secretary comes first."[100]

Differences among analysts from different agencies are supposed to be resolved at the National Intelligence Council, an interagency operation run by the DNI. Those differences should be fewer and narrower as intelligence agencies learn to switch from the pre-9/11 rule that limited information exchange to those with a need to know to the post-9/11 rule of responsibility to share. Analysts working with similar information should reach similar conclusions.

Among the INR analysts, civil servants outnumber FSOs by roughly three to one. "We'd like the ratio to be sixty-forty or even fifty-fifty," said the senior INR official, a civil servant. But many FSOs avoid INR because it has no overseas outposts and looks like a siding, not a main career track. Even so, the analysts build close relationships with FSOs in the field. Unlike the CIA, DIA, or other intelligence agencies, which have their own personnel abroad, INR cannot send orders to embassies, asking for particular kinds of reports or for the collection of particular kinds of intelligence. But INR analysts generally know who is doing what at posts in the countries they cover, and they use e-mail exchanges for informal queries. "Maybe 60 or 70 percent of the political and economic officers going out on assignment stop by INR to be briefed and make introductions," the official explained. "There's no requirement that they do so. It's really up to the INR analysts to build and maintain a network of contacts" overseas, in the department, in other agencies, and outside government.

Intelligence analysts are not policymakers and should not be advocates for particular policies. "Analysts who become advocates lose their advantage, their uniqueness," the senior INR official pointed out. "In a room full of policy people, the analyst has a special position. If he becomes an advocate, he joins the crowd." Pavitt gave an example. "You take analysts and put them in a meeting with ambassadors X and Y, assistant secretaries P and Q, and you ask, 'What if [former Thai prime minister] Thaksin comes back in a countercoup? What's the effect on Asian markets?' and watch them take over the room. That's when analysis serves policy best."[101]

FSOs serving as analysts in INR must check their policy hats at the door, but when they go abroad, the hat goes on again. Embassy reporting often does and should argue for or against particular policies and tactics, even strategies, and the embassy's point of view has weight. "The sense that comes from being in the place has great value, there's no other way to get it," the INR official said. "When the president gets his daily intelligence brief from the DNI, it's surprising how often he asks, 'What does the ambassador think?'"[102] A good ambassador has absorbed the intelligence from all sources available to him and formed a sound, well-reasoned opinion.

Part III

The Career

7

Stability and Change

Ask a member of the foreign service about the work, and it won't be long before you hear something like this: "Where else can you reinvent yourself every two or three years? There's always a different job, boss, country, or culture just ahead. You change posts, and you walk into the middle of a new adventure."

Change is only part of the story. Foreign service people don't talk much about it, but most of them take comfort in the stable framework that surrounds and cushions the constant change of foreign service life. That framework is the structure of a foreign service career, with its hierarchies and formalities; annual evaluations, periodic training, competitive promotions, regional and functional specialization, rotation through a variety of posts, and rising levels of responsibility, pay, and status. Retirement, which can come as early as age fifty with twenty years of service, is generous. So are health benefits. There are moving allowances, housing allowances, education allowances, hardship allowances, and other benefits, along with a reliable salary that keeps foreign service families comfortably in America's middle class. That, along with their diplomatic status and privileges, places them among the elites of most of the countries where they are assigned. Whether one serves in Afghanistan or Zimbabwe or Washington, D.C., there is the mixed but ever-present blessing of the same warm bureaucratic embrace. It is the relative security of the career that lets foreign service people thrive on the risk, tumult, and rootlessness of foreign service life.

Rank, Title, Pay, Benefits

Foreign service ranks run backward, like NASA countdowns. Classes nine, eight, and seven are noncommissioned classes. The classes from FS-06 to FS-01 are roughly equivalent to civil service grades GS-08 to GS-15, or to military ranks O-1 (second lieutenant, ensign) to O-6 (colonel, navy

163

captain). Above FS-01 is the senior foreign service, where the ranks have names. The lowest of the senior grades—the words *grade, rank,* and *class* are used interchangeably—is FE-OC (counselor), rising to FE-MC (minister-counselor), and FE-CM (career minister). FS designates foreign service, and FE mysteriously designates the senior or executive level. The senior grades are roughly equivalent to military flag ranks (general, admiral) or to the grades of the civil service's senior executive service.

Beyond these senior grades, the secretary of state may award the most distinguished members of the service the honorary personal rank of career ambassador. By custom, the number of career ambassadors on active duty is limited to five and rarely exceeds two or three. Some diplomatic ranks and titles, which are more or less standard across the diplomatic establishments of all countries, look like but are not related to the personal ranks used by the US senior foreign service (see chapter 4).

Base pay is established each year under a statutory formula that the president may decide not to follow. The pay schedules for 2010 are delineated in tables 7.1, 7.2, and 7.3, and the latest schedules are posted on the State Department's website (www.careers.state.gov). All federal salaries are adjusted to account for regional variations in living costs. The locality pay adjustment adds about 24 percent to the base for service in Washington, D.C., and about 9 percent for service overseas. Members of the senior foreign service, whose pay is linked to performance, do not receive a locality adjustment.

Benefits are many and varied; the State Department's website provides a summary.[1] Of special note are certain benefits paid only to foreign service employees assigned abroad: a housing allowance, which provides either furnished quarters or a stipend; an education allowance, which sends children to certified overseas American schools where available and pays a fixed stipend where they are not; and home leave, which pays travel from the post of assignment to a home leave address in the United States as well as paid leave that may amount to six weeks for every two years abroad. An employee assigned to a post where family members are not allowed receives a separate maintenance allowance. These and certain other allowances are not subject to federal tax. Base pay and hardship and danger differentials are fully taxable.

In the State Department, foreign service officers (FSOs) for the most part enter the foreign service as career candidates by passing written and oral examinations, followed by a medical exam and a security investigation. They will spend up to five years as career candidates. Then, if they are awarded

Table 7.1
Foreign Service Salary Table, 2010 (Base pay, US dollars)

Step	Class								
	1	2	3	4	5	6	7	8	9
1	99,628	80,728	65,413	53,003	42,948	38,394	34,324	30,684	27,431
2	102,617	83,150	67,375	54,593	44,236	39,549	35,354	31,605	28,254
3	105,695	85,644	69,397	56,231	45,564	40,732	36,414	32,553	29,102
4	108,866	88,214	71,429	57,918	46,930	41,954	37,507	33,529	29,975
5	112,132	90,860	73,623	59,665	48,338	43,213	38,632	34,535	30,874
6	115,496	93,586	75,832	61,445	49,789	44,509	39,791	35,571	31,800
7	118,961	96,393	78,107	63,288	51,282	45,844	40,985	36,638	32,754
8	112,530	99,285	80,450	65,187	52,821	47,220	42,214	37,737	33,737
9	126,206	102,264	82,863	67,143	54,405	48,636	43,481	38,870	34,749
10	*129,517	105,332	85,349	69,157	56,037	50,095	44,785	40,836	35,791
11	*129,517	108,492	87,910	71,232	57,719	51,598	46,129	41,237	36,865
12	*129,517	111,746	90,547	73,369	59,450	53,146	47,512	42,474	37,971
13	*129,517	115,099	93,263	75,570	61,234	54,741	48,938	43,748	39,110
14	*129,517	118,552	96,061	77,837	63,071	56,383	50,406	45,060	40,283

Source: US Department of State, www.state.gov/documents/organization/134927.pdf.
Note: * base pay cap = $129,517 (FS-01, Step 10, equivalent to GS-15, Step 10).

Table 7.2
Senior Foreign Service Pay Range, 2010 (Base pay, US dollars)

Minimum	Maximum
119,554	179,700

Caps	
OC (Counselor)	102% of Executive Level III
MC (Minister counselor)	107% of Executive Level III
CM (Career minister)	100% of Executive Level II

Source: US Department of State, www.state.gov/documents/organization/134927.pdf.

Table 7.3
Executive-Level Pay Scale, 2010 (US dollars)

Executive level I	199,700
Executive level II	179,700
Executive level III	165,300
Executive level IV	155,500
Executive level V	145,700
GS-15 Step 1	99,628

Source: US Department of State, www.state.gov/documents/organization/134927.pdf.

tenure, they will be appointed and commissioned by the president, by and with the consent of the Senate. They can then look forward to about twenty years in midcareer. If they are especially successful, they may spend another five years or more in the senior foreign service, at the top of their profession. Rank at entry depends on educational background and employment history, but most entrants begin at FS-06 or FS-05. Average time in grade and service at different ranks is presented in table 7.4.

State's foreign service uniquely includes foreign service specialists, who are not routinely commissioned and whose appointment and promotions do not routinely require Senate action. They serve in job categories that include security, financial management, human resources, general services, information management, and medicine. Specialists apply for employment in their specialties and, like the officers, enter the service after an oral examination and background and medical checks. Also like the officers, they are evaluated for tenure, but their careers are influenced more by the job opportunities and needs of the service in their fields of specialization. Rank at entry depends on the job being taken as well as on background and attainments. The same pay table, set by act of Congress, applies to officers and specialists, indeed to all members of the foreign service, whether they work at State, USAID, Commerce, or Agriculture.

Career Trajectory

An FSO or commissioned specialist can expect a career of close to thirty years in three parts, entry level, midlevel, and senior service. For those—the great majority—who begin their careers in classes six or five, the entry level usually lasts a bit more than four years, or two tours, and ends with tenure and promotion to class three. Passage through the middle grades—classes three, two, and one—may take a bit more than twenty years and end in voluntary retirement after age fifty, mandatory retirement for time in class or time in service, mandatory retirement at age sixty-five, or promotion into the senior foreign service.

The career path crosses two thresholds: one from career candidate to tenured employee, the other to gain entry to the senior foreign service. "It's a flow-through system," says Rob Nolan, a career FSO who headed both the career development and the performance evaluation offices in the bureau of human resources. "We hire bright people with the intention of keeping them for a finite period of time. If you're a generalist, we expect to keep

Table 7.4
Career Trajectory (Average)

Grade		Midpoint Base Salary ($)	Officers		Specialists	
			Years in Grade	Years in Service	Years in Grade	Years in Service
Entry level	06 to 05	50,000	—	—	4	6
	05 to 04	61,000	—	—	4	12
Midlevel	04 to 03	75,000	3	5	3	6
	03 to 02	94,000	3	8	5	9
	02 to 01	115,000	6	16	6	16
Senior foreign	01 to OC	144,000	6	22	4	16
service	OC to MC	155,000	5	24	4	14
	MC to CM	170,000	7	30	—	—

Source: Author's compilation.

Note: Salaries rounded to nearest thousand, years to nearest integer. Years in grade and service are counted at the time of promotion to the higher grade shown.

you around for twenty-seven years, maybe a year or two more if you learn a hard language. Those who make it into the senior foreign service do so on average after maybe twenty-one years of service, and they stick around for another nine years on average, for a career of thirty or thirty-one years total, not that much longer. Either way, you should leave with a decent annuity."[2]

The system is competitive but not cutthroat. Entry-level officers and specialists worry about gaining tenure, but 95 percent of them do. Midlevel personnel worry about being cut for failure to perform—what the service calls selection out, or involuntary separation. But more than 90 percent of tenured officers make it to FS-01, the highest rank before the senior foreign service, and most of those who do not reach that rank resign or retire voluntarily. Of those who reach FS-01, more than half go on to the senior ranks.

Careers don't necessarily follow a smooth path. Serendipity happens, and so does life. Bill Eaton rose rapidly but quit the service as a midlevel officer with ten years of service to become director of international operations for a struggling nonprofit organization. Within three years he had turned the organization around and become its executive director, but, he said, he missed the foreign service. "The way you come in every day and feel like you make a difference in the world, that you serve a higher purpose, something bigger than yourself. I missed the camaraderie, the excitement. I realized that working in your own country, in your own culture, wasn't nearly as much fun or as difficult as working overseas."[3]

Eaton was surprised to learn that the service would take him back. "The department treated [my time away] like a three-year sabbatical. I came back at the same grade, and a year later I got a promotion." As a management officer (see chapter 8), Eaton said he learned a lot in his time away from the service. "It was like a three-year MBA. I had a chance to learn from experts how to be a CEO. When we grow up in the foreign service, we tend to grow blinders, to think, this is the way things are done. But outside the service, we see other possibilities. The experience made me a better FSO."

The number of officers who resign is low, and the number who, like Eaton, resign and return is tiny. (The Byrds, foreign service specialists, also resigned and returned. Their story appears in chapter 9.) Perhaps that is because few FSOs understand what Eaton learned during his years in the private sector:

> On the outside, I realized how marketable we are, particularly in the management cone. We've learned to speak other languages, so we can translate what we do into business-speak or academic-speak. We're accustomed to handling odd problems, surprising situations. We're problem-solvers and quick thinkers. We can analyze people's thinking, their motives, pretty quickly, we do it all the time. . . . So I had no doubt that if I left again, I'd have lots of job offers. I had no fear about standing up for what I thought was right, speaking my mind. Ultimately that really helped my career.

Eaton rose to become assistant secretary of state for administration, ambassador to Panama, and dean of the language school at the Foreign Service Institute (FSI).

Professional Development

The performance of the service in Iraq exposed weaknesses in language skills that, as the Government Accountability Office showed, are widespread.[4] The foreign service agencies know they must improve and are determined to do so. "Languages," said a career development officer, "are our weapons systems, our rifles, our tanks."[5] As the foreign service grows in size, most of the additional hours of employee time will be absorbed by language training.

The service measures proficiency in a language on a six-point scale, with plus and minus signs to mark points between the integers. The following are the six points for the spoken language:

S-0   Unable to communicate

S-1   Elementary proficiency, basic courtesy requirements, able to conduct very simple conversations on familiar topics

S-2   Limited working proficiency, able to satisfy routine social demands and limited work requirements

S-3   General professional proficiency, able to participate effectively in most conversations on practical, social, and professional topics

S-4   Advanced professional proficiency, able to use the language fluently and accurately on all levels normally pertinent to professional needs

S-5   Functional native proficiency

A similar scale of R-0 to R-5 measures proficiency in reading.

Languages are categorized by difficulty, measured by the amount of full-time training normally required for a foreign service employee to progress from S-0, R-0 (no speaking or reading skills) to S-3, R-3. World languages (Western European languages related to English) like French, German, or Spanish require twenty-two weeks. Hard languages like Polish, Vietnamese, Hungarian, or Russian take forty-four weeks. The "superhard" languages—Chinese, Korean, Japanese, and Arabic—take longer. In addition, a language is called critical or supercritical if the service has a severe shortage of qualified speakers. In 2010, supercritical languages were Arabic (Modern Standard, Egyptian, and Iraqi); Mandarin Chinese; Dari and Farsi; Urdu; and Hindi. Languages merely critical were other forms of Arabic, Azerbaijani, Bengali, Cantonese, Kazakh, Korean, Kurdish, Kyrgyz, Nepali, Pashto, Punjabi, Russian, Tajik, Turkish, Turkmen, and Uzbek.

All these are among the seventy languages taught by native speakers at the remarkable language school on the Arlington, Virginia, campus of the Foreign Service Institute—the formal name of which is the George P. Shultz National Foreign Affairs Training Center. The native speakers double as cultural guides to their countries of origin, teaching by word and example the habits, customs, prejudices, and predilections that the students will encounter when they arrive at post. In addition, language training is typically combined with more formal area studies, covering geography, history, politics, economics, and culture. FSI, run by the Department of State, serves all foreign service and foreign affairs agencies. Spouses are included in language training where possible and when the budget allows.

Training should bring every FSO or specialist up to the level of proficiency in the local language that the position of assignment requires. But as good as the training is, the program falls far short of that ideal. The problem lies with the shortage of people, not with the quality of instruction. In 2008 almost one-third of the language-designated positions were either vacant or filled by people who lacked the proficiency required. The language gap was greatest in Afghanistan and Iraq, but the problem was global.

It won't be easy to close the gap. "We're going to have more language-designated positions," said Bill Eaton, dean of FSI's language school, "not just for officers, but for specialists too. Think about who needs the language. If you're speaking to the beat cop, the Customs official, service people, chances are they won't have English. You can use a translator, but you may not be sure what's going on."

Learning a language is more than a matter of good teaching and putting in the hours. "Some people can't learn a language," said Eaton, "or they can get to 2-2 [S-2, R-2] but not 3-3. We administer the Modern Language Aptitude Test, but it's not an iron-clad predictor of ability. Success in previous languages is a better guide."[6] And it can be hard to retain language skills not constantly refreshed. Ambassador Ron Neumann served in Iran from 1971 to 1973 and spoke some Farsi and Afghan Dari, but "when I started studying Arabic in 1980," he wrote, "it simply extinguished my Farsi within two months."[7]

Even fluent speakers need to know their limits. "Fluency is a great virtue," said Tom Pickering, who holds the rank of career ambassador and has been chief of mission in six different posts. "But conducting a negotiation in a foreign language—unless you were raised in it—is risky business. An interpreter brings precision."[8]

The S-3, R-3 level is the goal for most students, but as Eaton explains, "With a smaller group, we're working hard at building real fluency, with breadth and depth of vocabulary, so people can feel comfortable in a meeting or in front of a camera. For example, we have a pilot program to build a cadre of Chinese linguists. It starts with the second tour for junior officers. We send them here [to FSI] for one year of training, followed by assignment to China, where they are speaking Chinese, followed by another year of language training in Beijing or Taipei, followed by another assignment to

China—something like seven years in all. We may start a similar program in Arabic.

"It's a change in the whole approach to a career," said Eaton, whose own linguistic collection—Dutch, Russian, Italian, Turkish, and Spanish—reveals the old philosophy. "In the past, we'd be bouncing around from one part of the world to another. Now we're looking for much more sustained commitments."[9]

Language study takes much but not all of the time available for training during a foreign service career. In addition to the school of language studies, FSI provides training, most of it in courses lasting no more than a few weeks, in its schools of leadership and management, professional and area studies, and applied information technologies. The institute has created some two hundred courses for its distance learning program, and it offers another three thousand courses acquired from other sources. And in addition to the war colleges and the National Defense University (see chapter 6), about forty FSOs each year study at public or private universities, with their employing agency picking up the tab.

Some courses are mandatory, including the basic orientation (A-100) course for new officers, courses for first-time deputy chiefs of mission (DCMs) and first-time ambassadors, and courses in leadership and management at certain stages in a career. Active-duty FSOs may also have opportunities to teach, either at FSI, at the Department of Defense, or at other academic institutions. A number of senior officers, sixteen in the 2009–10 academic year, take assignments as diplomats in residence at colleges and universities around the country. Those assignments are directed primarily at recruitment, and the teaching load is light.

Moving Up

Members of the foreign service cannot cross the career thresholds until they can demonstrate a set of skills defined by the Bureau of Human Resources and measured objectively and subjectively. A career candidate begins with a five-year appointment. To gain tenure and enter the middle grades as an officer, the candidate must satisfactorily complete two tours of duty, at least one overseas and at least one in consular affairs, and must achieve a reasonable level of proficiency in at least one foreign language. Management has the flexibility to bend the rules or adapt them when individual needs are compelling. The standards are designed to ensure that tenured officers have the ability and potential to serve with full careers, through FS-01. An officer who needs a few extra weeks of language training, or who for some reason completed four years of service without exposure to consular work, will not necessarily be denied tenure for those reasons.

Tenure in the foreign service is not like tenure in the academic world. A tenured, midlevel officer or specialist faces up-or-out rules that restrict the amount of time that can be spent in any one grade, or in the service, without promotion. Officers who enter, as most do, in grade six, five, or four have a total time-in-service limit of twenty-seven years through grade one, with time-in-class (TIC) limits in each grade. Senior officers face a time-in-service limit of sixteen years, also with TIC limits in each grade (see table 7.5).

In accordance with the needs of the service, and when justified by outstanding performance, TIC limits for senior officers may be waived. Retirement at sixty-five is mandatory, although the director general can grant a five-year extension. The passage from the middle grades into the senior foreign service is not a random walk. There are six areas of competence—leadership, management, interpersonal skills, communication and foreign languages, intellectual skills, and substantive knowledge—used to measure performance, achievement, and potential as a career progresses. The office of personnel evaluation each year issues a set of precepts that define, in clotted, nearly unreadable prose, what the service expects of its members in each area as they progress from the entry level through the middle grades and into the senior service.

Some FSOs let their career just happen, but most try deliberately to acquire the mix of experiences, achievements, and skills that they need to be considered for the senior foreign service. Midlevel officers work on the steps, defined by the Bureau of Human Resources, that lead up to and across the senior threshold.

- Operational effectiveness
  - Geographic experience: Move around, but not too much. Senior officers must have three tours or six years dealing with one region (international organizations like the United Nations count as a region), plus two tours or three years in a second region, in the office of the secretary or one of the under secretaries of state, or in certain other functions. Long-term training at FSI's overseas facilities for languages like Arabic or Chinese counts as a regional tour.
  - Professional development: Brush up your skills or learn new ones. An academic year, cumulative, of training (other than language

Table 7.5

Up or Out (Years)

	Class	In Class	In Service
Midcareer	FS-04	10	
	FS-03	13	27
	FS-02	13	
	FS-01	15	
Senior foreign service	FE-OC	7	OC and MC
	FE-MC	14	together: 14
	FE-CM	7	

Source: Author's compilation. See 3FAM 6213.

training) is encouraged for midlevel officers. Teaching assignments at FSI, active military service (e.g., by reservists recalled to duty), and U.S government-funded employment in the private sector all count toward fulfilling this goal.

— Functional ability: Officers should look for ways to broaden their experience without straying far from their areas of specialization. An economic officer, for example, might take an assignment where the most important work is management of resources, perhaps overseeing an aid program. A consular officer might do a political tour in refugee policy. A management officer might take on an economic assignment negotiating rules to regulate trade in militarily useful products and technologies. A year of cross-functional or out-of-cone work during midcareer is recommended.

— Crisis response: Midcareer officers can show their mettle in a crisis by serving in the department's operations center, where crisis is a permanent condition, or in a tour in a country undergoing violent change or recovering from war or natural disaster. Without irony, the department also lists under this rubric service in support of a presidential visit or travel by the secretary of state.

- Languages: Officers will not be considered for the senior foreign service unless they speak and read two foreign languages, or one superhard language, well enough to use on the job (S-3, R-3). Mastery of just one language at the S-4, R-4 level (able to give interviews and converse on any topic) will also suffice.
- Leadership: Have at least one tour where you supervise a large staff and finish your training. Officers rarely reach the senior grades without having run a large staff, for example, as a deputy chief of mission

or top management officer in an embassy. One-week basic, intermediate, and advanced leadership courses at the FSI are required for
officers at grades FS-03, FS-02, and FS-01, and senior officers with
the rank of counselor must complete the senior executive threshold
seminar.

- Expeditionary energy: No one will enter the senior foreign service
without a tour, or two or three, in places that are difficult, dangerous,
and lonely. Officers who best handle the hardest assignments will be
best positioned to advance.

The Entrance Exam: Generalists

Members of the senior foreign service are at the top of their profession.
Nearly all of them, however, began at the bottom, with an experience powerful enough to create a bond among its survivors that lasts a lifetime—the
foreign service exam.

Officers are members of an elite corps, just 7,500 in number, that is largely
responsible for recruiting, hiring, assigning, promoting, and terminating its
own members. This element of self-selection, even more than the pressure-
filled and sometimes arcane nature of the work, gives the FSO corps a cohe-
siveness that has critics as well as supporters.

Choosing a Track

Officers follow one of five career paths, which the service calls tracks, or
cones. These are consular officer, economic officer, management officer,
political officer, and public diplomacy officer. Candidates choose their preferred track early, when they register for the foreign service exam. The
choice of track has a modest effect on the chance of a passing grade; it has a
major effect on the content of a foreign service career.

Candidates with scant knowledge of the service need to educate themselves before they choose their track. They should take a look at the State
Department's website, which offers a description of each track, and then
read chapter 8 of this book.

Taking the Test

The three-part entrance exam is a screening process so famously strenu-
ous that successful candidates look back on it as a rite of passage. The State

Department publishes a forty-page *Guide to the Foreign Service Officer Selection Process* on its website. The process has a clear objective: identify and hire the candidates best suited to a foreign service career and representative of the American people.

For those who give the test as well as for those who take it, the exam is a window into the service that reveals what the service prizes and rewards, and that can change. The department plans to convene a committee of experts to recommend changes in the selection process to better identify "innovative, entrepreneurial personnel."[10] Any changes adopted will appear on the department's website.

Part 1: The Written Exam

The written exam, the foreign service officer test (FSOT), is given usually three times a year at about two hundred locations around the country and at various embassies and consulates abroad. In 2009, about 1,600 people sat for the written exam, competing for about 1,300 job offers.

The exam has multiple choice and essay sections that test job knowledge and English expression. It includes a biographic section, designed to allow the testers to evaluate skills like problem solving and cultural sensitivity. The private company ACT (originally American College Testing) prepares and administers the test under contract.

The written exam is a source of constant controversy in the Department of State among active and former FSOs, and of course among candidates. The director general of the foreign service in 2007 questioned whether the written exam, which no other foreign service agency uses, still served a purpose for the Department of State. But McKinsey and Company, a human resources consultant contracted by the department to evaluate the selection process, as well as the department's industrial psychologist, reported that the written exam is the best single indicator of success in the foreign service. The department decided to retain it.

The exam has limits. It does not give a full picture of the candidate, which is why the testing process includes other elements. And the share of minority candidates who sit for the test is larger than the share that passes. The impact on minority candidates does not appear to be a function of the foreign service officer test (FSOT) in particular. Margaret Dean, a retired FSO who serves as a senior adviser to the board of examiners, said that "any cognitive test has the same impact." The department is acutely sensitive to the need to be fair and transparent and is careful to make sure that every element of the written exam is directly related to the evaluation of skills and attributes needed on the job.[11]

Part 2: Personal Narratives and the QEP

Those who pass the written exam—about the top 45 percent on recent tests—are asked to answer five personal narrative questions. In these answers the examiners are looking for evidence that the candidate understands the skills and qualities needed for the job and can show, by describing personal experiences, that he or she possesses them. The personal narrative should offer evidence of aptitude and skill in the six areas of competence used to measure performance throughout an officer's career (see appendix B).

A qualifications evaluation panel (QEP) looks at each candidate still in the hunt. This is the first part of the selection process directly related to the career track chosen at the time of registration. Multiple panels sorted by career track meet simultaneously and review about three thousand candidates in three weeks. The QEP reviews the total candidate file, which has the initial application with the work history and education experience (scrubbed to remove any legally proscribed information such as race or ethnicity), the written test scores, a copy of the essay, and the personal narratives. The panel looks for signs of experience that will bring strength to the job, or weaknesses or deficiencies that would have to be corrected, as well as for evidence that the candidate has skills and attributes that match the career track chosen.

This is one area where the candidate is in control of what the QEP knows. A candidate in the management cone will want to show, with examples drawn from personal experience, possession of management skills. A candidate in another cone might make different choices. Margaret Dean says that in the foreign service "most of the time we want candidates to follow the rules, do what they're told, deliver the démarche exactly as written. Except, when all of a sudden, we want them to throw off that Clark Kent clothing and show us their Superman logo. We need to see that they know the difference." The QEP looks for both personas.

Language skills come into play as well. The panel gives favorable attention to candidates who have knowledge of critical languages. Candidates who claim proficiency in a critical language take a test by telephone that consists of a conversation with a native speaker employed by the FSI. The FSI evaluation is part of the total candidate file.

A candidate's chances of getting through the QEP to the next stage, the oral assessment, depend on the choice of cone and the needs of the service.

Candidates are segregated by cone in the QEP review, and the number that passes in each cone is a function of the department's hiring needs in that cone, adjusted by other variables, such as the anticipated pass/fail rate at the oral assessment. In recent years the candidates with the best chance of passing through the QEP to the oral assessment have been those in the consular, economic, and management cones. The most oversubscribed or competitive cone is political affairs, followed by public diplomacy. This is largely why candidates in the three deficit cones have been given priority when scheduling a seat to register for the FSOT. The situation can change, however, so the best advice remains to pick a cone based on your personal skills and goals, not based on how you think it will affect your chances of getting through the QEP.

Some subjectivity enters into the process, but the panels are bound by guidelines set by the Bureau of Human Resources. The guidelines change from time to time as experience brings in information about indicators of future success and as the needs of the service for different types of skills and backgrounds evolve.

Part 3: The Oral Assessment

The oral assessment is a three-part tool that measures thirteen skills and qualities, or dimensions, essential to foreign service work (see table 7.6). Each of the three parts has equal weight in the scoring, and choice of career track has no effect on the outcome. The assessment takes the better part of a day to complete.

In the first stage, the group exercise, three to six candidates take on roles as an embassy task force charged with recommending to the ambassador an allocation of resources to various projects, with each candidate being responsible for one of the projects, and the group being collectively responsible for reaching a final decision. In the second stage, the structured interview, two examiners ask the candidate about his or her background and interest in the foreign service; they then ask the candidate to address some hypothetical situations that he or she might face overseas, such as a natural disaster or civil unrest. The examiners will also ask candidates to connect their experience to the skills and qualities they will need to succeed in the foreign service—as the candidates did in their personal narratives. The third stage is a case-management exercise, in which candidates have ninety minutes to read a narrative and quantitative brief on a complex management problem and write a two-page memo proposing how to deal with the issue.

When this assessment is over, the examiners provide immediate feedback. Successful candidates get a conditional job offer—conditional, among other things, on a security background investigation, medical clearance, and suitability clearance. Unsuccessful candidates may ask questions about the process but will probably be frustrated by the answers. Examiners will not tell candidates what they did well or badly because they do not want to give repeaters an advantage over first-time candidates.

All candidates who go through the oral assessment must sign a confidentiality agreement that constrains sharing information. However, everything a candidate needs to know about the test is on State's website, www.careers.state.gov, which gives a careful, detailed description of the entire examination process.

Table 7.6
Thirteen Dimensions of Foreign Service Work

Composure	To stay calm, poised, and effective in stressful or difficult situations; to think on one's feet, adjusting quickly to changing situations; to maintain self-control.
Cultural adaptability	To work and communicate effectively and harmoniously with persons of other cultures, value systems, political beliefs, and economic circumstances; to recognize and respect differences in new and different cultural environments.
Experience and motivation	To demonstrate knowledge, skills, or other attributes gained from previous experience of relevance to the foreign service; to articulate appropriate motivation for joining the foreign service.
Information integration and analysis	To absorb and retain complex information drawn from a variety of sources; to draw reasoned conclusions from analysis and synthesis of available information; to evaluate the importance, reliability, and usefulness of information; to remember details of a meeting or event without the benefit of notes.
Initiative and leadership	To recognize and assume responsibility for work that needs to be done; to persist in the completion of a task; to influence significantly a group's activity, direction, or opinion; to motivate others to participate in the activity one is leading.
Judgment	To discern what is appropriate, practical, and realistic in a given situation; to weigh relative merits of competing demands.
Objectivity and integrity	To be fair and honest; to avoid deceit, favoritism, and discrimination; to present issues frankly and fully, without injecting subjective bias; to work without letting personal bias prejudice actions.

Table 7.6 (*continued*)

Oral communication	To speak fluently in a concise, grammatically correct, organized, precise, and persuasive manner; to convey nuances of meaning accurately; to use appropriate styles of communication to fit the audience and purpose.
Planning and organizing	To prioritize and order tasks effectively, to employ a systematic approach to achieving objectives, to make appropriate use of limited resources.
Quantitative analysis	To identify, compile, analyze, and draw correct conclusions from pertinent data; to recognize patterns or trends in numerical data; to perform simple mathematical operations.
Resourcefulness	To formulate creative alternatives or solutions to resolve problems; to show flexibility in response to unanticipated circumstances.
Working with others	To interact in a constructive, cooperative, and harmonious manner; to work effectively as a team player; to establish positive relationships and gain the confidence of others; to use humor as appropriate.
Written communication	To write concise, well-organized, grammatically correct, effective, and persuasive English in a limited amount of time.

Source: US Department of State, *Guide to the Foreign Service Officer Selection Process, 2010–2011*, 29.

How to Prepare

There is no one best way to prepare for the entrance exam. The State Department publishes a study guide, available through the website, and a reading list weighted toward diplomacy, diplomatic history, and foreign service. No one needs to read it all. Old but still useful advice is to read the *New York Times*, the *Washington Post*, the *Economist*, or a similar publication—not just the international news, but politics, business, and cultural news as well. One successful candidate, applying after many years out of school, said his best move was to brush up with a high school advance placement American history textbook. Some candidates find the *Dictionary of Cultural Literacy* useful. The oral assessment will not yield to cramming, but a candidate should review the thirteen dimensions and reflect on how they are revealed in his or her biography, performance, and behavior. An exercise in empathy might also help—what are the examiners looking for, and how will they know when they've found it?

Candidates can get plenty of unfiltered advice—some good, some bad, and some bizarrely obsessive—from two Yahoo! groups, FSWE for the written exam, and FSOA for the oral assessment.

The most important single act of preparation is the one your mother recommended: Get some rest. It's a long day.

The Entrance Exam: Specialists

The 5,400 foreign service specialists work in one of nineteen jobs in seven job categories (see table 7.7). Like the generalists, the specialists of the foreign service pass through a written screening and an oral assessment. Unlike the generalists, specialists are hired to fill specific vacancies.

Candidates for specialist positions also start at the State Department's website, which lists what positions are available.[12] The Jobs USA site of the federal Office of Personnel Management carries much of the same information.[13]

To apply for a position, candidates complete an online form, provide any other documentation listed in the vacancy announcement, and send a two- or three-page biographic essay, including a section titled "Why I Want This Job."

Applications from candidates who meet the minimum standards for the position go to a panel of experts—not necessarily all foreign service specialists, but all experts in the field of work—for review. This QEP sends the likeliest candidates on to an oral assessment, which includes a written exercise as well as an interview. Two examiners conduct the assessment. At least one is a foreign service specialist in the relevant field. The assessment tests for the same skills and qualities that examiners look for in generalists, except for skills in quantitative analysis. So specialists can expect to be tested on twelve of the thirteen dimensions in table 7.6.

The written exercise is a forty-five-minute essay on a topic the candidate chooses from a list. The interview, which lasts about an hour, covers motivation, experience, and technical skills. Feedback is immediate. Those who pass are asked to make three commitments: to be willing to perform duties outside their field of expertise; to be available to serve anywhere in the world; and to support US policies in public, regardless of their personal convictions. They then receive a conditional offer of employment on the spot.

Table 7.7
Foreign Service Specialists: Jobs and Job Categories

Categories	Jobs
Administration	Facilities manager
	Financial management officer
	General services officer
	Human resources officer
Construction	Construction engineer
Information technology	Information management specialist
	Information management technical specialist
International information and	Regional English language officer
English-language programs	Information resource officer
	Printing specialist
Medical and health	Health practitioner
	Regional medical technologist
	Regional medical officer
	Regional medical officer–psychiatrist
Office management	Office management specialist
Security	Diplomatic courier
	Security engineering officer
	Security technical specialist
	Diplomatic security special agent

Source: Author's compilation.

Conversion Programs

Not all members of the foreign service enter through examination. "The State Department has many doors. Knock on them all, and one will open." Debi Fairman, who heard those words from a mentor, joined the State Department as a civil servant but got the itch to work abroad. Civil servants have few opportunities for assignment overseas, but if no FSO is available for a post, qualified and willing civil service officers have a chance. "They have to fill the hard-to-fill positions," she said. "If the foreign service pool is exhausted, and there's a civil service officer available, there can be a fit. For me it was a consular position in Georgetown, Guyana."[14] Her assignment to Guyana led to her eventual acceptance into the foreign service as a midlevel officer.

Debi Fairman's husband, Jimmy, went to Guyana as her dependent but found work in the embassy as an eligible family member. He started as the office management specialist (OMS) to the regional security officer and then filled in as OMS to the ambassador when the incumbent was away. He later took a course in general services at the FSI and eventually received an offer to join the foreign service as a general service officer (GSO) specialist. He then considered whether to seek conversion from specialist to officer status.

The rules that governed the Fairmans' case are fairly stringent. A candidate for conversion to the foreign service officer corps must be a career civil service officer or a foreign service specialist with at least seven years of service, with four of the last six years spent in foreign service positions abroad. It is hard for a civil servant, though usually not for a specialist, to meet the overseas service requirement. Then the candidate must undergo an oral assessment and be approved by the commissioning and tenure board (see chapter 9). The department plans to make more overseas positions available to civil service personnel and to expand the conversion program.[15]

The department is more aggressive in seeking officer recruits among foreign service specialists and civil servants at more junior levels. Under the department's Mustang program, specialists in grades FS-08 through FS-04 and civil servants in grades GS-5 through GS-12 can enter the officer corps as career candidates eligible for tenure, provided they

- are at least twenty-one years old, with at least three years of service in the Department of State;
- have a college degree in a relevant field, or take the written exam and reach an acceptable score;
- designate a career track and complete an FSI, university, or correspondence course in that field equivalent to a semester of college training;
- submit an autobiography of one thousand words;
- are recommended by the qualifications evaluation panel to take an oral assessment; and
- pass the oral assessment.

The Agency for International Development also offers opportunities for conversion from civil service to foreign service. If AID has overseas positions with no foreign service employees available to fill them, the agency may turn to civil service volunteers at grade GS-13 and above. These civil servants join the foreign service initially as noncareer candidates and become career candidates after two years of satisfactory work overseas; they become eligible for tenure a year after that. Like State, USAID plans to expand overseas opportunities for members of the civil service.[16]

From Job Offer to Job

Between a job offer and a job lie a few important details. In particular, the State Department's Bureau of Diplomatic Security must conduct a background check that looks for drug use, alcohol abuse, employment misconduct, financial irresponsibility, application fraud, criminal conduct, poor judgment, and questionable loyalty to the United States. The presence of any these factors may be disqualifying. The department's Office of Medical Services must decide whether to grant medical clearance based on a medical exam that looks for conditions that create severe risks or otherwise limit worldwide availability. The background check and medical clearance are typically completed within ninety days.

Candidates with medical and security clearances are placed on a registry, with those scoring highest on the entrance exam on top (additional points for veterans and for tested language skills are added here). How quickly names move from the registry to the employment rolls depends on how many officers and specialists are being hired and what tracks and specialties are most needed. Candidates not hired after eighteen months on the registry turn into pumpkins and have to start the entire process again. In 2007 the department set a goal for itself: cut the average gap between passing the orals and taking the oath from fourteen to three months, but in fact, in early 2010 the gap was nearly eighteen months. For officers, from written exam to induction averages twenty-eight months, ten months from test to registry and eighteen months from registry to swearing in.

How strait is the gate, and who passes through it? More than 100,000 people applied to become FSOs between September 2001 and February 2006. About 2,100 were sworn in. The new recruits had a median age of thirty-one. Four had earned an associate in arts degree; the rest had a bachelor's or graduate degree, 170 had master's degrees in business administration, and 86 had PhDs. More than 250 were lawyers, and three were medical doctors. Their work experience was too broad to allow categorization, but well over half had worked overseas. Many had completed State Department internships in Washington or at an embassy overseas. And though there is no foreign language requirement for entry, the 2,100 entrants had some degree of proficiency in ninety-six tongues.

Basic Training: A-100

The introduction to the service for new FSOs is a mandatory, five-week orientation course at the FSI campus in Arlington, Virginia, across the Potomac River from the State Department.[17] Foreign service specialists have separate orientation classes at FSI, as do State Department civil service employees, though the classes may meet together when schedules permit.

The officers' orientation course is called A-100, after the number of the basement room in the old State building where junior officers met for training in the late 1940s. The courses are individually and consecutively numbered; more than 150 classes have convened since the count began. In recent years classes have had sixty or seventy officers, sometimes more. Each course lasts five weeks; FSI hopes to expand the course to six or seven weeks in 2011 or 2012.

New officers are sworn in twice. An official from State's Bureau of Human Resources administers the oath of office on the first day of the first week of A-100 training, because until the oath is taken, new officers cannot draw their pay.[18] Then, on the last day of the fifth week, in a splendid room on the top floor of the State Department, the new officers are sworn in again. The secretary of state of usually attends and speaks at these occasions if she is in town; it is one of the few ceremonies in a service notoriously shy about pageantry. The moment is memorable, not least because the new officers may not see a secretary of state again for many years.

The oath is the same on both occasions:

> I do solemnly swear (or affirm) that I will support and defend the Constitution of the United States against all enemies, foreign and domestic; that I will bear true faith and allegiance to the same; that I take this obligation freely, without any mental reservation or purpose of evasion; and that I will well and faithfully discharge the duties of the office on which I am about to enter.

Between the first and second oath, the new recruits spend every workday, some evenings, and an occasional Saturday learning about what they have gotten into and what lies ahead. There are no papers, no exams, no grades. The sole requirement is perfect attendance, with some allowance for illness or emergencies, but not much else.

There's little training in the art or skills of diplomacy. (An exception: two days of work on "composure under fire," or how to address a hostile audience on a tough subject such as Iraq or US relations with Israel.) The A-100 is orientation, not training, which is done mostly on the job. Marcos Mandojana, an economic officer on his third tour of duty, recounted his impression: "To be honest, seven weeks of A-100 does very little to build diplomatic skills. Mostly it tells what State is. We did enjoy hearing the experiences of the people who came to talk to us, but there was nothing about démarches or writing well. And you get to know your classmates. It built esprit de corps."[19] Another officer, who entered when the course was longer, complained of FSI's fire hose approach: "My criticism then, and probably now, is that while each unit was useful, my mind was not big enough to handle all of them packed into eight or nine weeks. Two hours of this, two hours of that—it goes by too fast, it's a blur. It's like a European vacation when you're eighteen; you can't remember what happened in which country."[20] Once real work begins, the FSI lessons come back to mind. "What stuck with me," said Clayton Hays, "was dealing with foreign service nationals, the importance of cultural differences, gender roles, etc. At the time it seemed like a waste of time, but when I got to China I realized I wasn't in Kansas anymore. I had to be sensitive. A-100 was helpful that way."[21]

At some point during the course, the class goes to an off-site location for leadership and team-building exercises. And team-building works. Class members stay connected. They watch each other's progress throughout their careers and beyond in a spirit that is at once cooperative, competitive, and simply curious. As their paths cross and recross—which they will—they turn to each for inside information, support, gossip, and advice.

"I stay in touch with classmates, and like most A-100 courses, we have a group listserv," a first-tour officer explained. "There is almost daily information about people and where they are in life. It is a great support network, especially when it's time to bid on assignments."[22] Deborah McCarthy, an FSO with about twenty-five years of service, said, "There is an active networking system that begins with the people you entered with, the A-100 course. It's the essential network. I've maintained those contacts."[23] When the first member of the class becomes an ambassador, the others will say, "I knew her when."

The emotional energy of every new member of the service is focused on the first assignment. New officers get advice on available jobs from a career development officer in State's Bureau of Human Resources, and, with an active imagination and an atlas at hand, they picture life at each post:

Chengdu, Chennai, Chisinau, Gabarone, Guangzhou, Guayaquil, and so on. From the list of openings, they put in bids on the jobs they want, in order of preference. All this happens in the first two weeks.

Assignment anxiety ends in week five, on flag day, when the class meets in the FSI gym with a class mentor—one of four FSOs who work with each A-100 course—who announces the postings and gives each officer the flag of the country of assignment. Most people get what they want, or close to it. In the 132nd A-100 class, which graduated in February 2007, sixty-nine officers bid on seventy-two posts. Such is the variety of human desire, and the persuasive power of the career development advisers, that every officer was assigned to one of his or her top ten choices.

With assignments made, training has a sharper focus. Officers who need language skills stay at FSI. Officers heading to consular assignments, which await nearly all new FSOs, train at a mock American consulate. Within a few weeks, members of the A-100 class are dispersed around the world.

8

Foreign Service Functions: Five Tracks

FSOs are career candidates until approved for tenure by a commissioning and tenure board. New FSOs, whether they start at the entry level or (as some do) in the middle grades, have five years to make the cut. The first two tours, normally two years each, are critical. In most cases, the first tour is overseas, and the great majority of second tours as well. These first two tours give the candidates a chance to size up the service, and vice versa.

Entry-level officers don't always have the chance to spend time working in the track they chose when they signed up for the foreign service exam. The service must fulfill the demands that law and regulation place upon it to screen foreigners who want to come to the United States. Entry-level officers carry a lot of that load. So, for most new officers, the first tour, and sometimes the second, is largely or wholly in consular affairs. Work in the track of choice may not begin until tenure has been awarded.

Consular Affairs

Consular officers have two primary duties: to administer the visa provisions of US immigration law and to provide welfare and protective services to American citizens abroad. Consuls and vice consuls meet more people, and more kinds of people, than anyone else in an embassy, though usually under unfavorable conditions and rarely with time to chat. They see a society's middle class and underclass, not just its elites. They get little credit when things go right but lots of blame when things go wrong. They have commissions that allow them to perform consular functions, and most ambassadors don't, so if they hang tough on a decision they are hard to push around. They have tradition and history on their side, and also a flag, a white C surrounded by thirteen stars on a blue field, displayed in consular waiting rooms and offices. They put up with a lot of routine and drudgery, but they have some spectacular adventures and, always, the best stories.

No one enters the foreign service with a background in consular work. Training is extensive and essential. New officers heading out to consular assignments pass through FSI's courses at ConGen Rosslyn (ConGen for consulate general, Rosslyn for the Arlington, Virginia, neighborhood where the facility is located). The program gets high marks. Consular officer Marcos Mandojana explains, "I got consular training at FSI, and I thought that was good. They split it up into nonimmigrant visa [tourist, business, student], immigrant visa, and American citizen services, just like the posts. There were examinations for each phase. Lots of role play. We visited prisoners in jail with realistic settings, like rats in the cells. We did interviews. I think you know quite a bit about the rules when you finish. You know what the resources are, who to contact."[1]

Visas

Visa work absorbs the bulk of consular resources. A visa, usually in the form of a fraud-proof, machine-readable, printed photo ID stamped in a foreign traveler's passport, indicates a consul's approval of a request for permission to enter the United States. Possession of a visa does not guarantee entry, which is controlled at the port of entry by officers of the Department of Homeland Security (DHS), but it is extremely rare for holders of valid visas to be turned away on arrival.

In fiscal year 2009, foreign service posts issued close to half a million immigrant visas (for people who plan to stay in the United States) and close to 6 million nonimmigrant visas (for people who intend to leave after their visit). Nearly 2 million nonimmigrant applicants were turned down.[2] Under regulations issued after September 11, 2001, every one of these applicants must be interviewed in person by an American consular officer.[3]

The busiest visa post in the world is Manila, Marcos Mandojana's first post:

You spend the first couple of days observing another junior officer on the line. Nonimmigrant visas were the heaviest workload. Immigrant visas were mostly paperwork, but we often did over a hundred cases a day per person. It was grueling. Manila was number one in output that year. You start slow, but with a little experience you can speed up. You begin to recognize patterns of fraud. FSI had given me six months of training in Tagalog, and when the applicants whispered to each other, "cry now," they didn't know I understood.

Everything was done by appointment so we had to see everybody who came in. We stayed at work until we saw everybody with an appointment. It was like a machine. They were getting rid of backlogs; there were twenty-six officers doing consular work. We frequently worked Saturdays. We did get paid overtime—you can get overtime or compensatory time off until you're tenured.[4]

Nonimmigrant visa (NIV) work consists largely of trying to determine, in about a minute and a half, whether an applicant is likely to violate the terms of the visa he is applying for and stay or work in the United States illegally. The work can be depressing and frustrating. One NIV officer, a lawyer, explains it this way: "The law tells me to make a decision on whether they're coming back or not. But I don't know whether my country really cares who's coming back. There are people who stay two or three years illegally, and they get an automatic waiver from the Department of Homeland Security. I feel at times, what's the point? It's not my job to make policy, but this doesn't make a lot of sense."[5]

The workload can be daunting. At many posts, visa work provides employment opportunities for foreign service spouses or other family members, though only officers with consular commissions can conduct interviews and issue visas. A supervisory consular officer in Buenos Aires, a relatively low-pressure post for visa work, described the scene in 2005:

There are eight entry-level officers and one family member in the section. None of the officers is consular cone and all but one are on two-year assignments to the section. One is a rotational officer. I don't think any of them resent the work or the assignment, though a big part of my job, and the part I love, is to help them see the value and the challenges of the work they are doing. I try to get them to see that it's not just ticket punching. I know that some of it is grunt work and not intellectually stimulating, but I think that officers who resent the consular tour often suffer from poor senior management. I'm an evangelist for the consular cone, and I try to help the officers understand that their performance here will show their potential for leadership and performance in other jobs. We're fortunate because nearly all who've cycled through have played nice with the other kids and taken their jobs seriously. I take satisfaction in the fact that one officer, on a rotational tour, even asked to come back to the section. I think 9/11 showed that our work really matters.[6]

American Citizen Services

Consular officers will tell you that work on a visa line is "probably the same the world over."[7] But on the other side of the shop, the one serving American citizens, there is plenty of variety. Replacing lost or expired passports, notarizing legal documents, processing Social Security and veteran's benefits for persons living abroad, and other tasks may seem routine, but the legal puzzles of who is entitled to what can be fascinating. Every consular officer can tell stories of high drama involving Americans, not all innocent and not all victims, who are caught up in political strife, swindles and scams, or natural disasters, or are dealing with illness, accident, or unwelcome justice.

Besides his visa work, Marcos Mandojana handled welfare and protection for Americans in the Philippines.

> There were lots of Americans in jail. They were in for drug trafficking, murder. The prisons were very primitive, overcrowded. It was kind of scary to go there, really.
>
> What's it like to visit a murderer? At the maximum security prison there were five Americans, one in for murder. He had chopped up his wife's lover when he found them together. He was rich, he owned car dealerships in the Philippines. He had apparently bribed jail officials. He had donated computers to the jail. He didn't have to wear a prisoner's uniform, and he lived in one of the guard's quarters.
>
> There were shantytowns inside the jails, with huts, and that's where everyone else was, including the other Americans. A stark contrast. They had their own little economy in there, with little stores, kiosks, a little hospital. The prisoners protected each other. It was bizarre; there were thousands and thousands of people inside. These guys had been in jail for about eight years. Another guy was in jail for child molesting. One of the training exercises at ConGen Rosslyn was based on that individual.[8]

Mandojana saw the intersection of consular and political work when the violent Muslim separatist group Abu Sayyaf kidnapped first one and then three more Americans and held them hostage on a remote southern island. "I went down there three times with US Marines, accompanied a congressman down there. One day I got to my office and there was a towel with a femur and part of a skull—the remains of a hostage who had been beheaded."

Crisis Management

Responsibility for Americans in trouble often puts consular officers into central positions during times of crisis. Sean Murphy was chief of the consular section in Kuwait in 2002 and 2003, as the crisis with Iraq deepened and the war began. The American community in Kuwait numbered about twelve thousand, and, Murphy said, "everybody believed that Kuwait was going to be the main target" for Saddam Hussein's chemical and biological weapons.

Murphy recruited members of the community as wardens, to act as liaison between the community and the embassy, and rehearsed evacuation scenarios with the marines. In early 2003 the embassy established what it called authorized departure, triggering clauses in many employment contracts that allowed paid travel out of Kuwait for those who wished to leave. Many did, and Washington ordered evacuation of the rest in March.

We had a very small staff, four officers and nine foreign service nationals, but we kept track of departures and kept the community informed about how to get out, the state of the airport, the border with Saudi Arabia, what documentation the Saudis required, any guidance we had.

My family left five or six days before the war started. The work was intense, sixteen-hour days. I worked forty-five days in a row. I went into Iraq, to a base at the port of Um Qasr, in June 2003. Freelance American business people were popping up, running afoul of the military, and a national guard unit had detained a couple of them. The department wanted us to see what was going on. There were also Iraqis with relationships with the US military who for various reasons couldn't go home. Our military wanted State to take them to the United States, which wasn't going to happen. There were some very sad cases, but we couldn't do anything for them.

There was tremendous augmentation in the staffs of other agencies, but no increase in State's staff that I recall. The one big thing they did for us was to give us a six-week grace period for sending in personnel evaluation reports.[9]

Status

For many, if not most, officers, mandatory consular assignments were hard to get through but were ultimately beneficial. Even so, some fault the service for a one-size-fits-all approach to an increasingly diverse group of entry-level officers. David Caudill, a lawyer, joined the service in the management cone at age forty-one, after ten years in elective office in Clermont County, Ohio. His first tour was in consular affairs, and it was "a good experience," but, he added, "the foreign service doesn't know what to do with entry-level officers who have had previous careers. When I was thirty-one, I was running an office [county clerk] with more people, and spending more money, than most embassy section chiefs. There are a lot of people like me coming into the service now, but the service hasn't adapted. If the foreign service could harness the talent, instead of treating everyone like a twenty-two-year-old graduate, we would be a better service."[10]

For many officers the early consular assignments are a long and unexpected detour, sometimes a pleasure, but more often a pain. "I have a lot of respect for consular work, I even enjoy it. But it's about retaining talented people. 'Wow, this is going to be four years of my career that I'm going to dedicate to work that isn't what I planned for. It isn't what I signed up to do.' I think that's the biggest gripe."[11]

Consular officers are sensitive about how they are regarded inside the service. Officers in substantive political, economic, and public-diplomacy positions often look on those in management and consular affairs as engaged in work of a lesser order of importance. Marcos Mandojana saw the contrast when he transferred from the consular to the political section in Manila while continuing to work on the Abu Sayyaf kidnapping. "In the consular section you're in your own little world. You might have an occasional brown-bag lunch with the DCM. In the political section, however, I worked with everyone: the ambassador and DCM, the regional security officer, the drug enforcement administration, everyone."

Sean Murphy had a different view: "Initially consular work appears to be less prestigious to some, but these perceptions change as you rise through the ranks. When you compare one-level jobs [section chief] in an embassy, who supervises the largest staff? Since 9/11, visa work is seen as national security activity. We're first in line to get new equipment, we have some status and some clout."[12]

Economic Affairs

The only career FSO to serve as undersecretary for economic affairs is Alan Larson, who held that position from 1999 to 2005. Larson was also the only undersecretary of state appointed by President Clinton to survive the transition to the administration of George W. Bush. Larson holds a doctorate in economics from the University of Iowa, but he insists that "you don't need training at the doctoral level. You do need a grounding in core economic concepts. You want to be able to think like an economist, to use the tools of economic analysis. You need to know enough to recognize junk arguments."[13]

Economic officers deal with businessmen, bankers, investors, producers, bureaucrats, academicians, and real and phony experts in every field of human endeavor that can be turned into cash. They handle a broad and growing range of issues that have significant economic content: finance and monetary policy, of course, but also trade, intellectual property, energy, environmental protection, science and technology, prevention of AIDS, bribery, and money laundering. For the most part, it's hands-on work. "You should have practical knowledge of how business works, and you should think pragmatically," Larson explained. "We don't need the academic approach, the one that says, 'We know it works in practice, but does it work in theory?' If we know it works in practice, that's all we need. In much of the world, in its far reaches, American business has no one but the embassy to turn to. We need to know our stuff."

Economic work involves reporting, analysis, advocacy, and negotiation. Reporting and analysis are more fieldwork than desk work. Sitting in an office rarely answers questions about what drives markets, who owns what, or where the opportunities and risks are for exporters and investors. Nor does it answer questions about money laundering, bribery, environmental degradation, child labor, or any of the other issues that Americans care about. Senior officer Deborah Ann McCarthy remembers,

When I came into the foreign service, I expected to do economic analysis. I was a loan officer in a bank before I joined, and we had economists advising us on the economic situation, so that's what I thought I'd be doing. What I didn't expect, and really wasn't prepared for, was how to use my skills to promote a specific US agenda: pushing for trade agreements, pressing for protection of intellectual property, urging compliance with an IMF [International Monetary Fund] agreement. In practice, you do the analysis, but you have to be an advocate. You've got to market the US position and back it up with your analysis and knowledge of the situation.[14]

In Washington or overseas, economic officers rarely put on solo performances. Sometimes they are in the lead, but often they are supporting actors, with top billing going to the Treasury, the US Trade Representative's office, or some other agency with a claim to the issue. Teamwork is essential to success, overseas or in Washington.

Bill McCahill, an economic officer and Chinese linguist, was the deputy chief of mission in Beijing during the 1997–99 negotiations on Chinese accession to the World Trade Organization (WTO).

The focal point was the US Trade Representative, Charlene Barshefsky. The State Department in Washington wasn't much involved, and until the end of the process the Secretary did not seem interested. But the embassy was vital.

People all around the embassy were engaged, drawing energy from the sense that we were involved in something historic. Between negotiating sessions, we did reconnaissance. Everyone with contacts in the Chinese agencies involved would go out and gather information, so we could put together a picture of the whole Chinese side. Our economic section, about twenty officers, had some really good macro guys. They were plugged into what is now the State Planning Commission, the finance ministry, the central bank. We had about fifteen foreign commercial service officers, superb people, who worked the trade ministry and the ministry of information industries. And five or six agriculture guys. We used the consulates too, especially in Shanghai, Guangdong, and Guangzhou. Everyone who spoke Chinese contributed. I was the coordinator, the ringmaster. And I did reconnaissance of my own, with a back channel to Premier Zhu Rongji, through an aide whom I would meet on Saturday afternoons.

We had two young economic officers with really good Chinese. They would take a train out to the sticks, then hop on a bus and spend a couple of days in the countryside talking to farmers. Then they'd go back in six months or a year and do it again. They wrote some terrific stuff on rural China, where the migration of millions of peasants to the cities was already under way. Understanding the changes and the pressures on the government gave us insight into Chinese negotiating positions. It was great reporting.

We were deeply engaged with the American business community, through the local AmCham [American Chamber of Commerce] and meetings with a steady flow of visitors. We briefed the AmCham regularly, and sometimes there were three hundred people in the room. We were careful listeners and sturdy advocates. The administration was counting on the business community to lobby the deal through Congress, so government and business were hand in hand.[15]

Teamwork and coalition-building were also the keys to economic diplomacy after September 11. Within days of the attack, the State Department began to develop a plan to provide economic support to allies in the war on terrorism, tailoring support to the needs of each country.

The immediate center of attention was Pakistan, with which relations had long been strained.[16] The United States would need Pakistan's support for any challenge to the Taliban in neighboring Afghanistan, but giving that support would create costs and risks for Pakistan's then president, Pervez Musharraf, who faced constant pressure from Islamic extremists.

Musharraf sought, among other objectives, US help in reducing Pakistan's foreign debt and in improving its access to foreign markets. State immediately put together an interagency financial team, led by Undersecretary Larson, to reschedule the payments Pakistan was due to make to official foreign creditors. "We wanted to provide real relief as quickly as possible, without using appropriated funds," said Larson, who led a mission to Islamabad before the end of October 2001. "We faced a tough situation on the trade side, where customers for Pakistan's textile products were nervous that supplies would be disrupted. We met with buyers and told them that Pakistan was an ally, that we wanted orders to continue. We were using military transports to carry supplies into Pakistan, and we said we could consider using those aircraft to carry textile products out on return flights. That calmed things down."[17]

These measures were in place before the end of 2001. Later, with congressional approval and appropriations, Washington expanded debt relief, increased foreign assistance, and increased access to the US market for Pakistan's textiles.

The United States took a more multilateral approach to aid to other key allies. Even before the Taliban were driven from Kabul in November 2001, State's economic team had begun to rally global support for the new regime taking shape in Afghanistan. The State Department hosted the European Union at a November meeting on aid that worked out elements of a common approach. A follow-up meeting in Brussels in December, and the larger International Conference on Reconstruction Assistance to Afghanistan in Tokyo the following month, garnered pledges of $4.1 billion in support from sixty-one countries (including Iran), with roles for the World Bank and for various nongovernmental organizations. "Those pledges weren't all fulfilled," Larson said, "but there was a really big buy-in."

Support for Iraq after Saddam was harder to put together. As with Pakistan, debt relief was a major component. Larson explained,

> The Europeans were divided, but the United Nations Development Program hosted a meeting in June 2003 in the General Assembly room that got things moving. The United States set as a goal the cancellation—not the rescheduling, the cancellation—of 80 percent of Iraq's foreign debt by end of 2004. To get there, State led a collaborative interagency effort that, in my thirty-two years in the service, had no precedent. Every agency used its best contacts. [Treasury Secretary] John Snow and [Treasury Undersecretary] John Taylor went to the Germans. I went to the Japanese and brought them in, somewhat against their inclinations. The National Security Council dealt with the Russians, who were being asked to write down more than 80 percent of what they were owed, because of the changes in the value of the ruble. We brought in Saudi Arabia. We achieved our objective. In the end the cancellation of debt could not save Iraq's economy, but it was a great accomplishment for economic diplomacy.[18]

When the State Department polled FSOs to learn what skills they believed would be most in demand in the future, economics was their top choice.[19] The 2010 QDDR says that political officers as well as economic officers "must understand the economic dimensions of political challenges and the political dimensions of economic ones."[20] "I would agree with that," Larson said. "The latest wave of globalization is such a powerful force. It has been of tremendous benefit to the United States, but there is the sense in the country that our economic dominance is eroding. That places greater pressure on economic diplomacy. Economic issues are at the center of our most important international relationships, with China, Japan, Europe, Mexico, Saudi Arabia, the Gulf states. Foreign service officers without economic skills won't be up to the job in the years ahead."[21]

Management

Management officers are the inside guys of the foreign service: They take care of the money, the buildings, the data, and the people. They deal less with policy abstractions and more with the daily work of getting things done.

In Washington, management officers have natural homes in the department's Office of the Undersecretary for Management, the Bureau of Administration, the Bureau of Human Resources, and the Bureau of Resource Management. But every bureau in the department has an executive office, the management hub for the bureau's activities. Management officers posted abroad look to the executive office of their regional bureau, and specifically to a post management officer in that office, for support.

Overseas, management officers attend to the safety, health, and well-being of all staff and the hiring, training, assigning, paying, and dismissing of locally hired employees and contractors. They buy, sell, rent, and maintain all the civilian facilities used by the US government abroad and do the same with the equipment, from fleet vehicles to chemical toilets, that keeps an embassy in operation. They carry out IT tasks, including communications, network security, and record keeping. They pay the bills, keeping embassy sections and agencies inside their budgets. They know—or should know—where each dollar, ruble, peso, yuan, euro, lev, or ringgit came from, and where it went, and why. With the regional security officer, they control directly or indirectly essentially all of the embassy's resources.

Some foreign service candidates shy away from management because they think it is removed from policy. Bill Eaton, a former assistant secretary of administration, knows otherwise.

If you do your job right, and do your job well, you're involved in every single thing that happens in the embassy. You're involved in all the discussions about policy, because you can talk about operationalizing the policy. Lots of times we talk about policy in abstract terms, but at some point we have to say, OK, can we do that? Do we have the resources, do we have the capacity? Or can we modify the policy to make it more apt to achieve success with the resources we have? When I was management counselor in Ankara, the ambassador would consult me about how to tweak an initiative so we could carry it out. You have to know what's practical, what's possible.

As a management officer, I've traveled with presidents, organizing their trips. I traveled with Reagan, with Clinton. I was involved in negotiations with host government officials about what the president is going to do, where he's going to be, negotiating between what the host government wants him to do and what we want him to do. The White House came to me because as the management officer I had a reputation as a guy who gets things done. If you're an advance person in the White House, you want to talk about what you can get done, you don't want to talk about the theory of relativity.[22]

Management officers deal with foreign officials constantly, on issues such as employment law (for embassy employees and contract labor, and for American family members seeking jobs outside the embassy), taxes and exemptions, foreign exchange controls, customs clearances, building codes, and driving licenses and violations. Their work directly affects the quality of life for embassy employees and their families, and often for the broader American community as well. They have a supervisory or custodial role with regard to facilities run by or linked to the embassy that are a lifeline in many parts of the world—an American overseas school, an embassy clinic, a commissary. People look first to management officers when a physical crisis strikes—a natural disaster, a riot, a bomb, or an epidemic.

The four key people in an embassy are the chief of mission, the deputy chief of mission, the regional security officer, and the top management officer. If two of these four are first-rate performers, the embassy will be a well-run place; if three, it will be well run and happy; if all four, at least one must be due for a transfer.

A Real Foreign Service Experience

The first management job for Frank Coulter, later acting assistant secretary for management, came in his second tour, in Kaduna, Nigeria. Kaduna is closed now, but as many posts do today it offered what FSOs call "a real foreign service experience." Electric power was off nearly every day for three to six hours, maybe longer. Water supply was intermittent. Cobras, mambas, and malaria were real hazards, along with street crime and break-ins. Riots sometimes punctuated the tension between Muslims and Christians.

"We all rely on each other in a place like that. Everybody pitches in, and you learn a lot that you didn't know before. Generator maintenance on weekends, for example. Good management—taking care of the basics, responding quickly, and finding ways to improve the support platform—is the key to your post's success, because nothing happens if the support structure doesn't work."[23]

A small, stressed post is a great place to learn how to manage a crisis. Coulter's lesson came when three of the consulate's locally hired maintenance engineers were critically injured repairing a fuel line. Coulter and others at the consulate organized a local and international rescue effort in the hopes of saving the lives of the workers. "We worked out through concentric circles of support, doing what could be done in Kaduna and using phone patches through the State Department's operations center to the embassy in Lagos, the Bureau of African Affairs at State, the US Air Force in Germany for medevac support. Cooperation and teamwork are essential in a crisis. It was inspiring to see how it all worked, given how remote we were. In the end, though, we could not save the lives of our Nigerian colleagues."

Soon after, Coulter was put in charge of renovating a building, to replace the old consulate facility, said to be among the worst in the department's inventory. "For a second-tour junior officer, it was a thrilling ride. I had about three and a half months to get the plans drawn up and approved, contract the work, and complete the renovations. I had support from the embassy in Lagos, the Africa bureau's executive office, the foreign buildings office [now the Bureau of Overseas Building Operations], the Bureau of Administration, and security. I felt I had the authority to go with the responsibility, and I used it. It may have been the high point of my tour."

Specialists

Management is probably friendlier to specialists than other foreign service tracks. Eric Khant, a foreign service specialist in human resources now at grade FS-1, served six overseas tours and a tour in the department before he was assigned in 2006 as counselor for management affairs at a medium-sized embassy, one of the few specialists to head an embassy section. Russ King began his career in 1967 as a specialist working as a communicator before entering the officer corps through the Mustang program. He retired as a minister counselor in the senior foreign service and went on to fill management gaps around the world "when actually employed" (see chapter 3). There are scores of similar stories.

Responsibility in management can come early, as it did with Coulter. "Relatively junior people volunteering for places like Baghdad or Kandahar have opportunities for tremendous responsibilities, way beyond anything they can get on the outside," Russ King explained.[24]

The skills learned on the job in entry-level management tours overseas are resourcefulness, creativity, and leadership—meaning the ability to make a decision, act on it, and stand by its consequences. These skills get tested in the middle grades, when managers are often charged with meeting a rising workload and a more complex, challenging mission with no increase in resources—the hated "do more with less." Managers are tugged in opposite directions by contradictory imperatives. The department's Office of Management Policy, Rightsizing, and Innovation wants to keep our overseas presence down, but the assignments people want the family of an employee sent for a year to Iraq to be able to stay at their overseas post. The secretary wants more one- and two-person American presence posts, but security issues and the lack of a float for long-term language training make that decision hard to carry out. Managers have to strike the balance and get it right.

Serving Many Masters

Much of the diplomacy of management work is intramural, turning independent, suspicious, and often rivalrous agencies into a team. The Department of State typically is one among many US government agencies at an overseas post—when he served in Manila, Russ King counted fifty-two agencies with employees in the Philippines under the authority of the US ambassador—and at many posts State is not even the largest. Agencies at a post share support services such as communications, budgeting, personnel management, transportation, housing, building operations, contracting, and so forth, under the government-wide International Cooperative Administrative Support Services system (ICASS), which the Department of State administers.

ICASS is lunch with separate checks. Each agency, at least in theory, pays only for the costs of the services it uses. Washington provides a budget to the embassy's ICASS council, where every agency is represented, and the chairmanship rotates among them. The council decides what services will be provided, who will provide them, and who will pay.

"The ICASS council is your master," said Russ King. Making it work takes constant attention. There are jealousies. Better-funded agencies can take care of themselves and their people at a higher level than others. Because the ICASS council operates by consensus (or rarely by a two-thirds unweighted vote), small agencies can sometimes stop large agencies from doing what they want to do. A good management counselor has to know what needs to get done, how much things cost, and what rules and regulations apply. Then he or she has to apply this knowledge diplomatically, working with the council chairman and bringing the agencies together behind the chief of mission.

"We provide services to all agencies so they can do their job," said Eric Khant. "Ideally, good management is out of sight and out of mind, like the engine room in a ship. People shouldn't have to worry about what we do."[25]

Political Affairs

Political officers are still kings of the foreign service hill, despite repeated efforts to topple them. With their economic colleagues, they carry the burden of bringing foreign governments around to the US point of view. With their colleagues in public diplomacy, they present US views and values as persuasively as possible to local audiences. Their reporting and analysis of the situation in their country of assignment, along with reporting from clandestine sources, are often the starting point for policy. Calls for transformational diplomacy, for less reporting and more field work, are aimed mostly at them. Even so, their influence on policy formation is often strong, and when it is not, their frustration level rises. They are supposed to guard reality against wishful thinking. They need thick skins.

The political portfolio covers internal politics, relations with third countries, multilateral affairs, nuclear nonproliferation, environmental affairs, narcotics and crime, human rights, labor, refugees, and political-military affairs, including alliance relationships; military-to-military relations; manufacture, sale, purchase, and trade of weaponry and goods and technology with military application; arms trafficking; disarmament and de-mining; and international peacekeeping. In larger posts political work is divided among several officers, but in smaller posts one or two officers cover a great deal of ground.

Given the importance of their work and the prestige attached to it, it is surprising that political officers receive so little preparation. The training that consular officers receive before their first assignment has no parallel in the political track, or in economic affairs or public diplomacy for that matter. In these areas, on-the-job training, or OJT, is the rule. OJT? Call it SOS, for sink or swim.

"I kept thinking," said Richard Miles, "my boss is going to come in and tell me, 'Richard, this is how it's done. This is how we pick a subject to report on, this is how we make contacts.' Never happened. You learn by doing, or you don't learn. I think I probably just asked a colleague, or tried to copy what people I respected were doing."[26] Miles, a midlevel officer, had his first exposure to political work during his first tour (in Barbados, which is not what FSOs call "a real foreign service experience") and went on to political assignments in Berlin, the State Department, Buenos Aires, and the National Security Council (NSC) staff.

To make local contacts, Miles accepted every invitation that came his way. "I was pretty low on the totem pole, so I wasn't asked to glamorous events. The socializing wasn't easy. When I started out in the foreign service, the Myers-Briggs assessment marked me as a slight introvert. Now I'm a slight extrovert. It's part of the job. It doesn't come naturally to me, but I realized very quickly that it's one of the things—well, you've got to be that way or you're not going to succeed."[27]

Harry Kamian had better supervision but came to the same conclusion.

At my first post [in El Salvador during that country's long civil war in the 1990s], I had an outstanding adviser who took mentoring seriously. He explained why the job was important. He set it up as, here's our role, supporting the peace process here. He told me that Washington is interested in progress and setbacks in human rights, and how US programs are working (or not) to help institutions in El Salvador function. And what's the military up to? That's always a concern.

How do you get that information? Well, you have the press, political party contacts, UN officials, the NGOs. Mostly you go out and meet people. Rather than send me out on my own, he took me with him, so I got to see how he would ask questions and exchange information.[28]

Kamian learned his Spanish in school and gained fluency during a year as a visa officer. Miles had been an army intelligence officer in Germany before joining the foreign service and could work in German when he arrived in Berlin. Having the language and the courage to use it are important. In the Berlin embassy, said Miles, one supervisor stayed in his office, went nowhere and did little; sketchy language skills may have been the reason. Kamian experienced the reverse: "Other officers [in El Salvador] were absolutely first rate. I tried to learn from them."

Richard Miles didn't have the guidance that Kamian received in El Salvador. He found it hard to figure out what Washington wanted.

> In Barbados and Berlin, I thought I was a reporter, looking for interesting stories to tell. Only later, when I served in the department, did I realize that Washington has an agenda, for the world, for your region, for your country and for your post. Washington doesn't always make its needs clear, sometimes you have to figure it out. But if your reporting isn't relevant when it arrives, no one will read it. I mean, I knew that on an intellectual level, but I didn't really understand it until I saw it from the Washington end. You're not writing term papers, and you're not a stenographer. You have to pull out the important elements of information and put them together in a way that is useful.[29]

There can be tension in the political track between those who hope to shape events and those who observe, report, and wait for instructions. Miles's ambassador in Germany often said, "We're not just about reporting, we're about doing stuff. We have to figure out what to do and tell Washington we're going to do it unless they stop us." The careers section of the State Department's website describes political officers as "informed negotiators who interpret situations and advise on international issues."[30] It's a pretty gray description of what is really a vibrant and sometimes thrilling job.

Elsewhere in this book we've seen junior, midlevel, and senior political officers at the top of their game: Toby Bradley organizing local elections in a Shiite region of Iraq, Lynne Tracy trying to win friends for America in Peshawar, Steve Mann (a consular-cone officer who spent most of his career doing political work) negotiating pipeline politics in Central Asia, Jimmy Kolker organizing US government participation in the global struggle against AIDS. Every day in the news you can see career FSOs from the political track entrusted with and carrying out the nation's most delicate negotiations: Ambassador Christopher Hill and his successor James Jeffrey, using waning American influence to ensure that Iraq has a viable government as US troops leave; Ambassador Anne Patterson, who has guided our complex, conflicted relationship with Pakistan from Musharraf to Zardari;

or Ambassador Carlos Pascual, with a deep background in crisis management and national security affairs, maintaining a cooperative relationship between the United States and Mexico despite tempestuous domestic disputes in each country about the political, economic, and criminal influence of the other. These are the challenges that political officers aspire to take on and that the best will master.

Public Diplomacy

Public diplomacy, which goes over, under, around, and through governments to communicate a US message to a wider, less official audience, suffered more from the depredations of the 1990s than any other area of American representation abroad. When the Cold War ended, the executive and the Congress both seemed to conclude that the enterprise had lost its purpose. They cut funds, let staff go, closed American libraries and cultural centers overseas, and reduced the languages, hours, and reach of official broadcasting. In 1999 they abolished the US Information Agency (USIA) and folded it into the Department of State, where it was received like a cornerback on a baseball team. The office of undersecretary of state for public diplomacy, created in 1999, sat empty for three of its first six years. Integration is still imperfect.

"When you walk down the halls at Main State," said Marcia Bosshardt, "people don't say hello, they don't talk to anyone. That's the culture. A lot of FSOs are analytical, risk averse, introverted, maybe a little bit full of themselves. But for public diplomacy you need a different kind of person. In public diplomacy you talk to everyone." Bosshardt, an FSO who began her career in the USIA, teaches media tradecraft at the Foreign Service Institute. But, she says, "some things you can't teach. You have to recruit for the traits a public diplomacy officer needs: proud of our country, outgoing, a good listener, comfortable in any company, with the kind of fearlessness that is willing to make mistakes in a foreign language and keep going."[31]

Public diplomacy is a relatively new term. The website of the USIA alumni association traces it to 1965, but the expression was rarely used before the 1990s.[32] American officials define public diplomacy by its purposes: to understand, engage, inform, and influence foreign publics and policymakers, and to broaden the dialogue between American citizens and institutions and their counterparts abroad.[33] Public diplomacy officer Caryn Danz explained that these verbs are a progression:

First, you have to understand the people in the place where you are, their culture, their values, their history. Then you can engage them, establish a relationship, a dialogue. When you have a relationship of confidence, you can inform them, tell them things they may not know about the United States, our values, our foreign policy. You can explain things in a nuanced way, in a way that relates to their worldview, not ours. And then, hopefully, you can influence their thinking and their behavior. It's a long process, it can take years, but when it works it can be very powerful.[34]

American public diplomacy comes at this task from two sides: cultural affairs, and press relations and information. Cultural affairs include exchange programs that move in both directions, selecting and funding foreigners coming to the United States and, in smaller numbers, Americans going abroad. Information and media relations deal with the daily or hourly push and shove of the news. Many embassies will have a cultural affairs officer and an information officer, both reporting to a public affairs officer (PAO). At smaller posts, one American officer will cover both jobs. At every post, public diplomacy relies heavily on the skills, contacts, and bicultural understanding of foreign service nationals.

Public diplomacy is a tool in the service of policy. "In the last fifteen years there has been a tighter link between public diplomacy and policy," Betsy Whitaker, a senior FSO, said. "We expect public diplomacy officers to be part of the ambassador's inner circle and to work hand in glove with other embassy sections."[35] For example, to encourage adoption of legislation protecting intellectual property, public diplomacy officers identify performers, writers and publishers, film producers, and others who stand to benefit from stronger copyrights. Economic officers identify the scientists, engineers, and business owners who gain from patent and trademark protection. Political officers identify the legislators with the greatest influence over the issue, and the jurists whose opinions weigh most heavily. Cultural affairs officers invite these key players to the United States with US government support, for visits that may last five or six weeks, to meet with their US counterparts and with whomever they wish to see. "When they help design their own program, hear all points of view, and reach their own judgments, that's when these visits are most effective," said Caryn Danz.

Or so we think. In public diplomacy it is often hard to measure success. "We need to understand," said Betsy Whitaker, "that changing attitudes won't happen by next Tuesday."[36] The department uses extensive polls, surveys, and follow-up surveys to determine whether educational and other exchange programs do what they are intended to do.[37] On the press and information side, minutes of air time or website visits or column inches of print are easy to count, but their effect is rarely obvious. Some successes are hard to document, much less quantify. "There's a lot we keep out of the press and off the air," said Bosshardt. "When the press trusts you enough to check their stories with you, you can stop misinformation before it starts. You can't easily get credit for this."[38]

Public diplomacy officers should be well positioned to move into the senior ranks. They often have opportunities fairly early in their careers to manage programs with substantial budgets, to supervise large staffs of foreign service nationals, and of course to face the public and the press, in more than one language. They have increasing opportunities at the top as well: The department plans to establish new public diplomacy deputy assistant secretaries in every regional bureau.[39]

"There's not a lot that separates a public diplomacy officer from a political officer," Betsy Whitaker pointed out, "except perhaps the operational component, and understanding money and how to move it."[40] Public diplomacy officers with fifteen or twenty years of experience should have the skills and background the service looks for in making assignments as deputy chief of mission and promotions to the senior foreign service.

9

Assignments and Promotions

Three great mysteries of the foreign service are who gets in, who goes where, and who gets ahead. Who gets in and who gets ahead are vital to insiders, but who goes where is the hinge of the system. Whether the service can pass the day-to-day test of performing its mission depends on getting the right people to the right place at the right time.

If past recruitment, training, and promotion had been consistently wise, prescient, and fully funded, the service would always have individuals with the right skills, experience, and ambition to fill all its positions. And if recruitment, training, and promotion are wise, prescient, and fully funded today, assignments will be easy to make tomorrow. But wisdom and prescience are not always abundant, and money is scarce, so assignments are and will ever be a struggle.

Who Goes Where

FSOs and specialists are available for duty anywhere in the world—it is a condition of employment. The people and the positions, however, are not fungible. A consular officer who speaks Turkish may not work out as a security officer in Khartoum. A Russian-speaking political officer in Minsk may not be the right choice to deal with investment disputes in São Paulo or Guangzhou. A married, Arabic-speaking political officer who has served in Iraq may have exactly the skills and personal relationships that are needed there, but for how long should the service require separation from family? And in the course of a life in the service, events occur that may limit availability: a spouse's illness, a child's disability, an aging parent's need for care.

Assignments in today's foreign service are made through a formal process that is largely transparent and a parallel informal process that is largely opaque. In the formal process, the Bureau of Human Resources advertises positions that are coming open on the department's intranet, and members of the foreign service who are due for new assignments submit requests or bids for the positions in order of preference. Then a panel of officials of the Career Development and Assignments Office of the Bureau of Human Resources (HR/CDA) makes the assignments based on the needs of the service, the views of the bureaus, and the preferences of the employees. Panels meet weekly and dispose of hundreds of cases at each meeting, spending on average less than a minute on any one assignment. Any panel decision may be appealed to the director general.

The formal process is strongest where first- and second-tour officers and specialists are concerned. At middle levels and especially at senior levels, an informal process tends to preempt formal decisions.

Where entry-level officers and specialists go and what they do on their first and second tours depend heavily on the Bureau of Human Resources acting through career development officers (CDOs). Newcomers to the service get a list of available openings and have a chance to bid on their preferred assignments, but their CDO guides them and urges them to submit bids that are realistic. The CDO aims first to fill service needs, for example, for visa officers, and only then to make use of the talents that the new recruits bring into the service. From the point of view of the employee, the bidding process is one in which the best is the enemy of the good: Preferences will likely be accommodated if they are within the range of expectations that the CDO lays out. Those who buck the CDO's advice may find themselves headed for assignments they do not want, and with budding corridor reputations they may not want either.

CDO influence, however, ebbs quickly. New employees who take a hardship tour on the first or second assignment improve their chances of getting their first choice on the second or third assignment. By the third tour they have probably been awarded tenure and entered the middle ranks.

Officers and specialists in the middle grades need to do more work to line up the next assignment. Employees whose tours are coming to an end should not wait for the department to announce vacancies; they should check informally with friends and colleagues to advertise their availability and find out what opportunities are likely to be available. Those who hear of a job that appeals to them should go out and do a little self-promotion. They might introduce themselves by e-mail to the ambassador, the deputy chief of mission, and the immediate supervisor, explaining why they want the job, why they would be good at it, and why all concerned should want them at the post. They should also be in touch with the Washington office in charge, usually the executive office in the appropriate regional bureau, because the objective is a handshake (informal) agreement with the bureau that can be reported to the CDO. When the CDO is confident that both parties have agreed—no deal if there's only one hand shaking—the CDO marks the position unavailable on the intranet. The deal isn't closed until the formality of an assignments panel is complete, but it is rare for a handshake agreement to be broken without good cause.

Lobbying the posts and bureaus for a job is only half the game. The bureaus also go out and recruit, and they vet their prospects. For example, if the Beijing embassy needs an officer with a background in civil aviation, the Bureau of East Asia and Pacific Affairs (EAP) may scout around for active and former members of the Office of Aviation Negotiations who might be available. If it finds a suitable candidate, EAP pitches the glories of Beijing, or at least the opportunities for achievement and advancement that service in China presents. At the same time, EAP might ask the candidate's colleagues, supervisors, and subordinates to comment on his professional skills, work habits, and past performance—an exercise called a $360°$ review. All this bureau activity is outside the formal assignment process, but it plays a large and often decisive role.

To prevent the comfortable positions from disappearing early from the list of open slots, the department acknowledges handshake agreements only in a certain order, the same order in which formal assignments are made. In the summer of 2008 (most transfers take place in the summer, during school holidays), there were 3,577 positions to be filled, of which the 252 positions in Iraq were assigned first, followed by those in Afghanistan and other unaccompanied posts (i.e., posts where the employee's family members are not permitted to go). More than nine hundred overseas jobs—including those in Iraq and Afghanistan—met these criteria.[1] Because assignments to such jobs are normally for one-year tours, all these slots—more than 10 percent of all overseas positions—must be filled each year, and therefore account for close to 30 percent of overseas assignments. Only when these unaccompanied jobs are filled will the assignments process move on to a second group of positions, where dependents can join the employee but where the department pays a bonus for hardship and danger that totals 15 percent of base pay or more. About three thousand positions meet these criteria, and about one thousand must be filled each year. Within this group, posts that are historically hard to staff or that have critical needs get priority.

Table 9.1

Hardship Differentials, September 2008

Base Pay (%)	Posts	Positions	Examples
Low (0–10)	139	3,843	Buenos Aires, Paris (0)
			Amman, Bogotá, Windhoek (5)
			Istanbul, Kuala Lumpur (10)
Medium (15–20)	50	2,008	Lima, Mexico City, Moscow (15)
			Jeddah, Manila, Sofia (20)
High (25–35)	79	2,233	Beirut, Kathmandu, Lagos (25)
			Monrovia, Nairobi, Shenyang (30)
			Baghdad, Dushanbe, Kabul (35)
Total	268	8,084	

Source: US Government Accountability Office, *Department of State: Additional Steps*, 4.

Together, the unaccompanied and other hardship positions account for about half of all overseas positions. When they are filled, the other positions are processed. Handshake agreements on the second or third groups of posts have no effect until the first group of assignments is settled.

Midlevel officers and specialists can expect to serve two tours in posts that have a hardship-danger differential of 15 percent or more. A tour of duty in at least one such post is a prerequisite for promotion into the senior ranks. One of those tours will likely be without family, or with adult family members only. An employee who has done his fair share—a term of art with a squishy definition—is not likely to be required to serve in another hardship post.

The persistent notion that veterans of service in difficult and dangerous posts typically go on to Paris, London, and Rome is just wrong. Sylvia Bazala, the deputy chief of mission at the embassy in Sarajevo from 1998 to 2000, said that "when Kosovo blew up, some of the people in the embassy wanted to curtail to go to Kosovo. Many of the same people later went to Afghanistan, and to Iraq. They want to be in the front lines. I'm glad we have these people."[2] Assignment officers said the same thing: There is a contingent of FSOs and specialists, uncounted but sizable, that willingly takes on more than its fair share of the toughest jobs.

Senior officers are pretty much on their own. "By the time you're an FSO-1, if you haven't figured out how to go about getting an assignment, you're probably not qualified anyway," a member of the career development office observed.[3]

Deputy Chief of Mission

Assignments as deputy chief of mission (DCM) are handled differently. A DCM committee of senior department officers, chaired by the director general of the foreign service, identifies a slate of candidates for every vacant DCM position. The committee sends the names to the chief of mission, who makes the selection. Similarly, the deputy secretary of state chairs a committee—the D committee—that identifies candidates to be deputy assistant secretaries of state and sends the names to the secretary for approval. The D committee also identifies career FSOs as candidates for ambassadorial appointments and forwards those names to the secretary with a recommendation, usually accepted, that she send the names on to the White House office of personnel. That is where State's input ends. White House decision making, at least when viewed from the Department of State, is a black box.

In the trajectory of a typical foreign service career, assignment as DCM is a point of inflection, often the last overseas job for an officer at the top of the middle grades or the first for one newly promoted to the senior ranks. FSOs believe that promotion boards want to see that DCM ticket punched. Good performance as DCM is taken as evidence of broad substantive knowledge and leadership and management skills that are hard to demonstrate in narrower, smaller jobs. Poor performance often signals the end of the line.

Most FSOs who become chiefs of mission were a chief of mission's deputy for one or two tours. But not for three. "You shouldn't be a DCM more than twice," an ambassador said. "That's a bad sign." Of course, many DCMs are never named ambassador despite honorable service in the number two role.

It is an article of faith in the career foreign service that DCM is the toughest job in an embassy. The assertion may not stand up to scrutiny, but its widespread acceptance suggests that DCM is, as one ambassador said, "the quintessential foreign service job. It's coordination. If the institution is aiming at anything, it's aiming at producing ambassadors and DCMs."

The mating dance between an ambassador looking for a deputy and a would-be DCM looking for a post is *Animal Planet* material. Every DCM has a "how I got my job" story to tell. Emi Yamauchi's story shows the perseverance, luck, and old-boy networking that enter into most DCM assignments.

Yamauchi's first bid on a DCM position failed when the ambassador chose a civil service employee. (The American Foreign Service Association [AFSA] protested on principle the award of a foreign service position to a civil servant, to no avail.) Three years later, while serving as American consul general in Ho Chi Minh City, she received a call from the ambassador who had turned her down, offering to help with her next assignment. And he did, by putting in a good word for her with the front office of the Bureau of Western Hemisphere Affairs, which passed her name on to Secretary Powell's executive assistant Craig Kelly, who was then the likely future ambassador to Chile.

Kelly did not know Yamauchi, but he liked her background in public diplomacy and her mix of Asian and Latin American experience. That would be a good fit, he thought, with his own history as a political officer with service in Latin America and Europe. Chile was then preparing to host the summit-level Asia Pacific Economic Cooperation (APEC) forum, which lent importance to the Asian angle. Kelly checked out Yamauchi with people he knew who knew her: the assistant secretary for East Asian and Pacific affairs, the ambassador to Colombia, and her deputy in Ho Chi Minh City. When he was satisfied, he called her from Amman, Jordan, at 4 AM, and they had their first conversation. Eventually they met in Washington, where Yamauchi was taking soundings on assignments, including another promising DCM possibility. Two additional phone calls, the last from Colorado to Chicago, closed the deal. Yamauchi finally took up her post nine months later, almost a year after the mating dance began.

Tandem Couples

Assignments are critical moments in every foreign service life. Only ten or twelve assignments will fill thirty years. When husband and wife are both members of the service, each assignment can pose a challenge to a marriage as well as to a career. Tandem couples, as these spousal pairs are called, comprise about 10 percent of the foreign service, and they and the department have extra work to do at assignment time.[4]

First, each spouse in a tandem couple must tell the assignments office in writing of his or her desire to be assigned with the other spouse, if that is the case. The career development and assignments office is suspicious, or cautious, and won't let one spouse speak for the other. By its etymology, the word *tandem* means one in front of the other, like a tandem bicycle, not one alongside the other, like a yoke of oxen. Many tandem couples decide that one will lead and the other follow, sometimes taking turns tour by tour; in that case, couples need to tell the assignments office which spouse's career takes precedence. If one spouse is an entry-level officer (ELO), there is no choice. The department gives priority to ELOs to ensure that their assignments give them a fair shot at gaining tenure.

When a tandem wants to stay together, the department tries hard to accommodate by assigning them to posts that have two vacancies at the appropriate ranks and in the appropriate areas, but within the rules that prevent an employee from supervising a family member. That is easy enough to do for a Washington tour, but overseas it works only in the larger posts: There are no tandems at Recife or Bangui or Cebu or Chiang Mai. At the same time, the department promises not to allow marital status to give any employee an advantage in assignments or in chances for promotion. Taking care of tandems without denying desired assignments to others is difficult, and it grows harder as the number of unaccompanied posts is rising. Nevertheless, most tandems say they have managed well.

Philo Dibble and his wife, Elizabeth, rose to the senior levels of the service. In 2006, both were serving as deputy assistant secretaries of state, Philo in the international organizations bureau, which deals with the United Nations, and Elizabeth in the Bureau of Near Eastern Affairs, which deals with the Middle East. "We became a tandem couple in 1987," Philo said.

> We've been very lucky. We've played by the rules, we've made some compromises. We probably spent more time in Washington than either of us would have done if we were independent. We're both economic officers, and for most of our careers we've been at the same grade, so that limited our choices, given antinepotism requirements. We've been flexible. For example, in Pakistan, my wife did an economic job while I did narcotics work, because that's what was available. Had I insisted on an economics job, we couldn't have gone. Except for a year in Milan, where my wife took leave without pay to be with the kids, we've tried to do that all the way through. In senior positions it becomes more difficult. I don't think we'll be able to go out as a tandem again. Our choices are for one of us not to work, to separate, or to go to one of the three or four places where there is more than one mission.[5]

Like the Dibbles, the Byrds met overseas. Robin Byrd, whose father was a military attaché, joined the foreign service as an information management specialist in 1988 and was assigned first to Riyadh ("couldn't drive, but didn't have to wear a veil") and then to Moscow, where she met Lewis Byrd, a

Bechtel employee working on construction of the new Moscow embassy. They married, and in 1992 Lewis applied for a position as a foreign service facilities management specialist. Then Robin was posted to Santiago, Chile, and Lewis, still waiting to be called for an interview, went with her as an unemployed spouse. Lewis got his interview in January 1994, passed, and was assigned to Nairobi. About six months later, the department curtailed Robin's assignment in Chile and assigned her to Nairobi as well. They served as a tandem there and in Addis Ababa, returned to Washington in 1999, and soon thereafter left the service. It was a decision they came to regret. Lewis remarked, "every time I saw a plane go over I wondered where it was going." The department granted their request for reinstatement in 2001 and restored their sick leave and seniority. They have served as a tandem since.

Jim and Joleen Derham, both FSOs, had a different experience. The Derhams worked at different levels and in different tracks. Joleen entered the foreign service as a management officer when her husband, an economic officer, was already in midcareer, several grades above her. "The department has made it very difficult every time we've changed jobs, overseas much more than in Washington. At times it's very stressful. The two of us may have different views on the importance of careers and jobs, on the alternatives. In our situation, where I'm the senior officer—consul general in Rio de Janeiro, deputy chief of mission in Brazil and Mexico—there are nepotism problems" that are handled erratically.[6]

> In the case of Rio, I'm convinced the people who did the paperwork were not aware we were a tandem. I was consul general, she was the general services officer. Her boss was my subordinate, but no one said anything. In Brasilia, the ambassador agreed to review Joleen's performance evaluation, which would ordinarily be the DCM's job. Then the ambassador left post, and I was chargé for a year. But nobody checked, we handled things carefully to avoid favoritism, and everything worked out all right. When we went to Mexico, I was DCM, she was in the consular section, several layers below, and it should have been easy, but the department made it quite difficult.

Derham stressed two points about tandem couples. First, when the system is rigid, fight back. "If you're persistent enough, you're going to find a way. After Argentina we wound up coming back to the States, which is not what they wanted Joleen to do. 'Your career will be forever blighted,' they said, which was not the case.[7] The stakes are so much more important for the individual than for the system that the individual will fight harder and often prevail."

Second, "once you work it out, it's great. Getting up in the morning, you and your spouse going off to work, in interesting, reasonably remunerative jobs, it's great, it's definitely worth the effort."

More Positions Than People

The assignments system, like much else in the foreign service, is under some strain. "Since the mid-1970s," said Chris Midura of the career development and assignments office, "assignments have been employee driven. Management has pretty much lost the ability to steer the process." He added that an employee-driven system doesn't work when the number of positions to be filled and the number of people available to fill them are out of balance. "We have more positions than we have people to put in them." The assignment process is a devil's game of musical chairs, one with more chairs than players. And the least comfortable chairs are supposed to be filled first. But the Government Accountability Office found that, in September 2008, 17 percent of positions in high-hardship posts were unfilled, as opposed to 9 percent in posts with no hardship differentials.[8]

In April 2009 more than 20 percent of positions worldwide—about 1,650 of 8,100—were unfilled. It is hard to find a place where some officer or specialist isn't covering two positions. "Two of us are doing three jobs, because they gave one person to Iraq," said a midgrade officer without rancor. "I was here in the embassy until ten o'clock last night, and I got here at seven o'clock this morning, and I have to work [Saturday]. There's no crisis here, but Congress still requires the same number of reports."[9] The same situation is repeated all over the world.

Officers who entered the service in 2002 to 2004 under the Diplomatic Readiness Initiative (see chapter 2) have moved into the lower middle grades, but because the service took in so few new recruits in the 1990s, it has a serious shortage in the senior and upper middle ranks—for example, a deficit of 11 percent at FS-02 level in fiscal year 2010.[10] The deficits are most severe in management and public diplomacy. Officers in grades FS-05 and FS-04 often take jobs normally filled by FS-03s and FS-02s. These stretch assignments, which place relatively junior officers in relatively senior positions, are especially common in hardship posts. The GAO's survey of State

Department staffing in September 2008 found that officers on stretch assignments filled more than one-third of all officer positions in high-hardship posts, just under one-third in medium-hardship posts, and less than one-fifth in low-hardship posts.[11] A stretch assignment is a great opportunity for the up-and-coming, but the opportunity comes with the risk that, without experience and training, even abundant raw, natural talent won't be enough to get the job done.[12]

The increased foreign service hiring in State and USAID in FY 2009 and 2010 should relieve some of the pressure; so should an expected reduction in the number of foreign service positions in Iraq. But even if the administration continues to request and Congress continues to approve more foreign service hiring, the effects will not be widely felt until 2014 and subsequent years, as newly hired officers begin to enter the middle grades.

Who Gets Ahead

The foreign service puts a lot of time into its promotion system. Each member of the service, officer or specialist, receives a full and formal written performance evaluation every year, in addition to oral and less formal reviews and counseling with his or her supervisor. It takes several people to prepare each written report: one to rate, one to be rated, a third to review the other two, and a review panel to certify that the report complies with the department's rules and contains no inadmissible material. Each report becomes part of a personnel file, and five or six people on a promotion board review each personnel file each year. Members of the foreign service groan at the effort, especially in April, when most evaluation reports are due. They recognize, though, that time and effort are a price worth paying to keep a system in which the service picks its own winners by its own rules.

Evaluation

The promotion system, designed in part to avoid employee grievances, has three parts: counseling, evaluation, and selection. Counseling involves structured discussions between supervisor and subordinate to establish a clear understanding of what the job entails, what kind of performance is expected, and how well those expectations are being met. The supervisor (the rater), the subordinate (the rated employee), and a reviewer who is normally the rater's boss must certify in writing that they have discussed the work requirements. The rater and the employee must also document at least one of their counseling sessions.

Evaluation is a formal, even a rigid process, with rules and regulations. The centerpiece is the employee evaluation report, also called the EER or efficiency report, filled out each year for every American foreign service employee.

At the beginning of the rating period, the employee, the rater, and the reviewer agree in writing on work requirements that become part of the EER. At the end of the rating period, the rater checks off whether performance was satisfactory or unsatisfactory and then evaluates performance in a four-hundred-word narrative keyed to the work requirements. In a second narrative of similar length, the rater discusses the employee's potential, looking at the six areas of competence—leadership, management, interpersonal skills, communication and foreign languages, intellectual skills, and substantive knowledge—that the State Department's Bureau of Human Resources has defined and negotiated with the American Foreign Service Association (AFSA).

Because raters tend to overdo the positives (Brings order from chaos! Walks on water! Eats raw eggs with chopsticks!), the EER includes a block called areas for improvement. Here the rater indicates at least one of the six areas of competence in which the employee could do better. Examples are called for, but the block of space is mercifully small; fifty words or so will fill it.

The rater has someone looking over his shoulder. Every EER includes a review statement, prepared usually by the rater's boss and always by someone in the chain of command. Ideally, the reviewer has independent knowledge of the employee's work and is close enough to the scene to be able to comment on the relationship between the rated employee and the rater. The review is a place for fresh examples of work done well or ill, and it is a check on the prejudices or sloppiness of the rating officer.

When the rater and reviewer have finished, the rated employee must be given at least five days to comment in writing. Under privacy rules contained in the Foreign Service Act of 1980, the rater and reviewer have no access to the employee's comments. A promotion board member explained why the Rated Employee Comment Section (which may be left blank) is called the suicide box: "Statements that are too long, too short, whiny or filled with grammatical errors and typos hurt the employee more than most people appreciate. An example that always comes to mind is the employee who used three pages . . . to explain why a rater who described him as verbose was wrong."[13]

Finally, a review panel must certify that the rated, rating, and reviewing sections of the report comply with regulations, contain no inadmissible material, include examples to substantiate expressed judgments, and do not dispute matters of fact. When the panel signs off, the report is complete.

Efficiency reports can be a burden. They weigh most heavily perhaps on DCMs at large embassies. A DCM in most cases rates all the embassy's section chiefs, including those from agencies other than State, and reviews all the ratings that the section chiefs prepare. At a large embassy with several constituent posts—Beijing, New Delhi, Brasília—the DCM may well have twenty-five or thirty reports to write and dozens more to review. (In addition to his other duties, Henry Clarke, the sleep-deprived head of the Office of Provincial Affairs in Baghdad, had to write EERs on all of the FSOs in Iraq who were PRT team leaders and review statements on EERs for all of the FSOs who were deputy team leaders.) And with a few exceptions, all the reports are due at once, so there is no way to spread the work throughout the year.

Promotion

All the agony and effort that go into an evaluation report are aimed at a tiny audience. Commissioning and tenure boards have six members, as do selection (promotion) boards. Award of tenure and promotion in rank are separate actions, but the selection procedures in both cases are much the same.

Commissioning and Tenure Boards

Most candidates for tenure, called career candidates, are entry-level (junior) officers and specialists who have joined the service through a competitive process. A few career candidates start in the middle grades because of their specialized skills or employment history. Very few career candidates are senior officers, initially appointed as noncareer officers for limited periods, who decide to seek full career status. The commissioning of senior career candidates follows slightly different procedures than those described here, which apply to career candidates in entry-level and middle grades.

The director general of the foreign service appoints six members to each commissioning and tenure board. Five must be from the Department of State, including one from each career track, and the sixth must be from another foreign service agency. Regulations specify that at least one member of the board shall be a woman, and at least one shall be a member of a minority group.[14] All must be ranked FS-01 or above. Members serve two-year terms and meet quarterly, or more often if needed. AFSA gets a chance to comment on the names proposed for appointment, but it has no veto power.

New FSOs who come in at the bottom, in grades FS-06 or FS-05, have five years and three chances to make tenure. They are promoted administratively, by action of the Bureau of Human Resources, up to FS-04, where the work of the commissioning and tenure board begins. The board reviews all FS-04 career candidates (untenured officers) for the first time after they have completed thirty-six months of service, for a second time after forty-eight months, and for a third time, if necessary, six months before the five-year period runs out.

The board also reviews new officers who are in the middle grades—FS-03, FS-02, and FS-01—after thirty-six months and again after forty-eight months of service. A third review, if necessary, takes place about sixty days before the candidate's time expires. Midgrade officers, including untenured career candidates, also face selection boards, which consider them for promotion. Any untenured midgrade officer who is promoted goes before the commissioning and tenure board immediately, regardless of length of service.

Selection Boards

Most selection (promotion) boards meet from June to September and they feel the heat. They consider all candidates for promotion, except entry-level officers, who are administratively promoted from FS-06 to FS-05 and from FS-05 to FS-04.

Like commissioning and tenure boards, selection boards looking at officers through FS-01 have six members, including five from the Department of State, one from each career track. Tracks are not relevant for promotion above the rank of counselor (FE-OC), the lowest rank in the senior foreign service. The sixth or public member comes from outside the department. Members of a selection board must be at least one grade higher than the grade under consideration, so most are FS-01s (senior officers). Specialists have separate boards that are staffed by people knowledgeable in the specialty.

For officers in the middle grades, two boards screen every file. The first conducts a classwide competition and ranks members of a class, regardless of track, from top to bottom. The second goes track by track, looking for the best political, economic, consular, management, and public diplomacy officers. For officers at FS-04, there is no second board, because assignments in grades FS-06, FS-05, and FS-04 are often not linked to an officer's track. Promotions from FS-04 to FS-03 are by classwide competition only.

Boards typically read the files several times. In a first screening, a file may get no more than ten or fifteen minutes of consideration. That is usually enough to allow a sorting into one of three piles: review for possible promotion, review for possible low ranking, and don't review. "You're moving fast," said Ambassador Rob Nolan, a former head of the office of career development and assignments, "but there are six of you. Usually it takes only two people on a board to get someone reviewed, sometimes only one."[15]

The second screening is quite detailed. "We use a forced-distribution point system," Nolan explained:

> You look at people typically in batches of forty. You rate them ten, nine, eight, and so forth. You only have a certain number of tens to give, a certain number of nines. You have to use all your rankings, including the twos and ones. It depends on the size of the pool and the number of slots, of course, but typically if you're not getting fives and sixes you're not getting promoted. It's important that rating, reviewing, and especially rated officers do a good job. If your file is sloppy, with typos, that sort of thing, the board can be affected. The rated officer can insist on fixing typos, grammar, spelling. We tell officers, it's your file, you own it. Act accordingly.

The Bureau of Human Resources decides for each promotion cycle where to draw the promotion lines based on current and projected staffing needs and budgetary constraints. In recent years, classwide competition has produced about one-third of all officer promotions, excluding promotions into FS-03. The two-thirds of promotions that result from competition within tracks (e.g., FS-02 public diplomacy officer against other FS-02 public diplomacy officers) are allocated among the tracks in accordance with each track's share of total positions. This two-tier promotion system is intended to ensure that the service can identify and promote its best officers and still ensure that it has the distribution of skills it needs throughout its ranks.

Officers who are close but fall short of the promotion cut-off line get a consolation prize, a meritorious step increase, which means a modest raise in pay. For senior officers, the same board that considers promotions also recommends awards of performance pay and presidential awards, which include cash payments.

Promotion rates across the State Department's foreign service are fairly consistent: 26 percent of all officers and specialists were promoted in 2006, 26 percent in 2007, 25 percent in 2008, and 24 percent in 2009. Setting aside administrative promotions for junior officers, most promotions occur into and within the middle grades, FS-04 through FS-02. Each spring, after the promotion lists have been released, the in-house *State Magazine* publishes a detailed breakdown of promotions by class, cone, and specialist function, showing how many competed for promotion, how many succeeded, and how long it took them to advance.[16]

Selection boards look for the bottom as well as the top. For the middle grades, boards identify the bottom 5 percent classwide. (There is no low ranking of entry-level or senior officers. If entry-level officers do not get tenure, their appointments expire. Similarly, senior officers who are not promoted face time-in-class restrictions that may force their retirement before the mandatory age of sixty-five.) A single low ranking has no consequences. An officer who is ranked low twice in five years, in evaluations by different rating officers, faces review by a performance standards board and possible separation from the service, which is called selection out.

"Low ranking is controversial," said Rob Nolan. "The evaluation form isn't designed for it. Evaluation reports may reveal the bottom 2 or 3 percent, but the rest is a statistical exercise. The selection board ranks all the names in each class, counts them, divides by twenty and draws a line."[17] Across all the midlevel grades, fifty or sixty people face performance standards boards each year.

Part IV

The Future Foreign Service

10

Tomorrow's Diplomats

"Who needs the State Department?" a senior administration official said in 2004, echoing the speaker at the beginning of this book. He was speaking of reconstruction efforts in Afghanistan. "The military does a better job." But, paradoxically, the widespread dissatisfaction with the performance of the foreign service in Iraq and Afghanistan led to a rare moment when the administration—two successive administrations, in fact—resolved to rebuild the foreign service and equip it to perform its mission: to make America's way in the world.

The drive for change that began when Secretary Colin Powell's Diplomatic Readiness Initiative caught a second wind in Secretary Clinton's Diplomacy 3.0, and Congress accepted the need for a more robust, more agile, better-trained, and better-funded civilian force to carry out American policy. A hiring surge began in fiscal year 2009 that, by the end of 2010, had already increased the size of State's foreign service by 15 percent above FY 2008 levels. If the administration and the Congress stick with the plan, which, as of this writing, seems unlikely, the increase will reach 25 percent in FY 2013 (table 10.1).

In USAID, the planned surge is steeper and faster, a net doubling of the number of FSOs, from 1,200 at the beginning of fiscal year 2009 to 2.400 by the end of fiscal year 2012. The Department of Commerce and the Department of Agriculture expect to hire more FSOs during this period as well (see chapter 3).

The purpose of this surge is the interesting part of the story. It is meant to strengthen the foreign service as a component of national security, the agent of smart power and of two parts of the triad of defense, diplomacy, and development. This view of the mission of the foreign service, long held by many career diplomats, took hold more broadly across the executive branch in the midst of the failure of American force to bring stability or democracy to Iraq after the defeat and capture of Saddam Hussein.

Table 10.1
Foreign Service Projected Hiring and Attrition

Fiscal Year	2009 Actual	2010 Projected	2011 Projected	2012 Projected	2013 Projected
New hires	1,355	1,370	830	810	810
Attrition	398	400	400	400	400
Net gain	**957**	**970**	**430**	**410**	**410**
Net FSO	*567*	*646*	*322*	*310*	*310*
Net specialist	*390*	*324*	*108*	*100*	*100*

Source: US Department of State, Office of Resource Management and Organizational Analysis, 2010 Personnel Strategy Report, provided to the author.
Note: Italics are author's estimates.

Broadly, but also slowly, and by no means smoothly: Behind the cheery "whole of government" slogan are bureaucratic rivalry, resistance to change, aversion to risk, and loyalty to existing methods and institutions. The effort to build a unit in the State Department to plan and coordinate the US government response to dangerously fragile states has struggled. Its future, still uncertain, may determine the shape of the foreign service in which today's junior officers will spend their careers.

Stabilization, Reconstruction, and Civilian Response [S/CRS]

American forces entered Iraq in March 2003 and took control of Baghdad three weeks later. Within a year, however, an insurgency had taken hold in many parts of the country, with resistance to coalition forces combining with sectarian struggle to create a downward spiral of violence and economic collapse. In 2004 the National Security Council, tacitly acknowledging failures in planning, ordered the establishment of a US government office for stabilization and reconstruction, and after some strong debate placed that office in the Department of State.[1] The president a year later reinforced that decision—and tried to end interagency conflicts—by directing the secretary of state to "coordinate and lead integrated United States Government efforts, involving all US Departments and Agencies with relevant capabilities, to prepare, plan for, and conduct stabilization and reconstruction activities."[2]

To carry out the president's directive, Secretary Colin Powell created an Office of the Coordinator for Reconstruction and Stabilization (CRS) and placed it directly under his control, making it S (for secretary)/CRS in the department's alphabetic code. The new office and its coordinator were to blaze the trail into the new territory of smart power, Diplomacy 3.0, and whole-of-government operations. Congress endorsed the creation of S/CRS in Section 408 of the Consolidated Appropriations Act of 2005.[3]

Prepare, Plan, Perform

The new office was charged with three tasks:

- *Prepare* for civilian engagement in the full range of possible stabilization crises, drawing on the capabilities of all relevant US government agencies
- *Plan* for action in specific crises, which meant developing a civilian equivalent of military planning that links policy, strategy, and tactics to resources and logistics in a dynamic, flexible way
- *Perform* in Washington and in the field, coordinating interagency activity and deploying personnel abroad in teams with the skills to execute US policy or to reinforce US embassy and military personnel already in the region

Did they hit the ground running? No. The story shows how change comes slowly, if at all.

"It's been a very tough slog standing this thing up," said John Herbst. Herbst, a career FSO who had served as ambassador to Uzbekistan and later to Ukraine, became head of S/CRS in May 2006. "Carlos [Carlos Pascual, Herbst's predecessor][4] laid a good foundation, we had some sound ideas and good people" but no other assets except the president's directive and some funding from the Department of Defense, almost all for projects outside Iraq and Afghanistan.[5] Congress would not appropriate funds directly. "Opinion on the right," Dane Smith wrote, "fretted that the military would be dragged into peacemaking and policing, and on the left that aid was being militarized."[6]

"Our survival and ability to move forward were severely doubted," Herbst said. "The most difficult and unpleasant period in my thirty-year career was the first two or three months in this job. We had this grand vision, and we had spoken support from high levels, but we had no actual support. We had at best disinterest, if not skepticism and hostility, from the main centers of action in the State Department. In addition, we were regarded with suspicion in the interagency, especially in USAID," which saw a civilian response corps based in the State Department as a usurpation of its own authorities and responsibilities. At one point in July 2006, when an S/CRS staffer tried to assert the office's role by referring to the president's directive, an AID official replied, "Not all directives are meant to be used, and this administration will be gone in two years."[7]

But by late 2006, Herbst had reached an understanding with the AID administrator, and by early 2007 concerned agencies had agreed on organizational principles for managing interagency coordination during a stabilization crisis and for building a civilian expeditionary group—the Civilian Response Corps, with active, standby, and reserve elements—that would have or would learn to deploy to the field when needed.

"Now," said Herbst, "we had to shift from winning the interagency battle to winning the battle with Congress." President Bush in his state of the union address called for creation of a reserve corps, which S/CRS had envisioned as one element of the Civilian Response Corps, of "civilians with critical skills to serve on missions abroad when America needs them." The 2007 Iraq-Afghanistan supplemental appropriation set aside $50 million (in the State Department appropriation for diplomatic and consular programs) for such a reserve, but the money was conditioned on additional authorizing legislation that could not get through the Senate. "That cost us another year," Herbst said.

One step back, two steps forward. In a fiscal year 2008 supplemental appropriation and in the fiscal year 2009 budget, Congress continued to deny funds for the civilian reserve that the president had requested, but it provided money, split between State and AID, to start building the other two components of the Civilian Response Corps, the active and the standby. These two elements are staffed by federal employees, with the active element deployable within forty-eight hours and the standby within thirty days, for tours of up to one year. The active element, which Herbst calls the first responders, will number about 250 when fully staffed, and the standby about 2,000. Foreign service officers from USAID will be the largest contingent, making up close to 40 percent of the total in each element. The Department of State, with a mixed contingent of foreign service and civil service personnel, will provide close to 30 percent of each element. Civil servants from six other agencies make up the rest of the active and standby staff (see table 10.2). The reserve element was staffed by 2,000 experts from outside the federal government who would make a four-year commitment of availability for deployments of up to one year. Congress authorized but never funded the reserve.

Table 10.2
Smart Power at Work, Planned Staffing of Civilian Response Corps

Agency	Active	Standby
Agriculture	8	64
Commerce	5	40
Health and Human Services	5	40
Homeland Security	3	24
Justice	62	496
State	72	576
Treasury	2	16
USAID	93	744
Total	250	2,000

Source: Department of State, *Report to Congress on Implementation of Title XVI of P.L. 110-417, the Reconstruction and Stabilization Citizen Management Act of 2008*, May 9, 2009.

Note: The Department of Energy joined the Civilian Response Corps in September 2010 and plans to participate in the standby component.

After five years of PRTs in Iraq and Afghanistan, and earlier stabilization and reconstruction efforts in Bosnia, Kosovo, Haiti, Somalia, and elsewhere, the Civilian Response Corps is an easy idea to grasp. "Everyone gets it," said Herbst, and it has begun to prove itself with deployments and projects in the Democratic Republic of Congo, Sudan, Afghanistan, Ecuador, Uganda, Sri Lanka, and other hot spots. Recruitment is on the rise. "Our foreign service recruitments have been good, not great, a solid record," Herbst said. "With the civil service, they are breaking down the doors."

Training is under way. Herbst explained, "We've got some world-class trainers here. A foundations course, two weeks at the Foreign Service Institute on basic stability operations. A three-week introduction to planning, an intermediate planning course in the works, and a relationship with military planning—we have someone taking a one-year planning course at Fort Leavenworth. We're writing a SNOE course, on security in nonconventional operating environments. All CRC members are supposed to take the foundations, basic planning, and SNOE courses, then we put them in planning operations and they learn on the job."

The idea of planning and coordinating interagency operations out of the State Department remains a hard sell. In 2007, S/CRS developed a plan for a whole-of-government interagency management system (IMS) and secured its approval by the National Security Council.[8] The plan still sits on the shelf and has never been used. Ambassador David Greenlee, a senior adviser to S/CRS, explained it this way: "In a whole-of-government approach, you could run this place like a rheostat—turn up resources when you need them, turn them down when you don't, all from the same switch, without someone saying, wait a minute, that's my job. But it's hard for one part of government to coordinate capabilities and inputs with other parts of government."[9] Even within State, the ingrained reaction to a crisis is to toss it to the appropriate regional bureau. "My peers," said Herbst, "guys who've been around for twenty or thirty years, think the way the State Department does business is just fine. They think talented FSOs can manage a complex operation without new tools."[10]

State and USAID took up the issue in their quadrennial review. The QDDR noted the problems, reached familiar conclusions, and offered little more than new labels:

- Reconfigure S/CRS as a bureau for conflict and stabilization operations (CSO), elevating the coordinator to assistant secretary;
- Reinvent the Interagency Management System as an International Operational Response Framework;
- Present Congress with a two-year plan to strengthen the active and standby elements of the Civilian Reserve Corps. Abandon the unfunded reserve element and seek authorization and funding for a similar but slightly restructured Expert Corps.[11]

The resistance within State, coupled with the department's lack of experience in planning and its shortage of human and financial resources, has led many observers to conclude that responsibility in this area should be placed somewhere else. Stuart Bowen, the Special Inspector General for Iraq Reconstruction (SIGIR), recommends creating a US Office for Contingency Operations (USOCO) under the National Security Council.[12] Marine four-star general Anthony Zinni recommends creating a new military civil affairs command, comparable to SOCOM, the special operations command.[13] There is never a dearth of ideas for creating new bureaucracies.

"Everyone agrees," said Herbst, "that at the end of the day you need a civilian, whole-of-government approach to address breaking situations, so you don't have a vacuum that the military has to fill."[14] If the secretary of state succeeds in leading that approach, the stars of the future foreign service will be the officers and specialists who can prepare, plan, and perform in interagency operations in fragile states where conflict and anarchy pose risks to US security. "The protean foreign service officer," David Greenlee said, "will need in his or her career track to be part of an expeditionary, interagency, deployable outfit."[15]

The Institution, the Profession, the Career

The US Foreign Service as an institution, the diplomatic profession, and the foreign service career have changed profoundly over the past sixty years. Change has not come easily. The foreign service and its guardian, the Department of State, have in the main been slow to respond to new circumstances. They have rarely been adept at anticipating or preparing for shifting requirements or at examining recent experience, identifying shortcomings, and making corrections. Across a broad range of issues—treatment of minorities, adoption of advanced information technology, coping with terrorism—both have needed repeated collisions with failure before finding a path to change.

Events and political decisions now demand that the foreign service use a wider range of diplomatic tools and deal with a wider range of actors than in the past. The future is unknowable, but the service must prepare for whatever shape it may take. A recent interagency exercise posited five plausible scenarios:

- Asian megacorporations increasingly dominate a global economy at the expense of European and American military and economic powers.
- In a world of freedom, opportunity, and technological progress, the US government is overextended operationally, and activist democracies challenge the United States in unexpected ways.
- Persistent terrorism, nuclear proliferation, and economic turmoil present constant and changing threats, the most dangerous situation the United States has faced in more than fifty years.
- Political and economic power is increasingly organized on regional rather than national or global lines, creating a tense and highly competitive world with multiple points of friction.
- Hypercapitalism has created new and powerful forms of organization that leave public institutions increasingly weak by comparison, setting up potential global conflicts between profits and principles.

The scenarios are not forecasts but descriptions of the diverse environments in which the US government may have to operate. They share certain features with which the future foreign service must be equipped to deal:

- New connections between formerly segregated issues, such as health and national security
- Shorter decision cycles as global media extend their reach and reduce the time between event and reaction
- A rising importance of transparent global rules and standards, and growing (if temporary) advantages for those who abandon the norm
- The proliferation of strategically significant, networked, global actors, including profit-seeking corporations and religious and issue-based organizations
- New opportunities to counter traditional forms of power with disruptive technologies, strategic communications, and control of critical resources[16]

The Institution

At the institutional level, the response to these demands includes the integration of foreign assistance and foreign policy, the rediscovery of public diplomacy, the redeployment of resources, and the conscious expansion of connections between official and unofficial American pursuits abroad, often under the name of public-private partnerships. Functions such as information and propaganda, cultural diplomacy, commercial diplomacy, and foreign aid have sometimes been consolidated in the State Department and sometimes dispersed among several agencies (see chapter 2). Consolidation is the recent trend. The QDDR envisions a deep alignment of foreign assistance and diplomacy. Exchanges of officers between the two agencies are likely to expand. A convergence of their foreign service systems and personnel and even a merger of USAID into State are conceivable though unlikely. There has been no comparable effort to consolidate the Commerce Department's foreign commercial service and the State Department's economic officers, though the Commerce Department's relative neglect of its commercial service and the growing role of ambassadors in commercial advocacy keep State's FSOs heavily—and successfully—engaged in commercial work.[17]

All foreign service agencies are adjusting the way they use their foreign service members to match changes in the global distribution of economic and political power and the shifting location of strategic threats. The number of foreign service posts is growing, and if Baghdad and Kabul are excepted, the average size of a post is shrinking. Positions are moving from Western Europe to China, India, central Asia, and the Middle East. Redeployment by the Department of State includes greater use of one- and two-person "American presence" posts, which puts diplomats close to audiences that are far from urban elites, and of no-person "virtual presence" posts, where interactive computer kiosks let foreigners stay in touch with the United States between visits from circuit-riding FSOs.

Connections between America's official and unofficial presence overseas have been growing in breadth, depth, and complexity. The unofficial presence—investors; exporters; importers; charities; groups that preach, teach, or advocate; and purveyors of the globally pervasive American popular culture—dwarfs the official presence in almost every way. Foreign affairs agencies, American embassies, and the foreign service are still working out what kinds of relationships with these private entities best serve the public interest. For the resource-starved foreign service, the temptation is strong to see cooperation with the private sector as a way to spend private, unappropriated money for public purposes, but alignment of private and public interests can never be taken for granted. Relationships between embassies and the private groups operating in their countries are like diplomatic relationships between allies: they aim to maintain the alignment of interests and work in tandem where possible and, when interests diverge, stay in close touch, avoiding open conflict and finding areas of cooperation that can be expanded over time. Secretary Clinton announced a Global Partnership Initiative in April 2009 and named a special representative for global partnerships with ambassadorial rank.[18] The techniques of building and exploiting public-private partnerships are the subject of much study. The most successful examples are likely to be widely copied.[19]

The Profession

Changes at the professional level may be more fundamental. The foreign service did not have the skills required to perform the mission assigned to it in Iraq. Economic reconstruction required specialists in agronomy, sanitation, administration of justice, public finance, public health, and others not on the foreign service payrolls. The service turned to civilian contractors and military personnel, many drawn from the reserves, to do this work. The still unauthorized reserve element of the Civilian Response Corps would institutionalize this practice and make it far more efficient.

Economic and political reconstruction, in preconflict or postconflict situations, seems likely to be an essential feature of US foreign policy for many more years. The work is so far from the nineteenth- and especially twentieth-century conceptions of diplomacy that it will change the profession and its image, even if only a relatively small minority of practitioners is regularly engaged in it. At the same time, the geographic center of traditional diplomacy has shifted from Western Europe to places less comfortable and culturally more distant in east, south, and central Asia.

The skills and qualities required of professional diplomats in most ways have not changed. The sympathy with foreign cultures, the knowledge of foreign languages, the ability to explain America to foreign audiences, the quick grasp of one's own interests and how to advance them, the pragmatism that can chart a course through a negotiation to a satisfactory result, the ability to stay tethered to instructions and congressional mandates while moving forward—these are nothing new. The shifting demands of the job, however, are raising standards. The brilliant amateur and dashing dilettante are no longer models for the American FSO. Diplomacy American style can no longer be advertised as indoor work, no heavy lifting.

The Career

The foreign service career is changing too, in important ways. The law of supply and demand suggests that for the next ten years or so, officers and specialists who are prepared for service in dangerous, difficult, or isolated posts, or who are eager and able to learn a critical language, will find a seller's market. They will be rewarded with the assignments they want, the training they need, and the responsibility that creates opportunities for rapid advancement. But the pressure to take on hardship tours should not be exaggerated. Many, probably most, officers will spend no more than two or three years of a twenty-seven-year career in posts that take them away from their families.

In the past few years, the Department of State has come under pressure, from within as well as without, to lift its level of skill and bring more rigor and consistency to the professional development of FSOs. The model most often cited is the officer corps of the armed services.

Secretary Powell reportedly said that FSOs are better educated than military officers when they begin their careers, but military officers are better educated than FSOs at retirement. Because of its surplus of officers to billets, the military has more capacity for methodically upgrading and updating officers' skills as they rise through the ranks: A brigadier general with a twenty-three-year career has likely spent a total of four to six years in training, but an FSO with the same length of service and the rank of counselor has likely had only three years of training, including language training.

If the numbers in table 10.1 are met, and staffing patterns stay at roughly current levels, vacancies will be nearly eliminated, and training over the course of a career will increase. Distance learning will add to flexibility and open new opportunities.

The precepts that govern promotion to the highest levels of the service may have to change. Officers in midcareer are now encouraged to show their breadth with assignments outside their areas of geographic and functional expertise and, as they approach the senior ranks, to prove their mettle as managers with a tour as deputy chief of mission. But the service needs depth as well as breadth and, like USAID, may need to find a way to promote the people who are the best at what they do, without making them take unprofitable detours or unsuitable assignments.

Foreign Service Pride

The service is getting younger, not so much in age as in experience. In 2010 half of all members of the service in State, and 70 percent in USAID, had less than ten years of service.[20] These twenty-first-century diplomats recognize that the service is under stress, understaffed, inadequately trained for the missions assigned to it. They want change, and they will make sure it happens. The senior ranks have their traditionalists, but they are not filled with defenders of the status quo. On the contrary, some of the most carefully grounded proposals for reform come from some of the most experienced diplomats. Tomorrow's foreign service will not look like today's.

What will not change is the pride that members of the service can take in the career. FSOs and specialists feel that pride quietly. Inexplicably, neither the Department of State nor the US foreign service as an institution does much to foster what should be a formidable esprit de corps. There are no insignia of rank except for an ambassador's flag. There are few traditions or ceremonies. Promotions generally go unmarked. Awards may be conferred by mail or in perfunctory group presentations. New diplomats and new ambassadors get a gaudy swearing in, but otherwise a member of the service may pass a thirty-year career and see no pomp under any circumstance.

This public diffidence, and its obvious contrast with military display, emphasizes the difference between diplomats and soldiers. The foreign service may be America's first line of defense, but it relies on persuasion, negotiation, inducement, and threat, not on force. The army is fond of shock and awe and likes to describe its mission as "break things and kill people." The foreign service, with equal swagger, could counter, "We don't kill them, we bend them to our will."

"Diplomats," wrote David Newsom, "live in realms that are conspiratorial, cynical and devious."[21] They can be, but often are not, plain talkers and straight shooters. They seek clarity but are comfortable with ambiguity. Their most prized skills are verbal, psychological, and manipulative. As David Brooks observed, these are not talents that enjoy high honor among most Americans.[22]

The foreign service merits, but should not expect, the high esteem of the American public. Most diplomatic success is incremental, measured in small doses when it can be measured at all. Breakthroughs occur but they are rare. Americans are impatient. They want results, and they easily blame diplomats for failing to deliver. Neither the State Department nor the foreign service has anything like a grassroots constituency.

The greatest part of the work of the foreign service is done quietly. Its achievements often pass unnoticed, as do its sacrifices. Members of the service salute the flag but rarely wave it. Within the service, as its members will tell you, patriotism and passion for the job run deep. A life in the foreign service is its own emblem.

Appendix A. Department of State Organization Chart

United States
Department of State

Chief of Staff
(S/COS)

Under Secretary for Political Affairs (P)	Under Secretary for Economic, Business and Agricultural Affairs (E)	Under Secretary for Arms Control and International Security Affairs (T)	Under Secretary for Diplomacy and Affairs (R)

African Affairs (AF) Assistant Secretary	East Asian and Pacific Affairs (EAP) Assistant Secretary	Economic, Energy & Business Affairs (EEB) Assistant Secretary	International Security and Nonproliferation (ISN) Assistant Secretary	Education and Affairs Assistant Secretary

| European and Eurasian Affairs (EUR) Assistant Secretary | International Organizations (O) Assistant Secretary | | Political-Military Affairs (PM) Assistant Secretary | Public Affairs Assistant Secretary |

| Near Eastern Affairs (NEA) Assistant Secretary | South and Central Asian Affairs (SCA) Assistant Secretary | | Verification, Compliance and Implementation (VCI) Assistant Secretary | International Information (IIP) Coordinator |

| Western Hemisphere Affairs (WHA) Assistant Secretary | International Narcotics and Law Enforcement (INL) Assistant Secretary | | | |

Inspector General (OIG)	Policy Planning Staff (S/P) Director	Civil Rights (S/OCR) Director	Legal Advisor (L)	Legislative Affairs (H) Assistant Secretary	Intelligence and Research (INR) Assistant Secretary

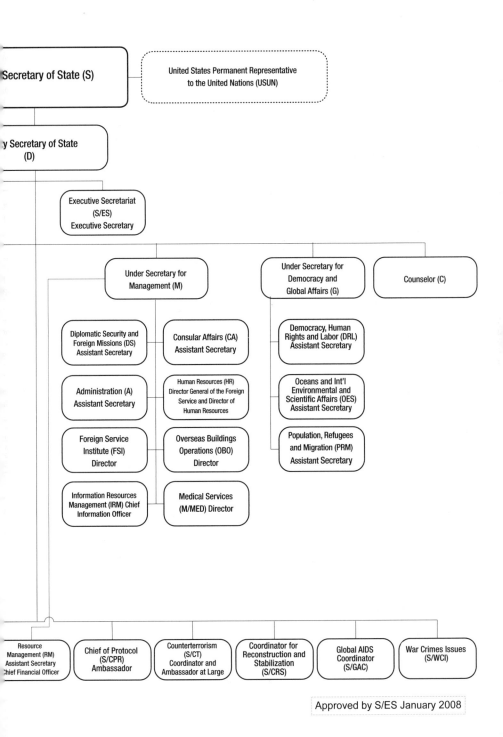

Secretary of State (S)

United States Permanent Representative
to the United Nations (USUN)

y Secretary of State
(D)

Executive Secretariat
(S/ES)
Executive Secretary

Under Secretary for
Management (M)

Under Secretary for
Democracy and
Global Affairs (G)

Counselor (C)

Diplomatic Security and
Foreign Missions (DS)
Assistant Secretary

Consular Affairs (CA)
Assistant Secretary

Democracy, Human
Rights and Labor (DRL)
Assistant Secretary

Administration (A)
Assistant Secretary

Human Resources (HR)
Director General of the Foreign
Service and Director of
Human Resources

Oceans and Int'l
Environmental and
Scientific Affairs (OES)
Assistant Secretary

Foreign Service
Institute (FSI)
Director

Overseas Buildings
Operations (OBO)
Director

Population, Refugees
and Migration (PRM)
Assistant Secretary

Information Resources
Management (IRM) Chief
Information Officer

Medical Services
(M/MED) Director

Resource
Management (RM)
Assistant Secretary
Chief Financial Officer

Chief of Protocol
(S/CPR)
Ambassador

Counterterrorism
(S/CT)
Coordinator and
Ambassador at Large

Coordinator for
Reconstruction and
Stabilization
(S/CRS)

Global AIDS
Coordinator
(S/GAC)

War Crimes Issues
(S/WCI)

Approved by S/ES January 2008

Appendix B. Foreign Service Core Precepts

The Qualifications Evaluation Panel (QEP) assesses the personal narrative with reference to six precepts that are predictors of success in the foreign service. These same precepts are used by the commissioning and tenure board and by promotion boards to evaluate potential throughout a foreign service career.

Leadership: Innovation, decision making, teamwork, openness to dissent, community service, and institution building

Interpersonal skills: Professional standards, persuasion and negotiation, workplace perceptiveness, adaptability, representational skills

Communication skills: Written communication, oral communication, active listening, public outreach, foreign language skills

Management skills: Operational effectiveness, performance management and evaluation, management resources, customer service

Intellectual skills: Information gathering and analysis, critical thinking, active learning, leadership and management training

Substantive knowledge: Understanding of US history/government/culture and application in dealing with other cultures. Knowledge and application of career track relevant information.

Source: US Department of State, http://careers.state.gov/officer/qep.html.

Appendix C. Interviews

The authors are grateful to all those who gave their time to this project, including those whose names have been withheld. Those interviewed spoke for themselves, not for their agencies or employers.

Charles Alexander	February 14, 2006
Frank Almaguer	November 6, 2009
Juan Alsace	August 28, 2006
Luis Arreaga-Rodas	November 13, 2009
Robert Batchelder	August 12, 2005
Davida Baxter	February 23, 2007
Sylvia Bazala	August 29, 2006
Barry Blechman	June 12, 2006
Marcia Bosshardt	August 6, 2007
Tobin Bradley	November 3, 2005
Rea Brazeal	January 26, 2006
Douglas Broome	January 31, 2006
John H. Brown	September 1, 2006
Jennifer Butte-Dahl	April 2, 2007; January 15, 2010
Lewis K. Byrd	August 10, 2006
Robin Byrd	August 10, 2006
Vincent Campos	February 15, 2007
Katherine Canavan	September 14, 2005
Joseph Castro	August 11, 2006
David Caudill	February 23, 2007
William N. Center	February 8, 2006
Andrew Chritton	June 23, 2005
Henry Lee Clarke	April 13, 2010
Marguerite Coffey	July 27, 2006
Frank Coulter	November 15, 2005; March 23, 2010
Keith Curtis	February 9, 18, 2010
Caryn Danz	July 25, 2007
Margaret Dean	April 21, 2010
Bill DePree	August 20, 2005
James Derham	July 10, 2005
Philo Dibble	October 26, 2005
Steve Dietz	April 27, 2007
David Dlouhy	January 27, July 20, 2007
William Eaton	April 15, 2010
Debi Fairman	February 23, 2007
Jimmie Fairman	February 23, 2007

Steve Gallogly	August 8, 2005
Robert Gallucci	June 9, 2007
David Greenlee	August 24, 2005; December 18, 2009
Marc Grossman	November 16, 2005
Linda Hartsock	June 23, 2005
Clayton Hays	August 12, 2005
John Herbst	January 11, 2010
Sheila Herrling	November 24, 2009; December 2009
L. Craig Johnstone	February 1, 2006
Harry Kamian	August 26, 2006
Sidney Kaplan	May 18, 2007; November 24, 2009
Steve Kashkett	August 29, 2006
Craig Kelly	August 29, 2006
J. Christian Kennedy	July 20, 2005
Deborah Kennedy-Iraheta	March 12, 2010
Kristie Anne Kenney	August 26, 2005
Eric Khant	February 23, 2007
Russ King	August 10, 2006
Jeremiah Knight	February 22, 2007
Jimmy Kolker	May 25, 2007
Alan Larson	July 13, 2007
Rose Likins	December 13, 2006
Dana Linnet	April 2, 2007
Hugo Llorens	August 12, 2005
Robert Loftis	September 19, 2006
Rudolph Lohmeyer	May 18, 2007
Mark Lopes	January 7, 2010
Philippe Lussier	December 9, 2009
Marcos Mandojana	February 8, 2006
Steven Mann	September 7, 2005
Kristine Marsh	March 3, 2007
John Marten	August 6, 2006
William McCahill	August 23, 2007
Deborah McCarthy	August 26, 2005
Sean McCormack	December 12, 2006
Christopher Midura	May 29, 2007
Richard Miles	March 10, 2006
Charnae Morris	March 8, 2006
Langhorne A. Motley	August 30, 2006
Sean Murphy	August 28, 2006
Marianne Myles	July 20, 2007
John Naland	May 17, 2007
Michelle Nichols	February 22, 2007
Robert Nolan	May 18, 2007

Cecilia Olea	August 10, 2006
Barbro Owens-Kirkpatrick	September 28, 2005
James Pavitt	January 25, 2007
W. Robert Pearson	June 27, 2006
Brian Polley	July 6, 2006
John A. Ritchie	October 28, 2005
Adele Ruppe	December 14, 2005
Gregory Schiffer	February 8, 2006
Henry Schmick	January 22, 2010
William Schofield	November 15, 2005
Susan Shea	June 27, 2005
Thomas Skipper	December 14, 2005
Timothy Slater	August 10, 2006
David Stephenson	February 23, 2007
Diana Tasnadi	October 23, 2006
Harry Thomas	August 13, 27, 2009
Lynne Tracy	January 27, 2010
Robert B. Waldrop	October 28, December 1, 2005
Betsy Whitaker	December 13, 2005
Loren Willet	July 6, 2006
Ann Witkowski	July 19, 2007
Bryan Wockley	March 6, 2007
Emi Yamauchi	May 16, 2007
Francisco Zamora	March 11, 2010
Ben Ziff	December 14, 2005

Appendix D. Websites and Blogs

The website associated with this book is www.careerdiplomacy.com.

Government

www.usda.gov/wps/portal/usda/usdahome	Agriculture Department home page
www.careers.state.gov	Careers at State
www.commerce.gov/	Commerce Department home page
http://foreignaffairs.house.gov/	House Foreign Affairs Committee
www.whitehouse.gov/omb/	Office of Management and Budget
http://foreign.senate.gov/	Senate Foreign Relations Committee
www.state.gov	State Department home page
http://blogs.state.gov	State Department official blog
www.youtube.com/statevideo	State on YouTube
www.usaid.gov/	USAID home page

Career Resources

www.commerce.gov/about-commerce/careers	Careers at Commerce
www.careers.state.gov	Careers at State
www.usaid.gov/careers	Careers at USAID
www.fas.usda.gov/admin/newjobs/fasjobs.asp	Careers with the Foreign Agricultural Service
http://fsot.wikidot.com/	Foreign service officer test wiki
www.usajobs.gov	Work for the federal government
http://groups.yahoo.com/group/fswe/	Yahoo groups for those planning to take
http://groups.yahoo.com/group/fsoa/	the foreign service officer test (written exam, oral assessment)

Foreign Service Websites

www.afsa.org	American Foreign Service Association
www.aafsw.org	Associates of the American Foreign Service Worldwide
www.fsyf.org	Foreign Service Youth Foundation
www.glifaa.org	Gays and Lesbians in Foreign Affairs Agencies

Foreign Service Blogs

http://diplopundit.blogspot.com	About the foreign service
www.thehegemonist.com	By a foreign service officer, about the foreign service

www.diplojournal.com — By a new FSO
www.twocrabs.blogs.com — By a new FSO (sworn in August 2010)
http://blogs.state.gov — DipNote, official State Department blog

Diplomacy and Diplomatic History

www.academyofdiplomacy.org — American Academy of Diplomacy
www.adst.org — Association for Diplomatic Studies and Training

http://thecable.foreignpolicy.com — Foreign service oral history transcripts at the Library of Congress

http://isd.georgetown.edu — Institute for the Study of Diplomacy
http://blogs.cgdev.org/mca-monitor — Rethinking US foreign assistance (Center for Global Development)

www.uscpublicdiplomacy.org — University of Southern California Center on Public Diplomacy

www.usdiplomacy.org — US Diplomacy—diplomatic history

Foreign Service Advocacy

www.publicdiplomacy.org — Public diplomacy and USIA alumni
www.uccoxfoundation.org — Una Chapman Cox Foundation
www.usglc.org — US Global Leadership Coalition

Notes

Chapter 1: What Is the Foreign Service?

1. Clinton, Statement before the Senate Foreign Relations Committee.
2. Ibid.
3. Clinton, Remarks before the House Appropriations Subcommittee.
4. Rice, Remarks at Georgetown School of Foreign Service.
5. Rice, Confirmation Hearings before Senate Foreign Relations Committee.

Chapter 2: History

1. Acheson, *Present at the Creation*, 303.
2. Grove, *Behind Embassy Walls*, 95.
3. Kissinger, *White House Years*, 11.
4. Conversation between Nixon and Kissinger, November 13, 1972, quoted in Humphrey, *Foreign Relations of the United States*, 768.
5. Foreign service officers in the Nixon White House included Frank Carlucci (later secretary of defense), Lawrence Eagleburger (secretary of state), Anthony Lake (national security adviser), Winston Lord (ambassador to China), John Negroponte (deputy secretary of state), Peter Rodman (assistant secretary of defense), and Harold Saunders (assistant secretary of state).
6. In 1792, when Congress passed the first law regulating consuls and their duties, the United States had five diplomatic and sixteen consular posts abroad. By 1860, the numbers had grown to 33 and 279. When no American was available, consular commissions were sometimes given to third-country nationals.
7. Consular salaries varied by post. At Cobiya, in the Mexican state of Tabasco, the salary was $500. At Liverpool, it was $7,500. Consuls receiving a salary greater than $1,500 were prohibited from engaging in mercantile business, although other private enterprise remained open to them. See Stuart, *American Diplomatic and Consular Practice*, 168.
8. Quoted by Ambassador Charles Freeman in a speech to the American Foreign Service Association Club, January 11, 1995, and provided to the author by the American Academy of Diplomacy.
9. Quoted in Stuart, *American Diplomatic and Consular Practice*, 174.
10. Some writers ridiculed consuls, but others benefited from consular appointments, which were a form of federal support for artistic achievement. A list of nineteenth-century writers who served as consuls includes Washington Irving, Nathaniel Hawthorne, James Fenimore Cooper, James Weldon Johnson, William Dean Howells, and Bret Harte. It was Howells's lobbying of President Rutherford B. Hayes, a relation by marriage, that secured the washed-up, alcoholic Harte the consulship in Munich. Kaplan, *Singular Mark Twain*, 335. Henry Adams served as private secretary to the minister of the American legation in London, his father, Charles Francis Adams. President Abraham Lincoln, who sent Charles Francis Adams to London, asked his secretary of state to use consular positions to "facilitate artists a little [in] their profession." Goodwin, *Team of Rivals*, 703.

11. Trask, *Short History*, 22.

12. Bierce, *Devil's Dictionary*, 18.

13. Adams, *Education of Henry Adams*, 1080.

14. Trask, *Short History*, 26.

15. Quoted in Barnes and Morgan, *Foreign Service of the United States*, 207. The U.S. Foreign Service is not alone in its image problem. A senior British career diplomat, Sir David Gore-Booth, remarked in 1999 that "one of the great failures of the Diplomatic Service has been its inability to cast off its image as bowler-hatted, pin-striped and chinless with a fondness for champagne." Cited in Bryson, "Ambassadors Going Out with a Bang."

16. Stimson's diary account of a conversation with FDR on January 9, 1933, cited in Morgan, *FDR: A Biography*, 368–69. Stimson was President Hoover's secretary of state before becoming Roosevelt's secretary of war; the conversation with Roosevelt cited here took place before Roosevelt's first inauguration.

17. Trask, *Short History*, 29.

18. LaRue Lutkins, interview by Charles Stuart Kennedy, cited in Morgan and Kennedy, *American Diplomats*, 46. George Kennan, too old for the draft himself, wrote that the department told foreign service officers to apply to their draft boards for deferments on their own; the department, for fear of congressional criticism, would not apply on their behalf. The press, he wrote, "repeatedly carried articles charging them, sometimes individually and by name, with being draft dodgers." Kennan, *Memoirs*, 140–41.

19. Mee, *Marshall Plan*, 215–16.

20. Kennan, *Memoirs*, 191–92.

21. Lauren, *China Hands' Legacy*, 13. Hiss was tried and convicted of perjury in 1950 but was never charged with espionage. Readers who wonder about the disparity between the large number dismissed for security concerns and the relatively small number believed to be involved with foreign powers may safely conclude that many were dismissed as security risks because they were believed to be homosexual.

22. There is no known recording or printed text of McCarthy's speech as delivered. This quote comes from an account by a reporter who was present. Desmond, "McCarthy Charges Reds Hold U.S. Jobs." Other accounts vary only in detail.

23. Cited in Acheson, *Present at the Creation*, 365.

24. See Davies, "The Personal Experience," 37–57.

25. See Kahn, *China Hands*, 174–75. The accuser quoted here is Patrick Hurley, named ambassador to China in 1944. Hurley tried to promote a Communist-Nationalist coalition to fight the Japanese. His professional staff, the China hands, did not believe such an approach had any chance of success. The quotation is from Hurley's letter of resignation to President Truman in November 1945.

26. Kennan, *Memoirs*, 216.

27. John S. Service, fired in 1951, was reinstated in 1957 after the U.S. Supreme Court ruled that the department, in dismissing him, had violated its own regulations.

28. Grove, *Behind Embassy Walls*, 41. The aide is identified as Bob Fearey.

29. Nathan and Oliver, *Foreign Policy Making*, 17.

30. Quoted in Trask, *Short History*, 35. The ambassador is Stanton Griffis, a businessman who served as ambassador to Poland, Egypt, Argentina, and Spain from 1947 to 1951.

31. For example, reserve officers had a separate pay scale, a source of continuing friction with the regular foreign service officers.

32. Bacchus, *Staffing for Foreign Affairs*, 201.

33. Ibid., 198–201. The 1980 act revived selection out for senior officers and extended it to secretaries, communications specialists, and other foreign service staff. Foreign service nationals (FSNs), local and third-country nationals employed by U.S. missions abroad, are by law members of the foreign service, but they are not subject to selection out. In this book, however, as in most usage, the phrase *members of the foreign service* means foreign service officers and specialists, not foreign service nationals.

34. For the early history, see Stuart, *American Diplomatic and Consular Practice*, chap. 1. Congressional efforts in 1995 to return the commercial service to the Department of State received wide support, but not wide enough: The measure died in committee.

35. The Trade Expansion Act of 1962 created the Office of the Special Trade Representative in the Executive Office of the President. The Trade Act of 1974 made the office responsible to both the president and Congress, the only such office in the U.S. government. An executive order changed the name to U.S. Trade Representative in 1979.

36. The staff of the USTR's office often includes a number of foreign service officers seconded from their home agencies. The U.S. ambassador, deputy chief of mission, and other officials at the U.S. mission to the World Trade Organization in Geneva are part of the office of the USTR.

37. An Economist/YouGov poll of the general population, taken in April 2010, showed that 71 percent of one thousand respondents would cut foreign aid first in any reduction of government spending. The next target for cuts was the environment, chosen by 29 percent, followed by agriculture, housing, and mass transit at 27 percent (www.economist .com/blogs/democracyinamerica/2010/04/economistyougov_polling).

38. Frumin, "Equipping USAID for Success: A Field Perspective," 9. Frumin calculates official development assistance using methodology adopted by the Organization for Economic Cooperation and Development.

39. The State Department's exercise, conducted jointly with USAID, was the first Quadrennial Diplomacy and Development Review (QDDR), patterned after the Defense Department's Quadrennial Defense Review (QDR). The QDDR was released in December 2010. The White House completed its Presidential Policy Directive 7 (PPD 7) on global development policy in September 2010 but did not release the text.

40. The *New York Times* reported on August 13, 1974, that all five black ambassadors, all seven black USAID mission chiefs, and seven of the ten black staff members who were USIA chiefs of section, were assigned in Africa. Johnson, "Black Envoys Seek More Non-African Posts," 4.

41. Quoted in *New York Times*, "Report on Minority Progress Still 'Distressing,'" June 28, 1983, B-6.

42. The position of director of personnel was at the time separate from that of director general. The officer who failed to win confirmation was Howard P. Mace. Welles, "Women Winning State Department Cases," 4.

43. U.S. General Accounting Office, *State Department: Minorities and Women*.

44. Name withheld, interview, January 2006.

45. Jordan, "'Hillary Effect' Cited for Increase in Female Ambassadors to U.S.," A1.

46. Luis Arreaga-Rodas, interview, November 13, 2009.

47. Marc Grossman, interview, November 16, 2005.

48. L. Bruce Laingen, correspondence with author, July 2005.

49. Vance, *Hard Choices*, 329.

50. Ibid., 340.

51. U.S. Department of State, *Final Report and Recommendations*, app. C. The seventy-two persons in the compound included thirty-seven Department of State employees, twenty-eight from the U.S. military (thirteen marines, six from the army, six from the air force, and three from the navy), four from the U.S. International Cooperation Agency, one from the FAS, one from the Department of Education, and one private businessman.

Three embassy officers, including the chargé d'affaires, were on their way to the foreign ministry building at the time the embassy was seized. They were effectively placed under arrest in the foreign ministry, where they stayed until their transfer to a prison in January 1981. Six people escaped the compound and took refuge in the Canadian embassy. Three months later they were smuggled out of the country under false identities provided by the Canadians, who then closed their embassy and withdrew all personnel. Thirteen were allowed to leave between November 18 and 20, after Khomeini ordered the release of "women and blacks." One hostage, Foreign Service Officer Richard Queen, was afflicted with multiple sclerosis and released in July 1980. Fifty-two hostages, including the three held in the foreign ministry, were released at noon on January 20, 1981, the last day of President Carter's term in office.

52. U.S. Department of State, *Final Report and Recommendations*, app. D. The murdered personnel include Ambassador John Gordon Mein, Guatemala, 1968; Public Safety Adviser Dan Mitrione, Uruguay, 1970; Ambassador Cleo A. Noel and Deputy Chief of Mission George Moore, Sudan, 1973; State Department employee John S. Patterson, Mexico, 1974; Ambassador Rodger P. Davies and administrative assistant Antoinette Varnava, Cyprus, 1974; consular agent John Egan, Argentina, 1975; Ambassador Francis E. Meloy Jr., Economic Counselor Robert O. Waring, and driver Zuhayr Mughrabi, Lebanon, 1976; Ambassador Adolph "Spike" Dubs, Afghanistan, 1979.

53. A group representing most of the hostages later tried to sue the government of Iran, but federal courts upheld the validity of the renunciation clause of the agreement with Iran and rejected their case. Kessler, "Administration Blocks Ex-Hostages' Bid for Damages from Iran," A1. The most recent federal court ruling came in 2002. The Supreme Court refused to hear an appeal in 2004. The Department of State repeated its opposition to claims by the hostages against Iran at a meeting with a group of former hostages in 2006.

54. Steigman, *Foreign Service*, 2.

55. U.S. Department of State and Inman, *Report of the Secretary of State's Advisory Panel.*

56. For OSAC's membership, see www.osac.gov.

57. The predecessor of the DS was the smaller Office of Security, which reported to the assistant secretary for administration.

58. The Bureau of Human Resources counted 5,119 foreign service specialists on June 30, 2009. Of these, 1,745 were diplomatic security special agents. Office-management specialists were the next largest category, numbering 795.

59. U.S. Department of State, Bureau of Diplomatic Security, *Diplomatic Security 2009 Year in Review*, 23.

60. For the distinction between ambassador and chief of mission, see chapter 5.

61. See www.state.gov/m/ds/about/overview/c9004.htm.

62. Langehorne A. (Tony) Motley, interview, August 30, 2006.

63. Gib Lanpher, telephone conversation with author, August 2007. Ambassador Lanpher noted that "a six-week ARB on Iraq, including salaries, travel, and per diem, costs less than one armored Suburban. Pretty good value provided the recommendations are given serious consideration."

64. U.S. Department of State, U.S. Agency for International Development, *Leading through Civilian Power: The First Quadrennial Diplomacy and Development Review* (QDDR), 71.

65. Gates, Landon lecture.

66. Marquardt, "The DRI Rides to the Rescue," 21.

67. U.S. Department of State, *America's Overseas Presence*, 5.

68. Marc Grossman, interview, November 16, 2005.

69. Grossman's inner circle included Bill Eaton, David Dlouhy, and Mike Polt. The original skunk works was a secret engineering department set up at Lockheed Aircraft Company in 1943 to develop jet aircraft. The name came from the "Skonk Works," a hidden still where denizens of Dogpatch, the fictional mountain community in Al Capp's Li'l Abner comic strip of the era, produced the stupefying Kickapoo Joy Juice.

70. U.S. Government Accountability Office, *Staffing and Foreign Language Shortfalls*, 5. Looking back, the GAO calculated the cost of the DRI at $197 million.

71. Or very nearly. Of the 1,158 foreign service positions requested, the department obtained 1,069.

72. Foreign Affairs Council, *Secretary Colin Powell's State Department*, 3–4. See also Marquardt, "DRI Rides to the Rescue." The Foreign Affairs Council is an umbrella group of eleven organizations, including the American Academy of Diplomacy, the American Foreign Service Association (AFSA), the Associates of the American Foreign Service Worldwide, the Association for Diplomatic Studies and Training, the Association of Black American Ambassadors, the Business Council for International Understanding, the Council of American Ambassadors, the Una Chapman Cox Foundation, the Nelson B. Delavan Foundation, and the Public Members Association of the Foreign Service, USA.

73. Foreign Affairs Council, *Secretary Colin Powell's State Department*, 4.

74. Henrietta Fore was undersecretary for management, John Negroponte was deputy secretary, Richard Boucher was assistant secretary for South and Central Asian affairs, Nicholas Burns was undersecretary for political affairs, Chris Hill was head of the U.S. delegation to the six-party talks with North Korea, Brian Gunderson was chief of staff to Secretary Rice, General Peter Pace was chairman of the joint chiefs of staff, and Admiral Edmund Giambastiani was vice chairman.

75. Harry Thomas, interview, August 27, 2009. The figure of 22 percent includes those who were on temporary duty lasting ninety days or more. In correspondence with the author, Thomas noted that the department was required to ramp up staffing so quickly that many who went in the early years were never formally assigned.

76. Luis Arreaga-Rodas, interview, November 13, 2009. The plan includes about 5,700 new hires and projects attrition at about 3,600.

77. Grossman interview, November 16, 2005.

Chapter 3: The Foreign Service Today

1. Foreign Service Act of 1980, sec. 3904.

2. See chapter 6 for a detailed discussion of foreign service ranks.

3. The original building, which faces 21st Street, NW, was constructed before World War II to house the War Department, which until then had shared space with the State Department in what is now the Eisenhower Executive Office Building on 17th Street, NW, next to the White House. The War Department, however, moved instead to the much larger Pentagon, built in haste in 1943 and 1944, leaving the building at 21st and C streets vacant. State moved there instead in 1947 under pressure from the White House, which wanted to expand into the space that State occupied. State's new home was cramped, however, and was soon incorporated in a new and much larger building completed in 1960, with its main entrance on C Street, NW, at 22nd Street, NW. See Acheson, *Present at the Creation*, 213. The new building was named for President Truman in 2000, and the original building, renovated between 1999 and 2007, was named the George C. Marshall wing.

4. See www.afsa.org/plaquelist.cfm. The American Foreign Service Association (AFSA) erected the first plaque in 1933 and the second in 1972. Names on the plaques are chosen by the AFSA governing board.

5. For a full list of State Department office designations and abbreviations, see www .state.gov/documents/organization/86890.pdf.

6. Excluding about 125 chiefs of mission from the denominator, and about 41,000 foreign service nationals and other locally engaged staff from the numerator. If these are included, the ratio is about 1 high official for every 340 employees. For a list of State officials based in Washington with a rank equivalent to assistant secretary or higher, see www.state.gov/r/pa/ei/biog/c7647.htm.

7. Foreign service nationals are subject to the employment laws of the jurisdiction in which they work.

8. The word *attaché* defines an official assigned to an embassy to perform a specific task. Although U.S. military personnel assigned to a U.S. embassy still use the title *attaché*, the term is slowly passing out of use, along with other terms from French diplomatic usage, like *démarche*, *aide-mémoire*, and *note verbale*. In diplomatic rank, an attaché is ordinarily below a counselor.

9. "Executive Order 13534," *Federal Register*, vol. 75 (March 11, 2010): 12433–35.

10. Figures are for fiscal year 2009. Deborah Kennedy-Iraheta, interview, March 12, 2010.

11. Figures for fiscal year 2009 include the Supplemental Appropriations Act, 2008; the American Recovery and Reinvestment Act of 2009 (the stimulus bill); the Omnibus Appropriations Act, 2009; and the Supplemental Appropriations Act, 2009. See U.S. Department of State, *Congressional Budget Justification*, vol. 2, *Foreign Operations, FY 2011* 1–2. AID hires contractors to carry out many of its programs. The costs, including the

contractor's salaries and other operating costs, are charged to AID's program budget. Not all foreign assistance flows through the AID budget, and what is budgeted in one year is generally spent in other years, so published figures on U.S. foreign assistance, as calculated, for example, by the Organization for Economic Cooperation and Development (OECD), may bear little or no relation to the AID budget.

12. Douglas Broome, interview, January 31, 2006.

13. National Security Strategy, May 2010, 15.

14. Ibid., 5.

15. White House Fact Sheet, U.S. Global Development Policy, September 22, 2010. The text of the directive was not made public.

16. *Leading through Civilian Power: The First Quadrennial Diplomacy and Development Review*, December 15, 2010, 6.

17. Ibid., 21.

18. Francisco Zamora, interview, March 11, 2010.

19. Clinton, Remarks to the Center for Global Development.

20. L. Craig Johnstone, interview, February 1, 2006.

21. Frank Almaguer, interview, November 6, 2009.

22. Luis Arreaga-Rodas, interview, November 13, 2009.

23. Deborah Kennedy-Iraheta, interview, March 12, 2010.

24. Ibid.

25. Ibid.

26. The U.S. and Foreign Commercial Service is commonly called the Commercial Service (CS), with the overseas, foreign service component called the FCS, and the domestic, civil service component called the Office of Domestic Operations, or ODO.

27. These numbers are drawn from the president's fiscal year 2011 budget request, which at the time of this writing awaits congressional action. See www.osec.doc.gov/bmi/budget/11BiB/2011_BiB.pdf for details.

28. Keith Curtis, interview, February 9, 2010.

29. Ford, "Final Thoughts on the Foreign Service at the Commerce Department," 4. Ford, who joined the foreign service in the Department of State and transferred to the FCS in 1980, later served as U.S. ambassador to Honduras.

30. Figures are from 2009 and do not include about 50 foreign service officers in USDA's Animal and Plant Health Inspection Service (APHIS). In addition, about 150 foreign service nationals work for FAS, and 200 work for APHIS.

31. Chuck Alexander, interview, February 14, 2006.

32. Henry Schmick, interview, January 22, 2010. The WTO is the World Trade Organization, the OIE is the World Organization for Animal Health (the initials come from its former name in French, Office International des Epizooties), the Codex is the Codex Alimentarius or food code (international guidelines on food safety), and the IPPC is the International Plant Protection Convention.

33. Henry Schmick interview, February 14, 2006.

34. Henry Schmick interview, January 22, 2010.

Chapter 4: Form and Content

1. See Seitzinger, *Conducting Foreign Relations without Authority.* The Logan Act of 1799 does in fact provide sanctions—fines and possible imprisonment—for unauthorized efforts by private U.S. citizens or residents to influence the behavior of foreign governments engaged in disputes with the U.S. government. A recent study by the Congressional Research Service found only one indictment (in 1803) and not a single prosecution under the Logan Act in its history.

2. Sometimes the second of these credentials is skirted. President Lincoln (according to his secretary of state William Seward, who revealed the story in 1868) had a "secret diplomatic service" of envoys he sent abroad, without Senate confirmation or even knowledge, to counter Confederate efforts to win foreign support and recognition. See Bridges, "A Massive Tome but Still Lacking."

3. AFSA's "Statement on Ambassadors" is available online at www.afsa.org/ambassadors.cfm, with links to AFSA's count of career and noncareer ambassadorial appointments, from which the figures on the administration's appointments are taken. The statement by the Academy of Diplomacy is at www.academyofdiplomacy.org/media/Ambassadorial_Qualifications_Sen_Obama_6_2008.pdf. For the administration's promise to adhere to the historical ratio, see the statement by White House spokesman Vietor in "Top Obama Fundraisers Get Posts," A1.

4. See http://history.state.gov. The historian's page on the Department of State website lists all former chiefs of mission and principal officers of the department and distinguishes between career and noncareer appointees.

5. Robert Kimmitt (1989–91), Arnold Kanter (1991–93), and Peter Tarnoff (1993–97).

6. Lewis, "Gates Is a Big Draw for Visiting World Leaders," 1.

7. Nicolson, *Evolution of Diplomatic Method,* 2, 51–68. See also Berridge, *Diplomacy,* 111–12. This discussion deals only with European diplomacy, because U.S. diplomatic practice is entirely derived from European traditions.

8. Quoted in Nicolson, *Evolution of Diplomatic Method,* 68.

9. Sharp, *Diplomatic Theory of International Relations,* 58.

10. See http://untreaty.un.org/ilc/texts/instruments/english/conventions/9_1_1961.pdf and http://untreaty.un.org/ilc/texts/instruments/english/conventions/9_2_1963.pdf.

11. United Nations, *Vienna Convention,* 1961, art. 41, para. 1.

12. For a description of immunities and privileges enjoyed by U.S. diplomats posted abroad, see www.state.gov/documents/organization/22243.pdf.

13. *Agrément* is for chiefs of mission only. Others assigned to an embassy are simply reported to the host government as either diplomatic or administrative and technical staff. Some governments, however, reserve the right to approve military attachés in advance.

14. Berridge notes that before the Congress of Vienna the reference point for precedence was a list of primacy among sovereigns promulgated by the papacy in 1504 (the pope came first). In practice, diplomats had to negotiate precedence before each meeting. Berridge, *Diplomacy,* 110–11.

15. See Transition Center of the Foreign Service Institute, *Protocol for the Modern Diplomat.*

16. See www.royal.gov.uk/RoyalEventsandCeremonies/Audiences/Ambassadorscre dentials.aspx.

17. See www.state.gov/s/cpr/rls/dpl.

18. Sharp, *Diplomatic Theory of International Relations*, 299.

19. Ibid., 204. The term *moral clarity* has an interesting history, traced by William Safire in his "On Language" column in the *New York Times Magazine.* See www.nytimes .com/2002/05/12/magazine/12ONLANGUAGE.html.

20. Many ambassadors, including the coauthor, have attested to this story. One written account is in Grove, *Behind Embassy Walls*, 262.

21. Attributed to Sir Henry Wotton, British ambassador to Venice (1651). Freeman, *Arts of Power*, 4; *Random House Unabridged Dictionary of the English Language*, 2nd ed., s.v., "diplomat." The dictionary's definition wrongly excludes persons who work for no national government—the UN secretary general, for example—or who deal not with countries but with international organizations—for example, the U.S. ambassador to the World Trade Organization.

22. Kissinger, *Diplomacy*, 683.

23. Neumann, *Other War*, 28.

24. Kennan wrote his long telegram, as it was called, while bedridden with fever. In his *Memoirs*, he says that "the effect produced in Washington by this elaborate peda- gogical effort was nothing less than sensational. . . . It was one of those moments when official Washington, whose states of receptivity or the opposite are determined by sub- jective emotional currents as intricately imbedded in the subconscious as those of the most complicated of Sigmund Freud's erstwhile patients, was ready to receive a given message" (294). The telegram, Kennan explains, was the basis for his article "The Sources of Soviet Conduct," which he signed *X*, in the July 1947 issue of *Foreign Affairs* (354–67 and 547–59).

25. Barbro Owens-Kirkpatrick, interview, September 28, 2005.

26. Brent Scowcroft, remark to author, November 1992.

27. Comparisons to advertising are common. See, for example, Cohen, "Democracy as a Brand," *New York Times.* The comparison gained currency when Charlotte Beers, an advertising executive known for successful brand development, was named undersecre- tary for public diplomacy at the Department of State in October 2001. She served until March 2003.

28. Shultz, *Turmoil and Triumph*, 28–31. Shultz held a doctorate in industrial econom- ics from MIT and worked as an arbitrator and mediator of labor disputes before joining the Nixon cabinet as secretary of labor in 1969.

29. The U.S. Institute of Peace has published a series of studies on cross-cultural ne- gotiating behavior, including volumes on Iranian, Chinese, Russian, North Korean, Japa- nese, French, German, Israeli, Palestinian, and U.S. negotiating practices.

30. Robert Gallucci, interview, June 9, 2007. Gallucci described the negotiations with North Korea in a book he wrote with the two other members of the negotiating team. See Gallucci, Poneman, and Wit, *Going Critical.*

31. Destler, Fukui, and Sata, *Textile Wrangle*, is a cautionary tale of what can hap- pen when negotiators outrun their domestic constituents. What began as a dispute over

square yards of cloth built to a clash over control of Okinawa and led to the fall of the Japanese government.

32. Perkins, "Department of State and American Public Opinion," 282–83.

33. Neumann, *Other War*, 168.

34. Kissinger, *Years of Renewal*, 628.

35. Carlucci, interview by Charles Stuart Kennedy, in Lutkins, *Frontline Diplomacy*.

36. Ibid.

37. Ibid. Kissinger's account of these discussions, written after Carlucci's interview, does not mention Carlucci's appointment with the president but otherwise supports Carlucci's account. Kissinger calls Carlucci "extremely astute" and notes, "I had urged Carlucci's appointment and took his views very seriously." Kissinger, *Years of Renewal*, 629–34.

38. Carlucci, interview by Charles Stuart Kennedy, *Frontline Diplomacy*.

39. Steve Gallogly, interview, August 8, 2005.

40. For perhaps the first time in a negotiation of this type, many of the scores of agreements negotiated between the governments, and between the governments and the private participants, were made public on a now defunct website.

41. Steven Mann, interview, September 7, 2005.

42. White House, *National Security Strategy*, September 2002, 1.

43. White House, *National Security Strategy*, March 2006, 1. The words echo President Bush's second inaugural address, given January 21, 2004: "It is the policy of the United States to seek and support the growth of democratic movements and institutions in every nation and culture with the ultimate goal of ending tyranny in our world."

44. President Woodrow Wilson coined the phrase on April 2, 1917, in his address to Congress seeking a declaration of war.

45. Adams, *Education of Henry Adams*, 852.

46. Rice, Remarks at Georgetown School of Foreign Service.

47. Rice, Opening Remarks before the House Committee.

48. Quoted in Harris, "New Order," 31.

49. Rea Brazeal, interview, January 26, 2006; Katherine Canavan, interview, September 14, 2005; Betsy Whitaker, interview, December 13, 2005.

50. Harry Thomas, interview, August 13, 2009.

51. Nye, "Soft Power," 153–71; Anonymous, "Think Again: Soft Power," Suzanne Nossel used the term *smart power* in an article in the March–April 2004 edition of *Foreign Affairs*. The three D's of American policy appeared as "defense, democracy, and development" in the 1984 *Report of the Bipartisan Commission on Central America* (the Kissinger Commission). Secretary Rice sometimes referred to "diplomacy, defense, and development" and sometimes to "democracy, defense, and development," for example, in connection with issuance of the Interagency Counterinsurgency Guide on January 13, 2009 (see http://2001-2009.state.gov/secretary/rm/2009/01/113933.htm). Secretary Clinton discussed "smart power" in a foreign policy address to the Council on Foreign Relations on July 15, 2009 (www.state.gov/secretary/rm/2009a/july/126071.htm), and has used the phrase, along with references to the three D's, on many other occasions. See www.state.gov/secretary/rm/index.htm. The term "civilian power" made its debut on p. 3 of

the QDDR, where Secretary Clinton defined it as "the combined force of civilian personnel across all federal agencies advancing America's core interests in the world."

52. The fifteen focus countries are Botswana, Cote d'Ivoire, Ethiopia, Guyana, Haiti, Kenya, Mozambique, Namibia, Nigeria, Rwanda, South Africa, Tanzania, Uganda, Vietnam, and Zambia. In those countries, PEPFAR's objectives were summarized and quantified as "2-7-10": treat 2 million people suffering from AIDS, prevent 7 million new infections, and care for 10 million people affected by HIV/AIDS, including orphans. All three objectives were to be and in fact were met by fiscal year 2008.

53. Jimmy Kolker, interview, May 25, 2007.

54. U.S. Department of State, *Leading through Civilian Power: The First Quadrennial Diplomacy and Development Review*, 32.

55. Kolker interview, QDDR, 32.

56. Quoted in Gilbert, *Churchill: A Life*, 75–76.

57. The consulate was upgraded to a consulate general on February 9, 2010.

58. Lynne Tracy, interview, January 27, 2010.

59. USIA was the U.S. Information Agency, which was responsible outside the United States for U.S. government public affairs, press relations, international exchanges, educational and cultural diplomacy. The agency was closed in 1999 and its functions were transferred to the Department of State.

60. Tracy interview, January 27, 2010.

61. "Present Secretary's Award for Heroism to Lynne Tracy," December 7, 2009, www.state.gov/secretary/rm/2009a/12/133238.htm. An *iftaar* is the evening meal that breaks the daily fast during Ramadan.

62. Tracy interview, January 27, 2010. Pakistani guards and security forces repelled an attack on the consulate in Peshawar on April 5, 2010. Two guards were killed. Four attackers, two with unexploded suicide vests, died in the attack, which failed to penetrate the consulate's perimeter.

Chapter 5: The Foreign Service at War

1. George Kennan, a political officer at the Berlin embassy in December 1941, gives an account of his arrest, internment, and repatriation in *Memoirs*, 135–41.

2. Clark, "No Formulas: Bosnia, Haiti, and Kosovo," in *Commanding Heights*, ed. Miklaucic, 55.

3. Dobbins, "Retaining the Lessons of Nation-Building," in *Commanding Heights*, ed. Miklaucic, 73. The Defense Department eventually recognized stability operations as a "core U.S. military mission" with "priority comparable to combat operations," but not until November 28, 2005, in Department of Defense Directive No. 3000.05.

4. Bodine, "Pre-Emptive Post-Conflict Stabilization and Reconstruction," in *Commanding Heights*, ed. Miklaucic, 33. The Pentagon office was the Office of Reconstruction and Humanitarian Assistance, headed by Army Lieutenant General Jay Garner.

5. A careful account of the CPA prepared for the RAND Corporation concludes that it did "reasonably well . . . in most areas for which it had lead responsibility, but it failed in the most important task [security], for which it did not." Dobbins et al., *Occupying Iraq*, 327.

6. Per NSPD-44, December 7, 2005, "The Secretary of State shall coordinate and lead integrated United States Government efforts, involving all U.S. Departments and Agencies with relevant responsibilities, to prepare, plan for, and conduct stabilization and reconstruction activities" (www.fas.org/irp/offdocs/nspd/nspd-44.html).

7. U.S. Department of State and Broadcasting Board of Governors, *Report of Inspection: Embassy Baghdad, Iraq*, and *Report of Inspection: Embassy Kabul, Afghanistan*. The numbers for Baghdad include 1,330 employees at the embassy (chancery) proper and 543 employees in 29 provincial reconstruction teams, two regional embassy offices, and one regional reconstruction team. The numbers do not include 140,000 U.S. troops and 150,000 Department of Defense contractors in country at the time of the inspection, February–March 2009. The numbers for Kabul include 558 U.S. direct hires, 548 locally employed staff, and about 100 U.S. staff hired under other authorities, mainly Title 5, Section 3161 of the U.S. Code, which allows agencies to hire outside experts under certain circumstances.

8. Clinton, Remarks before the House Appropriations Subcommittee.

9. Perito, *U.S. Experience with Provincial Reconstruction Teams in Afghanistan*, 2.

10. Ibid., 31; USAID's "Provincial Reconstruction Teams—FAQs," http://afghanistan .usaid.gov/en/Program.31f.aspx. Additional civilians, including many experts brought in as temporary government employees (not consultants), were expected to arrive in 2010.

11. Neumann, *Other War*, 70–71. Ambassador Neumann, a career FSO, was ambassador to Algeria (1994–97) and Bahrain (2001–4) before joining the Coalition Provisional Authority in Baghdad (2004–5). He served as ambassador to Afghanistan from 2005 to 2007. His father had also been ambassador to Afghanistan in 1967–73.

12. Neumann, *Other War*, 26.

13. Stevens, "PRT Team Transfer of Authority Ceremony Held in Panjshir Valley."

14. Frumin, "Equipping USAID for Success," 17.

15. Ibid., 13, 17; Neumann, *Other War*, 215.

16. Frumin, "Equipping USAID for Success," 13–16.

17. Ibid., 23; Neumann, *Other War*, 25–26.

18. Neumann, *Other War*, 39–41, 109–10.

19. Frumin, "Equipping USAID for Success," 7–8.

20. David Satterfield, interview 17, by Barbara Nielsen, February 15, 2008, in *Oral Histories*.

21. Perito, "U.S. Experience with Provincial Reconstruction Teams in Iraq and Afghanistan."

22. A full complement of civilians, not always available, would include one from the Department of State, one from USAID, and one from the Department of Agriculture, as well as an official from the Afghan Ministry of the Interior. See U.S. Department of State, Joint Center for Operational Analysis, and U.S. Agency for International Development, *Provincial Reconstruction Teams in Afghanistan*, 9n; and Perito, *U.S. Experience with Provincial Reconstruction Teams in Afghanistan*, 5.

23. Rick Olson, interview 5, by Marilyn Green, March 12, 2008, in *Oral Histories*.

24. Tobin Bradley, interview, November 3, 2005.

25. Support from the CPA in Baghdad for the development of locally elected governing bodies is open to question. A 2009 RAND Corporation study, *Occupying Iraq*, notes

that the CPA, to protect its own authority, preferred to appoint local officials. In May 2003 the CPA asked the military commander of coalition forces not to "initiate election activity . . . for any office whatsoever" (137). The study found that "although more than 600 neighborhood, city, district, and provincial councils had been established" by July 2003, "they lacked any formal authority or money and enjoyed questionable legitimacy" (138).

26. Vincent Campos, interview, February 15, 2007.

27. See Perito, "Provincial Reconstruction Teams in Iraq." The civilian leadership of the PRTs in Iraq stands in contrast to Afghanistan, where the PRTs have a military commander (usually a lieutenant colonel) and a staff in which military personnel outnumber civilians. The PRTs in Afghanistan report, effective 2007, to the International Security Assistance Force, a NATO operation.

28. Stephenson, Presentation at the U.S. Institute of Peace, Washington, DC, February 22, 2007; U.S. Department of State, Bureau of Public Affairs, "Provincial Reconstruction Teams."

29. See, for example, U.S. Department of State, *FY 2008 Budget in Brief.*

30. Speckhard, "Provincial Reconstruction Team Leaders Discuss Progress."

31. U.S. Department of State, "On-the-Record Briefing," March 30, 2007.

32. Ibid.

33. U.S. Department of State, *FY 2008 Budget in Brief,* 175: "Funds will be used to stand up new PRTs and to support and augment existing PRTs. The funds requested will be used to cover the costs of salaries, life and other operational support, offices and housing (and furnishings for both), vehicles, communications, and leases not covered by other agencies. This funding also will cover security costs for the stand-alone PRTs that will not be co-located with a brigade combat team or on a forward operating base."

34. U.S. Department of State, Satterfield, "On-the-Record Briefing," March 30, 2007.

35. Tyson, "Applying Diplomacy to Conflict," A19. "Ex-Envoy Says Iraq Rebuilding Plan Won't Work," *Reuters,* February 17, 2007.

36. U.S. Department of State, Satterfield, "On-the-Record Briefing," March 30, 2007.

37. Ibid.

38. Ibid.

39. U.S. Department of State, Buckler et al., "Briefing on Reconstruction Progress."

40. The bibliography lists those studies that are cited in this text. Other studies are identified in Luehrs, "Provincial Reconstruction Teams: A Literature Review." See also the websites of Center for Army Lessons Learned (CALL) and the Special Inspector General for Iraq Reconstruction (SIGIR).

41. Henry Clarke, interview, April 13, 2010.

42. Center for Army Lessons Learned, *PRT Playbook,* annex C, app. 1.

43. Clarke, "Reconstructing Iraq's Provinces," 142.

44. Neumann, *Other War,* 182, 200.

45. U.S. Congress, House of Representatives, Committee on Armed Services, Subcommittee on Oversight and Investigations, *Agency Stovepipes,* 28.

46. Clarke, "Reconstructing Iraq's Provinces," 142 (emphasis in original).

47. Special Inspector General for Iraq Reconstruction, *Hard Lessons,* 333.

48. U.S. Department of State and Broadcasting Board of Governors, *Report of Inspection: Embassy Baghdad, Iraq*, 17; U.S. Government Accountability Office, *Department of State: Comprehensive Plan*, 10.

49. See Williamson, "How Much Embassy Is Too Much?" A11; U.S. Department of State, Satterfield, "On-the-Record Briefing," February 7, 2007.

50. U.S. Government Accounting Office, *Department of State: Comprehensive Plan*, 3.

51. Numbers from U.S. Department of State, *Department of State's Goal for Arabic Speakers*. Forty percent is a reasonable figure, assuming a twenty-seven-year career with five years spent in entry-level positions and two years spent in Arabic language training.

52. U.S. Department of State, Sean McCormack, Daily press briefing.

53. Cooper, "Few Veteran Diplomats Accept Mission to Iraq."

54. U.S. Department of State, "Foreign Service Assignments," provided to the author by the AFSA.

55. U.S. Government Accountability Office, *U.S. Public Diplomacy: Strategic Planning Efforts*, 14. As of March 31, 2007, 199 of 887 public diplomacy positions in the United States and abroad were vacant.

56. U.S. Department of State, McCormack, Daily press briefing, response to taken question.

57. DeYoung, "U.S. to Cut Ten Percent of Diplomatic Posts Next Year," A26. According to AFSA president John Naland, the effect of Thomas's order is to remove about eighty positions, mainly FS-3 and FS-2 generalist (officer) positions, from the list of jobs opening in the summer of 2008. Private communication with the author, December 2007.

58. U.S. Government Accountability Office, *Persistent Staffing and Foreign Language Gaps Compromise Diplomatic Readiness*, 2–3. Officers serving in positions above their grade filled 34 percent of the midlevel positions in posts of greatest hardship (40% in Iraq and Afghanistan), according to the GAO.

59. Reuters, "State Department to Order 250 to Iraq Posts."

60. DeYoung, "Envoys Resist Forced Iraq Duty"; Cooper, "Foreign Service Officers Resist Mandatory Iraq Postings"; Stockman, "Diplomats Angry over Forced Posts in Baghdad"; U.S. Department of State, McCormack, Daily press briefing.

61. Peters, "Strip for Action."

62. Cooper, "Few Veteran Diplomats Accept Mission to Iraq."

63. Boot, "Send the State Department to War."

64. See www.blogs.state.gov.

65. See chapter 2, note 75.

66. The department can order foreign service officers and generalists to any post, in accordance with the needs of the service, but such directed assignments are rare. Anyone who accepts an assignment without being ordered to do so is considered a volunteer.

67. Andy Passen, private communication, November 5, 2007.

68. Gates, Landon lecture.

69. See U.S. Department of State, *FY 2008 Budget in Brief*, 22–24. Specifically, 104 positions for training enhancement, 57 for reconstruction and stabilization programs, 73 to handle increased overseas workload, and 20 to represent the United States in new and nontraditional locations.

70. Leahy, "Statement of Senator Patrick Leahy, Chairman, State Foreign Operations, and Related Programs Subcommittee."

71. Gingrich, "Rogue State Department," 45. Gingrich was a member of Secretary Rice's Advisory Committee on Transformational Diplomacy and made similar recommendations in that context.

72. Dorman, "Iraqi Service and Beyond," 37.

73. Name withheld, private correspondence, August 2006.

Chapter 6: Politics and Professionalism

1. Johnstone, "Strategic Planning and International Affairs."

2. Kissinger, *Years of Upheaval*, 445.

3. Gingrich, "Transforming the State Department."

4. Kissinger, *Years of Upheaval*, 434. Dr. Kissinger speaks on this point with authority. As President Nixon's national security advisor in the years before he became secretary of state, Kissinger traveled secretly to China in 1971 and arranged President Nixon's visit there that ended twenty years of isolation. Secretary of State Rogers was not told of Kissinger's trip until after it had been successfully concluded.

5. Acheson, *Present at the Creation*, 162–63.

6. Baker, with DeFrank, *Politics of Diplomacy*, 31–32.

7. Haig, *Caveat*, 62.

8. Kissinger, *Years of Upheaval*, 445.

9. Ibid., 442.

10. Haig, *Caveat*, 27.

11. Schedule C positions are excepted from the competitive service because they have policy-determining responsibilities or require the incumbent to serve in a confidential relationship to a key official. Appointments to Schedule C positions require advance approval from the White House Office of Presidential Personnel and OPM, but appointments may be made without competition. OPM does not review the qualifications of a Schedule C appointee—final authority on this matter rests with the appointing official. See www.opm.gov/transition/trans20r-ch5.htm.

12. Kissinger, *Years of Upheaval*, 442–43.

13. Marshall, *Armed Forces Officer*, 8.

14. Tony Motley, interview, August 30, 2006.

15. Freeman, *Arts of Power*, 127.

16. Name withheld, interview, 2006.

17. Mark Fitzpatrick, quoted in Kessler, "Administration Critics Chafe at State Dept. Shuffle," A4.

18. Craig Kelly, e-mails to author, September 28 and October 7, 2006.

19. Gates, Forrestal lecture, April 7, 2010, www.defense.gov/speeches/speech.aspx ?speechid=1444.

20. McWilliams, "They Spoke Out," 54.

21. The 2009 awards related to an objection to a requirement that diplomatic couriers flying with a certain carrier sign a waiver of their right to sue before boarding; a proposal to introduce web-based technology to human-rights reporting; and a challenge to

established U.S. policy toward Ethiopia. The AFSA awards are not necessarily related to use of the dissent channel. See "Rivkin Award," 50–51.

22. See http://careers.state.gov/specialist/faqs.html; http://careers.state.gov/officer/faqs.html.

23. Deborah Ann McCarthy, interview, August 26, 2005.

24. Name withheld, interview, 2006.

25. The Bureau of Human Resources says annual attrition is under 6 percent—that is, fewer than 6 percent of foreign service members leave each year through retirement, resignations, or other causes.

26. Resignations over Balkan policy included Steven Walker, desk officer for Croatia; Marshall Freeman Harris, desk officer for Bosnia; and George Kenney, deputy head of the Yugoslav desk. Jon Western, a State Department civil servant, also resigned over Balkan policy. John Brady Kiesling, a political officer in Athens; Mary Ann Wright, deputy chief of mission in Mongolia; and John Brown, a cultural affairs officer in Moscow, resigned over Iraq. Matthew Hoh, a political officer serving as senior civilian representative in Zabul province, Afghanistan, resigned over Afghanistan.

27. Interview, name withheld, August 2006. For a different view, see Bill Eaton's story in chapter 7.

28. See www.state.gov/r/pa/e/speeches/index.htm.

29. Some appointees on special temporary missions may be accorded the personal rank of ambassador without Senate confirmation, for a period not to exceed six months. See U.S. Department of State, *Foreign Affairs Handbook,* vol. 3, *Personnel Operations Handbook,* 3FAH-1 H-2432.1-2.

30. Representative Jeff Fortenberry, comments to meeting of Diplomatic and Consular Officers Retired, Washington, D.C., September 26, 2006. The term *A committee* is one of art. By custom, members do not serve on two A committees. In the Senate, unlike the House, the Committee on Foreign Relations is considered an A committee.

31. Name withheld, interview, January 2010.

32. See www.state.gov/s/h/org/css.

33. Melia, "Congressional Staff Attitudes," 16–17.

34. Name withheld, interview, January 2010.

35. Jennifer Butte-Dahl, interview, January 15, 2010. Libyan agents bombed the LaBelle discotheque in Berlin in 1986 and in 1988 blew up Pan Am 103 over Lockerbie, Scotland. The Libyan Claims Resolution Act was signed into law on August 4, 2008. The secretary of state certified on October 31, 2008, that the United States had received funds sufficient to compensate the victims of Libyan terrorism, and the U.S.-Libyan Claims Settlement Agreement was implemented by executive order.

36. Name withheld, interview, 2006.

37. The Pearson program also includes one-year assignments to state and local government offices. The American Political Science Association also provides congressional fellowships that are open to foreign service personnel.

38. Name withheld, interview, January 2010.

39. Authorizing legislation for entitlement programs like Social Security usually does include budget authority, called direct or mandatory spending. Mandatory spending,

which also covers interest on the national debt, does not require separate appropriation. Although mandatory spending now amounts to about 60 percent of all federal outlays, it is a trivial element in spending on international affairs, coming into play only with regard to pensions for foreign service personnel.

40. The statutory language is 22 USC. 2680.

41. Ibid.

42. Philippe Lussier, interview, December 9, 2009.

43. For the State Department's budget presentations, see www.state.gov/s/d/rm/rls/. For AID's budget presentation, see www.usaid.gov/policy/budget.

44. James W. Morhard, remarks at a forum for business leaders organized by the Business Council for International Understanding, Rosslyn, VA, May 5, 2003.

45. Steve Dietz, interview, April 27, 2007.

46. For a more detailed presentation, see www.state.gov/f/releases/iab/2008.

47. State receives appropriations for U.S. participation in international border and fisheries commissions under Function 300, Natural Resources and Environment; the rest of State's budget and all of AID's is in Function 150. Other government agencies in Function 150 include Export-Import Bank, the Overseas Private Investment Corporation, the Trade and Development Agency, and the Peace Corps. Nongovernmental organizations include the U.S. Institute of Peace, the Inter-American Foundation, the Asia Foundation, the National Endowment for Democracy, and the Millennium Challenge Corporation. Agencies principally funded elsewhere that receive some funds through the 150 account include the Department of Agriculture for food aid, the Treasury for international technical assistance and debt relief, and the Department of Defense for support for foreign military sales and international exchange and training programs.

48. QDDR, 120.

49. Craig Johnstone, interview, February 1, 2006.

50. Steve Dietz, interview, April 27, 2007.

51. Katherine Canavan, interview, September 14, 2005.

52. Shultz, *Turmoil and Triumph*, 35. Shultz served in four cabinet posts (secretary of state, secretary of labor, secretary of treasury, and director of the OMB). He was also chief executive officer of Bechtel Corporation, a global construction and engineering company with forty thousand employees.

53. Presidential Policy Directive 1 of February 13, 2009, established the current organization of the NSC (see www.fas.org/irp/offdocs/ppd/ppd-1.pdf).

54. QDDR, 5.

55. Barbro Owens-Kirkpatrick, interview, September 28, 2005.

56. Hugo Llorens, interview, August 12, 2005.

57. James Derham, interview, July 10, 2005.

58. Ibid.

59. Name withheld, interview, August 2005.

60. John Ritchie, interview, October 28, 2005.

61. Illegal immigration has dropped since 2005, due to improved enforcement and economic recession. The Pew Hispanic Center estimated successful illegal immigration from Mexico at 175,000 persons in the year ending March 2009. The Border Patrol

apprehended 662,000 Mexicans in the year ending September 2008. Passel and Cohn, *Mexican Immigrants*, 3–4.

62. John Ritchie, interview, October 28, 2005.

63. Jim Derham, interview, July 10, 2005.

64. Sean Murphy, interview, August 28, 2006.

65. Name withheld, interview, August 2005.

66. Foreign Service Act of 1980, sec. 207.

67. QDDR. 28.

68. U.S. Department of State, *Foreign Affairs Manual*, 2 FAM 113.1.

69. Ibid., 2 FAM 111.1-5.

70. National Security Decision Directive 38, June 2, 1982, www.state.gov/m/pri/nsdd/45148.htm.

71. U.S. Department of State, *Foreign Affairs Manual*, 2 FAM 112.

72. See U.S. Congress, Committee on Foreign Relations, *Embassies as Command Posts*, 9.

73. State Department inspectors found that "in Somalia, for example, the Embassy had $30,000 to spend on public diplomacy while the MIST team [AFRICOM Military Information Support Team] had $600,000." U.S. Department of State and Broadcasting Board of Governors, *Report of Inspection, Bureau of African Affairs*, August 2009, 14. The Department of Defense reported to Congress in 2009 that it "does not engage directly in public diplomacy, which is the purview of the State Department," but that statement is valid only if public diplomacy is defined as excluding activities not originating with or approved by the Department of State. See the Department of Defense Report on Strategic Communication, submitted to Congress under Section 1055(b) of the Duncan Hunter National Defense Authorization Act for FT 2009, http://mountainrunner.us/files/dod/1055_Dec2009.pdf. Undersecretary of State for Public Diplomacy Judith McHale has talked of "rebalancing the respective roles, responsibilities, and resources of State and Defense in the public diplomacy and strategic communications arenas" in U.S. Congress, Committee on Foreign Relations, Subcommittee on International Operations and Organizations, Human Rights, Democracy, and Global Women's Issues, *Statement for the Record by Under Secretary for Public Diplomacy and Public Affairs Judith McHale*, 5.

74. U.S. Congress, Committee on Foreign Relations, *Embassies as Command Posts*, 7.

75. Frank Almaguer, interview, November 6, 2009.

76. *First Line of Defense*, by Keeley, is the title of a book about ambassadors and embassies published by the American Academy of Diplomacy in 2000, and the subtitle of Andrew Steigman's 1985 book about the foreign service. Both books are cited in the bibliography. An internet search cites the metaphor as early as 1924, when it appears in an article by Navy Captain Frank H. Schofield in the Annals of the American Academy of Political Science. It has been used by secretaries of state Warren Christopher, Madeleine Albright, and Colin Powell and secretaries of defense Bill Perry and William Cohen. In a similar vein, the Foreign Affairs Oral History Collection of the Association for Diplomatic Studies and Training at the Library of Congress has the title *Frontline Diplomacy* (http://memory.loc.gov/ammem/collections/diplomacy/).

77. Priest, *Mission*, 71n. The sixth area command, AFRICOM, was announced in 2007 and established in October 2008.

78. Frumin, "Equipping USAID for Success," 5.

79. U.S. Congress, *Embassies Grapple to Guide Foreign Aid*, app. 1, 1. The programs, called Section 1206 programs after the relevant clause of the National Defense Authorization Act, are aimed at strengthening the capacity of foreign militaries to interdict terrorists and drug traffickers. In the president's budget, Section 1206 programs are in Function 050 (national defense), not Function 150 (international affairs), which shifts congressional authorization, appropriations, and oversight away from committees that deal with State and USAID to committees that deal with the Department of Defense.

80. U.S. Department of the Army, *Counterinsurgency*, 2–9.

81. Ibid. Anne Witkowski of the Center for Strategic and International Studies alerted the authors to this publication. David Galula is the author of *Counterinsurgency Warfare: Theory and Practice* (Praeger, 1964), in which this citation originally appeared.

82. Szayna et al., *Integrating Civilian Agencies in Stability Operations*, 98–104.

83. Barry Blechman, interview, June 12, 2006.

84. Richard Miles, interview, March 10, 2006.

85. Steve Dietz, interview, April 27, 2007.

86. Name withheld, interview, April 2007.

87. Vincent Campos, interview, February 15, 2007.

88. See http://policy.defense.gov/common/Policy_Leadership_Slate.pdf; and www.jcs.mil/page.aspx?id=20.

89. See www.state.gov/t/pm/polad/index.htm for a description of the POLAD program and the State-DOD Officer Exchange Program. Expansion plans are discussed in QDDR, 54.

90. Robert Loftis, interview, September 19, 2006.

91. U.S. Department of the Army, *Counterinsurgency*, A-3.

92. Loftis refers to Robert Kaplan's book *Imperial Grunts*.

93. President Truman to Secretary James F. Byrnes, October 1945, cited in Acheson, *Present at the Creation*, 158.

94. Acheson, *Present at the Creation*, 127, 157–63. The description of OSS personnel as collectivists and do-gooders is a citation in Acheson from 1954 testimony by Spruille Braden, a three-time ambassador who in 1945 was assistant secretary for Latin American affairs (160).

95. James Pavitt, interview, January 25, 2007.

96. Ibid.

97. Newsom, *Diplomacy and the American Democracy*, 39.

98. See the official website of the intelligence community, www.intelligence.gov.

99. Pavitt, interview, January 25, 2007.

100. Name withheld, interview, June 2007.

101. Pavitt, interview, January 25, 2007.

102. Name withheld, interview, June 2007.

Chapter 7: Stability and Change

1. See http://careers.state.gov/officer/compensation.html.

2. Rob Nolan, interview, May 18, 2007.

3. William Eaton, interview, April 15, 2010.

4. U.S. Government Accountability Office, *Department of State: Persistent Staffing,* and *Department of State: Comprehensive Plan.*

5. J. Christian Kennedy, interview, July 20, 2005.

6. William Eaton, interview, May 15, 2010.

7. Neumann, *Other War,* 219n.

8. Pickering, Oral presentation, "American Negotiating Behavior and the Transformation of U.S. Diplomacy." Pickering was ambassador to Nigeria, El Salvador, India, Russia, Israel, and the United Nations.

9. William Eaton, interview, April 15, 2010.

10. QDDR, 165–66.

11. Margaret Dean, interview, April 21, 2010.

12. For vacancy announcements, see www.careers.state.gov/specialist/opportunities.

13. See www.usajobs.opm.gov.

14. Debi Fairman, interview, February 23, 2007.

15. QDDR, 165–67.

16. Ibid.

17. The Arlington campus of the FSI is the George P. Shultz National Foreign Affairs Training Center. Secretary Shultz worked hard with the Congress to obtain the funds to create the center, on a campus that was once a girls' school (Arlington Hall), and later, during World War II, the home of the Army Security Agency, the forerunner of today's National Security Agency (NSA).

18. Salary and allowances are paid every two weeks, in arrears, so long as the Congress appropriates the necessary funds.

19. Marcos Mandojana, interview, February 8, 2006. The A-100 course was cut from seven weeks to five weeks in 2009 to accommodate the larger intake of new officers.

20. Richard Miles, interview, March 10, 2006.

21. Clayton Hays, interview, August 12, 2005.

22. Name withheld, interview, March 2006.

23. Deborah McCarthy, interview, August 26, 2005.

Chapter 8: Foreign Service Functions—Five Tracks

1. Marcos Mandojana, interview, February 8, 2006.

2. Report of the Visa Office, 2009, at www.travel.state.gov/visa/statistics/statistics _1476.html.

3. Under a visa waiver program that started in 1986, visitors from twenty-seven countries may enter the United States without a visa if they meet certain requirements. Without this program, the demand for visas would be dramatically greater.

4. Marcos Mandojana, interview, February 8, 2006.

5. Name withheld, interview, June 2007.

6. Robert Batchelder, interview, August 12, 2005.

7. Gregory Schiffer, interview, February 8, 2006.

8. Marcos Mandojana, interview, February 8, 2006.

9. Sean Murphy, interview, August 28, 2006.

10. David Caudill, interview, February 23, 2007.

11. Name withheld, interview, March 2006.

12. Sean Murphy, interview, August 28, 2006.

13. Alan Larson, interview, July 13, 2007. The full title of the position is undersecretary for economic, business, and agricultural affairs.

14. Deborah Ann McCarthy, interview, August 26, 2005.

15. William McCahill, interview, August 23, 2007.

16. Aid and military sales to Pakistan were restricted under the Symington (1978), Pressler (1990), and Glenn (1998) amendments, which imposed sanctions aimed at curtailing Pakistan's nuclear weapons program. President Bush waived these restrictions after the September 11 attacks.

17. Alan Larson, interview, July 13, 2007.

18. Ibid.

19. Maryanne Myles and David Dlouhy, interviews, July 20, 2007. See chapter 10.

20. QDDR, 42.

21. Alan Larson, interview, July 13, 2007.

22. William Eaton, interview, April 15, 2010.

23. Frank Coulter, interview, November 15, 2005.

24. Russ King, interview, August 10, 2006.

25. Eric Khant, interview, February 23, 2007.

26. Richard Miles, interview, March 10, 2006.

27. The Myers-Briggs Type Indicator is a psychological or personality test administered to entering foreign service officers during their basic A-100 training. Whether the test, based on Jungian ideas, offers more insight than a skillful reading of the tarot is a matter of debate.

28. Harry Kamian, interview, August 26, 2006.

29. Richard Miles, interview, March 10, 2006.

30. See http://careers.state.gov/officer/career-tracks political.

31. Marcia Bosshardt, interview, August 6, 2007.

32. See www.publicdiplomacy.org.

33. See www.state.gov/www/global/general_foreign_policy/rpt_981230_reorg6.html; and www.state.gov/s/d/rm/rls/bib/2008. The same words appear almost verbatim in part III of the reorganization plan President Clinton submitted to Congress in 1998 and on page 14 of the department's budget in brief for fiscal year 2008.

34. Caryn Danz, interview, July 25, 2007.

35. Betsy Whitaker, interview, December 13, 2005.

36. Betsy Whitaker, interview, December 2005.

37. See http://exchanges.state.gov/programevaluations/program-evaluations.html.

38. Marcia Bosshardt, interview, August 2007.

39. QDDR, 63.

40. Betsy Whitaker, interview, December 13, 2005.

Chapter 9: Assignments and Promotions

1. U.S. Government Accountability Office, *Department of State: Additional Steps*, 1.

2. Sylvia Bazala, interview, August 29, 2006.

3. Name withheld, interview, April 2007.

4. In April 2007, according to the Bureau of Human Resources, there were 589 tandem couples (1,178 employees) in the foreign service agencies of State, USAID, the FCS, and the FAS. The total includes couples in which husband and wife work for different agencies.

5. Philo Dibble, interview, October 26, 2005. Places with more than one mission include Brussels, home to the U.S. Mission to the European Union, the U.S. Mission to NATO, and the U.S. Embassy to the Kingdom of Belgium; Geneva, home to the U.S. missions to UN agencies and to the World Trade Organization; Vienna, home to the embassy to Austria, a mission to UN organizations, and a mission to the Organization for Security and Cooperation in Europe; and Paris, with an embassy and a mission to the Organization for Economic Cooperation and Development.

6. James Derham, interview, July 10, 2005.

7. Not at all. Jim Derham later became ambassador to Guatemala.

8. U.S. Government Accountability Office, *Department of State: Additional Steps*, 6. Because of limitations in the data produced by the State Department's Global Employee Management System, the GAO did not include positions in Iraq in calculations of vacancy rates.

9. Name withheld, interview, June 2007. Required reports are a major headache. The Congress mandated at least 310 reports in FY 2010, and the department itself required 108 (QDDR, 73).

10. Bradley, "Timely Data," 29.

11. Ibid., 7.

12. The department's inspector general noted some of the problems with stretch assignments in "Strengthening Leadership and Staffing at African Hardship Posts," referenced in U.S. Department of State, Office of the Inspector General, *Semiannual Report to Congress*, 18.

13. Ray, "One-Two-Three," 25.

14. U.S. Department of State, *Foreign Affairs Handbook*, 1 (composition).

15. Rob Nolan, interview, May 18, 2007.

16. Data for 2009 were published in April 2010. Bradley, op. cit.

17. Rob Nolan, interview, May 18, 2007.

Chapter 10: Tomorrow's Diplomats

1. Smith, *Expanded Mandate*, 18.

2. U.S. National Security Council. "Management of Interagency Efforts Concerning Reconstruction and Stabilization," NSPD-44, December 7, 2005.

3. P.L. 108-447, December 6, 2004. See also the Reconstruction and Stabilization Civilian Management Act of 2008, incorporated as Title XVI of the Duncan Hunter National Defense Authorization Act for 2009, P.L. 110-417, October 8, 2008.

4. Carlos Pascual had an ideal background for S/CRS. He was a career FSO who had served in USAID as well as State. He had three years' experience on the staff of the National Security Council. He had been ambassador to Ukraine and coordinator for U.S. Assistance to Europe and Eurasia (2003), another job requiring interagency skills. Nevertheless, he struggled with lack of support at S/CRS, and he resigned from the job and the

foreign service in January 2006 to become director of foreign policy studies at the Brookings Institution. He returned to government service in 2009, when he was nominated and confirmed as U.S. ambassador to Mexico.

5. John Herbst, interview, January 11, 2010. The funding came under Section 1207 of the 2006 National Defense Authorization Act, which allowed the Department of Defense to transfer up to $100 million per year in services or funds to the Department of State for specific stabilization and reconstruction projects. Section 1207 was renewed as Section 1210 of the 2008 Defense Authorization Act.

6. Smith, *Expanded Mandate*, 22.

7. John Herbst, interview, January 11, 2010.

8. Smith, *Expanded Mandate*, 24. Herbst sent an "Overview of the Interagency Management" to all U.S. posts overseas by unclassified message, State 006691 of January 22, 2008, provided to the author.

9. David Greenlee, interview, December 18, 2009.

10. John Herbst, interview, January 2010. Herbst retired from the foreign service at the end of June 2010 and became director of the Center for Complex Operations at the National Defense University. His successor on an interim basis is Bob Loftis.

11. QDDR, 140–44. Turning the office into a bureau, or the coordinator into an assistant secretary, would require congressional approval.

12. Special Inspector General for Iraq Reconstruction, *Applying Iraq's Hard Lessons*, 23–27.

13. Magnuson, "Integrating Civilian Agencies."

14. John Herbst, interview, January 2010

15. David Greenlee, interview, December 2009.

16. Sidney Kaplan, interviews, May 18, 2007, and November 24, 2009. The exercise, called Project Horizon, engaged fifteen agencies in joint strategic planning.

17. Kopp, *Commercial Diplomacy*, 5–7.

18. Clinton, Remarks at the Global Philanthropy Forum Conference. The special representative for global partnerships is Elizabeth Frawley Bagley.

19. See, for example, Slaughter, "America's Edge." Ms. Slaughter is director of the State Department's office of policy planning.

20. QDDR, 167.

21. Newsom, *Diplomacy and the American Democracy*, 74.

22. Brooks, "Truck Stop Confidential."

Glossary

13 dimensions Traits and skills measured during the oral assessment of foreign service candidates (State)

150 account Section of the federal budget, as prepared by the Office of Management and Budget, dealing with international affairs

360° review Evaluation by superiors, subordinates, and peers

A-100 Basic training and orientation course for new foreign service officers (State)

AEP Ambassador Extraordinary and Plenipotentiary—full diplomatic title of an ambassador sent by one head of state to another and commissioned to represent and act on behalf of the sending state

AFRICOM See *Combatant command*

AFSA American Foreign Service Association—the professional association and collective bargaining agent (union) for members of the foreign service. www.afsa.org

AID, USAID US Agency for International Development

Aide-mémoire Text summarizing a document or (more often) an oral presentation, often left with officials after a démarche

Ambassador Highest diplomatic rank

Ambassador at large Ambassador not accredited to any foreign state or international organization

APEC Asian Pacific Economic Cooperation

ARB Accountability Review Board, panel convened by the secretary of state to investigate incidents at US posts abroad that result in loss of life or serious injury

Area combatant command See *Combatant command*

Assistant secretary At the Department of State, the official in charge of a bureau. Assistant secretaries and higher officials require Senate confirmation; deputy assistant secretaries and below do not.

Attaché An official assigned to an embassy to perform a specific task (e.g., military attaché, agricultural attaché)

Backstopping Bureaucratic jargon for providing support

Base pay Basic salary prescribed by law for a given rank or pay grade, may be increased by various allowances and bonuses

BBG Broadcast Board of Governors

Bid list A list of preferred assignments that a member of the service submits to the Bureau of Human Resources

Bureau Basic organization unit of the Department of State; headed by an assistant secretary

Cable Electronic communication sent through official channels requiring *clearance*, also called telegrams—those originating at an overseas post bear the signature of the officer in charge, those originating in the Department of State bear the signature of the secretary of state or acting secretary

CDO   Career development officer

CENTCOM   See *Combatant command*

CERP   Commanders Emergency Response Program

Chancery   Embassy building in which the ambassador's office is located

Chargé, chargé d'affaires   Diplomatic title given to an embassy official in charge of a mission in the absence of an ambassador; if temporary, chargé d'affaires ad interim

Chief of mission   Head of a diplomatic mission

Chief of party   Project leader (USAID)

CIA   Central Intelligence Agency

Civil service   Corps of civilian public employees, other than members of excluded services (such as the foreign service)

Clearance   Approval of a document by offices with an interest in the topic; whoever drafts a document obtains the clearances

Coalition Provisional Authority   Governing body in Iraq from April 2003 until June 2004

Codel   State Department jargon for a congressional delegation on official overseas travel

COIN   Counterinsurgency

COM   Chief of mission

Combatant command   One of ten US military unified combatant commands involving more than one service; six are area commands—AFRICOM (African), CENTCOM (central), EUCOM (European), NORTHCOM (northern), PACOM (Pacific), and SOUTHCOM (southern). SOCOM, the Special Operations Command, is one of four functional commands.

Cone   One of five functional specializations for foreign service officers: consular affairs, economic affairs, management, political affairs, and public diplomacy; also called *track*

ConGen   Consulate general, a relatively large post headed by a consul general; subordinate to an embassy

Constituent post   Overseas post separate from and subordinate to an embassy

Consul   Diplomat accredited to perform consular functions, including protection and welfare of citizens of the sending state, representation of commercial interests, and administration of travel controls (visas)

Control officer   Member of embassy or consular staff designated to take care of an official delegation or important visitor

COPs   Country operating plans

CORDS   Civil Operations and Revolutionary Development Support, an element of the US pacification program during the Vietnam War

Counselor   (1) Diplomatic title of an embassy officer responsible for supervising the work of a section (such as agricultural counselor, political counselor, counselor for consular affairs); (2) lowest rank in the senior foreign service; (3) title of a confidential adviser to the secretary of state, the highest-ranking office in the Department of State not requiring Senate confirmation. Not to be confused with consular, which pertains to the work of consuls.

CPA   See *Coalition Provisional Authority*

CRS See *S/CRS*

DACOR Diplomatic and Consular Officers Retired, a private association. www.dacorba con.org

DATT Defense attaché, normally the senior military member of an embassy

DCM See *Deputy chief of mission*

DEA Drug Enforcement Administration

Demarche An official diplomatic representation to a foreign government, conducted in person

Deputy chief of mission Second-highest-ranking official in a diplomatic mission

Desk officer An officer in a regional *bureau* of the Department of State responsible for a specific country or group of countries

DG See *Director general*

DIA Defense Intelligence Agency

Diplomacy 3.0 Diplomacy, defense, and development

Diplomatic corps All the accredited diplomats at a post or in a country

Diplomatic immunity Protection from taxation, arrest, or prosecution accorded to accredited diplomats as representatives of sovereign powers; see *Vienna Conventions*

Diplomatic list Official list of all the accredited diplomats in a country

Diplomatic note Formal written communication between governments, generally from a foreign ministry to a diplomatic representative, or from a diplomatic representative to a foreign ministry

Director general (DG) Head of the US Foreign Service and of the State Department's Bureau of Human Resources, by law must be a career foreign service officer

DNI Director of national intelligence

DOD Department of Defense

DOJ Department of Justice

Drafter Principal author of a document

DRI Diplomatic Readiness Initiative

DS Bureau of Diplomatic Security (State)

DSS Diplomatic Security Service (State)

EAP Bureau of East Asia and Pacific Affairs (State)

EEOC Equal Employment Opportunity Commission

EER Employee evaluation report, also called efficiency report

ELO Entry-level officer

EO Executive order, a presidential document establishing or implementing regulations

ESF Economic support funds

EUCOM See *Combatant command*

FAH Foreign affairs handbook with procedures of the *Foreign Affairs Manual*

FAM Foreign affairs manual setting out the regulations and procedures of the foreign service

FAS Foreign Agricultural Service, the foreign service of the Department of Agriculture

FBI Federal Bureau of Investigation

FCS Foreign Commercial Service, the foreign service of the Department of Commerce, part of the US Commercial Service

FMF, FMS   See *Foreign military financing, foreign military sales*

Foreign military financing, foreign military sales   US government programs to support the sale of US-made weaponry abroad

Foreign Service Act   Unless otherwise stated, the 1980 legislation

FSI   Foreign Service Institute, the training arm of the foreign service

FSN   Foreign service national—non-American employee of the US service, ordinarily a national of the country in which employed

FSO   Foreign service officer

FSOA   Foreign service oral assessment

FSOT   Foreign service officer test

FSR   Foreign service reserve, a personnel category (1946–80, State)

FSWE   Foreign service written exam

FY   Fiscal year—in the US government begins October 1 and ends September 30; designated by its ending date (FY 2010 is the year ending September 30, 2010)

GPOI   Global Peace Operations Initiative, program run by the Department of Defense to provide training for foreign forces engaged in international peacekeeping

GS   General schedule, pay schedule for members of the civil service

GSO   General services officer—an embassy officer responsible for the housing stock, transportation, contracts and procurement, supplies, and the like

GWOT   Global War on Terrorism

Hardship allowance, differential   Supplemental pay, a percentage of base pay, for members of the foreign service serving in places designated by the Department of State

HR/CDA   Bureau of Human Resources, Career Development and Assignments Office (State)

ICASS   International Cooperative Administrative Support Services

IDCA   International Development and Cooperation Agency, an umbrella agency that included *USAID* (1979–98)

IED   Improvised explosive device

IMET   International Military Education and Training, a US military-to-military exchange program

IMS   Interagency management system

INR   Bureau of Intelligence and Research (State)

Inspector general   Senior official in an agency, authorized to conduct internal reviews and investigations to promote good management and prevent waste, fraud, and abuse

ITA   International Trade Administration—unit of the Department of Commerce that is home to the US Commercial Service, formerly the US and Foreign Commercial Service

IV, NIV   Immigrant visa, nonimmigrant visa

JAG   judge advocate general (US Navy)

JCS   Joint chiefs of staff

KGB   Internal security and foreign intelligence service of the Soviet Union (acronym for Committee on State Security, in Russian)

L   Bureau of Legal Affairs (State Department)

Legal attaché   Title used by an FBI agent assigned to an embassy abroad

LES   Locally engaged staff, includes foreign service nationals and other persons hired locally by a US mission, including third-country nationals, resident US citizens, and family members of foreign service or other embassy personnel

Locality pay   Adjustments to base pay to account for local differences in living costs

Main State   The Harry S Truman Building at 22nd and C streets NW, Washington, D.C.

MCC   Millennium Challenge Corporation, a US provider of foreign assistance

Midlevel officer   Foreign service officer in grades 3, 2, or 1

Mission   (1) The broadest word for a diplomatic post, the US mission to a country includes the embassy, all subordinate posts, and all personnel subject to the authority of the chief of mission (ambassador); (2) US representation to an international organization, such as the US Mission to the United Nations or the US Mission to the European Union; (3) the AID presence in a country, headed by a mission director

MOU   Memorandum of understanding

NATO   North Atlantic Treaty Organization

NEA   Bureau of Near East Asian Affairs (State Department)

NFATC   (George P. Shultz) National Foreign Affairs Training Center, the Arlington, Virginia, campus of the Foreign Service Institute

NGO   Nongovernmental organization

NIV, IV   Nonimmigrant visa, immigrant visa

Nodel   State Department jargon for members of Congress traveling abroad unofficially; see *Codel*

Noncareer   See *Political appointee*

NORTHCOM   See *Combatant command*

Note verbale   An unsigned diplomatic note in the third person, less formal than a signed note, more formal than an aide-mémoire

NSA   National Security Agency

NSC   National Security Council

NSPD   National Security Presidential Directive

OECD   Organization for Economic Cooperation and Development

OEO   Office of Economic Opportunity, a US domestic agency closed in 1974

OER   Officer evaluation report, subsumed in EER (employee evaluation report)

Office of Personnel Management   Federal agency that operates the civil service

OJT   On-the-job training

OMB   Office of Management and Budget

OMS   Office management specialist

OPAP   Overseas Presence Advisory Panel (State, 1999)

OpenNet   State Department intranet

OPM   See *Office of Personnel Management*

OSAC   Overseas Security Advisory Council, a federal advisory committee promoting cooperation between private entities and the Department of State on security matters. www.osac.org

OSS   Office of Strategic Services, the wartime predecessor of the *CIA*, closed in 1945

OUDS(P)   Office of Undersecretary of Defense for Policy

PACOM   See *Combatant command*

PAO   Public affairs officer

PCS   Permanent change of station (not temporary duty), transfer

PEPFAR   President's Emergency Program for AIDS Relief

PNG   Persona non grata. Literally, unwelcome person, a designation applied by a receiving government when it strips a diplomat of accreditation and evicts him or her from the country

POLAD   Political adviser

Political appointee   Office holder named by and serving at the pleasure of the president or the agency head and exempt from the rules of competitive service; positions designated by law, executive order, or action of the Office of Personnel Management; see *Schedule C*

Post   Any US diplomatic or consular establishment

Principal officer   Senior officer at a post

Protocol   Accepted way of doing things

Provincial Reconstruction Team   Mixed military-civilian unit engaged in civil affairs, economic reconstruction, and political stabilization in Iraq and Afghanistan

PRT   Provincial reconstruction team

Public diplomacy   Diplomatic action intended to affect public opinion in a foreign country

QDDR   Quadrennial Diplomacy and Development Review

QEP   Qualifications Evaluation Panel

QRF   Quick Response Fund, civilian version of the CERP

REO   Regional embassy office (State, Iraq)

Residence   Ambassador's living quarters

RIF   Reduction in force, federal employment jargon for layoffs

RNet   Intranet for State Department retirees

Rotational tour   For entry-level foreign service officers, includes service in more than one section of an embassy

RSO   Regional security officer

Schedule C   Personnel category designating a *political appointee* serving at the pleasure of the agency head and not subject to Senate confirmation

SCO   Senior commercial officer, title used by the senior foreign commercial service representative at an overseas post

S/CRS   Office of the Coordinator for Reconstruction and Stabilization (State Department)

Security clearance   Authorization of access to classified information

SES   Senior executive service, the top grades of the civil service

Seventh floor   Leadership of the Department of State, location in *Main State* of the offices of the secretary, deputy secretary, and undersecretaries of state

SFS   Senior foreign service, the top grades of the foreign service

SIGIR   Special Inspector General for Iraq Reconstruction

SOCOM   See *Combatant command*

SOUTHCOM   See *Combatant command*

Special envoy   Person appointed to represent the United States with respect to a particular topic, not accredited to any government or international organization (e.g., special envoy for Holocaust issues, special envoy for Korean peace talks)

Staffdel   Congressional staff delegation on official travel

Tandem   Foreign service employees on active duty who are married to each other

TDY   Temporary duty (not permanent change of station)

Three D's   Diplomacy, defense, and development

TIC   Time in class

Track   See *Cone*

Undersecretary   Subcabinet rank below deputy secretary and above assistant secretary

UNODIR   Unless otherwise directed—*you know, dear*

USAID, AID   US Agency for International Development (1961)

USDA   Department of Agriculture

USIA, USIS   United States Information Agency, the locus of US public diplomacy from 1953 to 1999. Outside the United States, USIA was called the US Information Service, apparently to reduce confusion with the Central Intelligence Agency (CIA).

USICA   US Information and Communications Agency (1978–82)

USOCO   US Office for Contingency Operations

USTR   US Trade Representative

Vienna Conventions   1961 and 1963 conventions on diplomatic relations and consular relations, respectively, codifying international law with respect to treatment of diplomatic and consular personnel and property. Signatories to the conventions agree that diplomats and property covered by the conventions are immune from arrest, prosecution, taxation, and similar forms of state coercion.

WAE   When actually employed—a retired member of the foreign service available to work under a short-term contract

WTO   World Trade Organization

Bibliography

Acheson, Dean. *Present at the Creation.* New York: W. W. Norton, 1969.

Adams, Henry. *The Education of Henry Adams.* 1918. Reprint, New York: Library of America, 1983.

Anonymous. "Think Again: Soft Power." *Foreign Policy,* online exclusive, February 23, 2006. www.foreignpolicy.com/articles/2006/02/22/think_again_soft_power.

Bacchus, William. *Staffing for Foreign Affairs: Personnel Systems for the 1980s and 1990s.* Princeton, NJ: Princeton University Press, 1983.

Baker, James A., III, with Thomas M. DeFrank. *The Politics of Diplomacy: Revolution, War, and Peace, 1989–1992.* New York: G. P. Putnam's Sons, 1995.

Barnes, William, and John Heath Morgan. *The Foreign Service of the United States: Origins, Development, and Functions.* Washington, DC: U.S. Department of State, Historical Office, 1961.

Berridge, G. R. *Diplomacy: Theory and Practice.* 3rd ed. Basingstoke, Hampshire, UK: Palgrave Macmillan, 2005.

Bierce, Ambrose. *The Devil's Dictionary.* 1911. Reprint, New York: Dover, 1993.

Bodine, Barbara K. "Preemptive Post-Conflict Stabilization and Reconstruction." In *Commanding Heights: Strategic Lessons from Complex Operations,* edited by Michael Miklaucic, 31–38. Washington, DC: Center for Complex Operations and Center for Technology and National Security, National Defense University, July 2009.

Boot, Max. "Send the State Department to War." *New York Times,* November 14, 2007.

Bradley, Monica. "Timely Data: HR Releases 2009 Foreign Service Promotion Statistics." *State Magazine,* April 2010, 28–31.

Bridges, Peter. "A Massive Tome, but Still Lacking." Review of *Abraham Lincoln: A Life,* by Michael Burlingame. *California Literary Review,* October 15, 2009. http://calitreview.com/5017.

Brooks, David. "Truck Stop Confidential." *New York Times,* August 14, 2007.

Bryson, Andrew. "Ambassadors Going Out with a Bang." *BBC News,* October 16, 2009. http://news.bbc.co.uk/2/hi/8307273.stm.

Carlucci, Frank C., III. Interview by Charles Stuart Kennedy, December 30, 1996. *Frontline Diplomacy: The Foreign Affairs Oral History Collection of the Association for Diplomatic Studies and Training.* Library of Congress, Manuscript Division. Arlington, VA: ADST, 1998. http://hdl.loc.gov/loc.mss/mfdip.2004car03.

Center for Army Lessons Learned. *PRT Playbook: Tactics, Techniques, and Procedures.* Handbook 07-34. Arlington, VA: U.S. Department of Defense, September 2007. http://usacac.army.mil/cac2/call/docs/07-34/07-34.pdf.

Clark, Wesley. "No Formulas: Bosnia, Haiti, and Kosovo." In *Commanding Heights: Strategic Lessons from Complex Operations,* edited by Michael Miklaucic. Washington, DC: Center for Complex Operations and Center for Technology and National Security, National Defense University, July 2009.

Clarke, Henry L. "Reconstructing Iraq's Provinces, One by One." *Joint Forces Quarterly* 52 (2009). http://ndupress.ndu.edu.

Clinton, Hillary R. "Remarks at the Global Philanthropy Forum Conference." April 22, 2009. www.state.gov/secretary/rm/2009a/04/122066.htm.

———. Remarks before the House Appropriations Subcommittee on State, Foreign Operations, and Related Programs, "National Security through Diplomacy," Washington, DC, April 23, 2009, www.state.gov/secretary/rm/2009a/04/122098.htm

———. Remarks to the Center for Global Development. "Remarks on Development in the 21st Century." Washington, DC, January 6, 2010. www.state.gov/secretary/rm/2010/01/134838.htm.

———. Statement before the Senate Foreign Relations Committee. "Nomination Hearing to Be Secretary of State." Washington, DC, January 13, 2009. www.state.gov/secretary/rm/2009a/01/115196.htm.

Cohen, Roger. "Democracy as a Brand: Wooing Hearts, European or Muslim." *New York Times*, October 16, 2004.

Cooper, Helene. "Few Veteran Diplomats Accept Mission to Iraq." *New York Times*, February 8, 2007.

———. "Foreign Service Officers Resist Mandatory Iraq Openings." *New York Times*, November 1, 2007.

Davies, John Paton. "The Personal Experience." In *The China Hands' Legacy: Ethics and Diplomacy*, edited by Paul Gordon Lauren, 37–57. Boulder, CO: Westview, 1987.

Desmond, Frank. "McCarthy Charges Reds Hold U.S. Jobs." *Wheeling Intelligencer*, February 10, 1950. www.wvculture.org.history/government/mccarthy.html.

Destler, I. M., Haruhiro Fukui, and Hideo Sata. *The Textile Wrangle: Conflict in Japanese-American Relations, 1969–1971.* Cornell, NY: Cornell University Press, 1979.

DeYoung, Karen. "Envoys Resist Forced Iraq Duty." *Washington Post*, November 1, 2007.

———. "U.S. to Cut Ten Percent of Diplomatic Posts Next Year." *Washington Post*, December 13, 2007.

Dobbins, James. "Retaining the Lessons of Nation-Building." In *Commanding Heights: Strategic Lessions for Complex Operations*, edited by Michael Miklaucic. Washington, DC: Center for Complex Operations and Center for Technology and National Security, National Defense University, July 2009.

Dobbins, James, and Seth G. Jones, Benjamin Runkle, and Siddharth Mohandas. *Occupying Iraq: A History of the Coalition Provisional Authority.* Santa Monica, CA: RAND Corporation, 2009.

Dorman, Shawn. "Iraqi Service and Beyond." *Foreign Service Journal* 83 (March 2006): 17–41.

Ford, Charles A. "Final Thoughts on the Foreign Service at the Commerce Department." *AFSA News*, May 2005, 4.

Foreign Affairs Council. *Secretary Colin Powell's State Department: An Independent Assessment.* Task Force Report. Chapel Hill, NC: American Diplomacy, 2004. www.diplomatsonline.org/taskreport0303.html.

Foreign Service Act of 1980, PL 96-465, as amended, 22 U.S.C. sec. 3901 et seq. www.usaid.gov/policy/ads/400/fsa.pdf.

Freeman, Charles W., Jr. *The Arts of Power: Statecraft and Diplomacy.* Washington, DC: U.S. Institute of Peace Press, 1997.

Frumin, Amy B. "Equipping USAID for Success: A Field Perspective." PCR Project Special Briefing. June 2009. Washington, DC: Center for Strategic and International Studies.

Gallucci, Robert, Daniel Poneman, and Joel Wit. *Going Critical: The First North Korean Nuclear Crisis.* Washington, DC: Brookings Institution Press, 2004.

Gates, Robert M. Forrestal lecture, April 7, 2010, www.defense.gov/speeches/speech .aspx?speechid=1444.

———. Landon lecture. Kansas State University, November 22, 2007. www.defenselink .mil/speeches/speech.aspx?speechid=1199.

Gilbert, Martin. *Churchill: A Life.* New York: Henry Holt, 1991.

Gingrich, Newt. "Rogue State Department." *Foreign Policy* 137 (July–August 2003): 42–48.

———. "Transforming the State Department: The Next Challenge for the Bush Administration." Speech at the American Enterprise Institute, Washington, DC, April 22, 2003. www.aei.org/publications/pubID.16992,filter.all/pub_detail.asp.

Goodwin, Doris Kearns. *Team of Rivals: The Political Genius of Abraham Lincoln.* New York: Simon & Schuster, 2005.

Grove, Brandon. *Behind Embassy Walls: The Life and Times of an American Diplomat.* Columbia: University of Missouri Press, 2005.

Haig, Alexander M., Jr. *Caveat: Realism, Reagan, and Foreign Policy.* New York: Scribner, 1984.

Harris, Shane. "New Order." *Government Executive* 38 (August 1, 2006): 30–39. www.gov exec.com/features/0806-01/0806-01s1.htm.

Herrling, Sheila, and Steve Radelet. "Modernizing U.S. Foreign Assistance for the Twenty-First Century." In *The White House and the World: A Global Development Agenda for the Next U.S. President,* edited by Nancy Birdsall, 273–98. Washington, DC: Center for Global Development, 2008.

Humphrey, David C., ed. *Foreign Relations of the United States, 1969–1976.* Vol. 2, *Organization and Management of U.S. Foreign Policy, 1969–1972.* Washington, DC: Government Printing Office, 2006. www.state.gov/documents/organization/77830.pdf.

Johnson, Thomas. "Black Envoys Seek More Non-African Posts." *New York Times,* August 13, 1974, 4.

Johnstone, L. Craig. "Strategic Planning and International Affairs in the 21st Century." Remarks at opening session of the Conference Series on International Affairs in the 21st Century. U.S. State Department, Dean Acheson Auditorium, Washington, DC, November 18, 1997. www.state.gov/www/policy_remarks/971118_johnstone_strat plan.html.

Jordan, Mary. " 'Hillary Effect' Cited for Increase in Female Ambassadors to U.S." *Washington Post,* January 11, 2010, A1.

Kahn, E. J. *The China Hands.* New York: Viking, 1972.

Kaplan, Fred. *The Singular Mark Twain: A Biography.* New York: Doubleday, 2003.

Kaplan, Robert. *Imperial Grunts: The American Military on the Ground.* New York: Random House, 2005.

Keeley, Robert V., ed. *First Line of Defense: Ambassadors, Embassies and American Interests Abroad.* Washington, DC: American Academy of Diplomacy, 2000.

Kennan, George. *Memoirs.* Boston: Little, Brown, 1972.

Kessler, Glenn. "Administration Blocks Ex-Hostages' Bid for Damages from Iran." *Washington Post,* March 19, 2006, A1.

———. "Administration Critics Chafe at State Dept. Shuffle." *Washington Post,* February 21, 2006, A4.

Kissinger, Henry. *Diplomacy.* New York: Touchstone, 1995.

———. *White House Years.* Boston: Little, Brown, 1979.

———. *Years of Renewal.* New York: Simon & Schuster, 1999.

———. *Years of Upheaval.* Boston: Little, Brown, 1982.

Kopp, Harry W. *Commercial Diplomacy and the National Interest.* Washington, DC: American Academy of Diplomacy and Business Council for International Understanding, 2004.

Lauren, Paul Gordon, ed. *The China Hands' Legacy: Ethics and Diplomacy.* Boulder, CO: Westview, 1987.

Lawson, Marian Leonardo, Susan B. Epstein, and Kennon H. Nakamura. *State, Foreign Operations, and Related Programs: FY2011 Budget and Appropriations,* Congressional Research Service, Washington, May 5, 2010.

Leahy, Patrick. "Statement of Senator Patrick Leahy, Chairman, State Foreign Operations, and Related Programs Subcommittee." Hearing on FY 2008 State, Foreign Operations Budget Request, May 10, 2007. http://leahy.senate.gov/press/200705/051007 .html.

Lewis, Mike. "Gates Is a Big Draw for Visiting World Leaders." *Seattle Post-Intelligencer,* April 17, 2006.

Luehrs, Christoff. "Provincial Reconstruction Teams: A Literature Review." *Prism* 1 (December 2009). www.ndu.edu/inss/press/prism/1/Prism_issue%201%20for%20 web.pdf

Lutkins, LaRue R. Interview by Charles Stuart Kennedy, November 17, 1989. *Frontline Diplomacy: The Foreign Affairs Oral History Collection of the Association for Diplomatic Studies and Training.* Library of Congress, Manuscript Division. Arlington, VA: ADST, 1998. http://hdl.loc.gov/loc.mss/mfdip.2004lut01.

Magnuson, Stew. "Integrating Civilian Agencies into Military Operations Remains Difficult." *National Defense,* December 2009.

Marquardt, Niels. "The DRI Rides to the Rescue." *Foreign Service Journal* 81 (April 2004): 20–28.

Marshall, S. L. A. *The Armed Forces Officer.* Department of the Army Pamphlet 600-2. Washington, DC: Government Printing Office, 1950.

McWilliams, Edmund. "They Spoke Out." Review of *Dissent: Voices of Conscience* by Ann Wright and Susan Dixon. *Foreign Service Journal* 56 (May 2009): 53–55.

Mee, Charles L., Jr. *The Marshall Plan: The Launching of the Pax Americana.* New York: Simon & Schuster, 1984.

Melia, Thomas O. "Congressional Staff Attitudes toward the Department of State and Foreign Service Officers: A Report Based on 25 One-on-One Interviews with Key

Congressional Staff." Unpublished paper prepared for the Una Chapman Cox Foundation, Washington, DC, 2002.

Morgan, Ted. *FDR: A Biography.* New York: Simon & Schuster, 1985.

Morgan, William, and Charles Stuart Kennedy, eds. *American Diplomats: The Foreign Service at Work.* Lincoln, NE: iUniverse, 2004.

Nathan, James, and James Oliver. *Foreign Policy Making and the American Political System.* 3rd ed. Baltimore: Johns Hopkins University Press, 1994.

Neumann, Ronald E. *The Other War: Winning and Losing in Afghanistan.* Washington, DC: Potomac Press, 2009.

Newsom, David. *Diplomacy and the American Democracy.* Bloomington: Indiana University Press, 1988.

Nicolson, Harold. *The Evolution of Diplomatic Method.* London: Constable and Co., 1953.

Nye, Joseph S., Jr. "Soft Power." *Foreign Policy,* Autumn 1990, 153–71.

Olsen, Rick. Interview 5. By Marilyn Green, March 12, 2008. *Oral Histories: Iraq Provincial Reconstruction Teams.* Washington, DC: U.S. Institute of Peace and Association for Diplomatic Studies and Training, 2009. www.usip.org/resources/oral-histories-iraq -provincial-reconstruction-teams.

Passel, Jeffrey S., and D'Vera Cohn. *Mexican Immigrants: How Many Come? How Many Leave?* Washington, DC: Pew Research Center, July 22, 2009. www.pewhispanic.org.

Perito, Robert M. "Provincial Reconstruction Teams in Iraq." Special Report 185. Washington, DC: U.S. Institute of Peace, March 2007. www.usip.org/pubs/specialreports/ sr185.pdf.

————. *The U.S. Experience with Provincial Reconstruction Teams in Afghanistan: Lessons Identified.* Special Report 152. Washington, DC: U.S. Institute of Peace, October 2005.

————. "The U.S. Experience with Provincial Reconstruction Teams in Iraq and Afghanistan." Testimony before the House Armed Services Subcommittee on Oversight and Investigations. Washington, DC: U.S. Institute of Peace, October 18, 2007. www.usip.org/resources/us-experience-provincial-reconstruction-teams-iraq-and -afghanistan.

Perkins, Dexter. "The Department of State and American Public Opinion." In *The Diplomats: 1919–1939.* Vol. 1, *The Twenties,* edited by Gordon A. Craig and Felix Gilbert, 282–308. New York: Atheneum, 1963.

Peters, Ralph. "Strip for Action." *New York Post,* December 26, 2006.

Pickering, Thomas R. Oral presentation. "American Negotiating Behavior and the Transformation of U.S. Diplomacy." U.S. Institute of Peace, Washington, DC, May 12, 2010.

Priest, Dana. *The Mission.* New York: W. W. Norton, 2003.

Ray, Charles A. "One-Two-Three: Penetrating the Promotion Process." *State Magazine,* February 2007, 24–25.

Rice, Condoleezza. Confirmation hearings before Senate Foreign Relations Committee, opening statement as prepared for delivery. Washington, DC, January 18, 2005. www .state.gov/secretary/rm/2005/40991.htm.

————. Opening remarks before the House Committee on Appropriations Subcommittee on Science, State, Justice, and Commerce, and Related Agencies, as prepared for delivery. *President's FY 2006 Budget Request.* Washington, DC, March 9, 2005. www .state.gov/secretary/rm/2005/43184.htm.

———. Remarks at Georgetown School of Foreign Service. "Transformational Diplomacy." Washington, DC, January 18, 2006. www.state.gov/secretary/rm/2006/59306 .htm.

———. Remarks at Town Hall Meeting. U.S. State Department, Dean Acheson Auditorium, Washington, DC, January 31, 2005. www.state.gov/secretary/rm/2005/41414 .htm.

"Rivkin Award." *Foreign Service Journal* 86 (July–August 2009): 50–51.

Safire, William. "On Language." *New York Times Magazine,* May 12, 2002.

Satterfield, David. Interview 17. By Barbara Nielsen, February 15, 2008. *Oral Histories: Iraq Provincial Reconstruction Teams.* Washington, DC: U.S. Institute of Peace and Association for Diplomatic Studies and Training, 2009. www.usip.org/resources/oral -histories-iraq-provincial-reconstruction-teams.

Schouten, Fredreka. "Top Obama Fundraisers Get Posts." *USA Today,* October 29, 2009.

Seitzinger, Michael V. *Conducting Foreign Relations without Authority: The Logan Act.* CRS Report for Congress RL33265. Washington, DC: Government Printing Office, February 1, 2006. http://opencrs.cdt.org/rpts/RL33265_20060201.pdf.

Sharp, Paul. *Diplomatic Theory of International Relations.* Cambridge Studies in International Relations 111. New York: Cambridge University Press, 2009.

Shultz, George P. *Turmoil and Triumph.* New York: Scribner, 1993.

Slaughter, Anne-Marie. "America's Edge: Power in the Networked Century." *Foreign Affairs* 88 (January–February 2009). www.foreignaffairs.com/articles/63722/anne -marie-slaughter/americas-edge.

Smith, Dane F., Jr. *An Expanded Mandate for Peace Building: The State Department Role in Peace Diplomacy, Reconstruction, and Stabilization.* Washington, DC: Center for Strategic and International Studies, April 2009.

Special Inspector General for Iraq Reconstruction. *Applying Iraq's Hard Lessons to the Reform of Stabilization and Reconstruction Operations.* Washington, DC: Government Printing Office, February 2010. www.sigir.mil/files/U.S.OCO/ApplyingHardLessons.pdf.

———. *Hard Lessons: The Iraq Reconstruction Experience.* Washington, DC: Government Printing Office, February 2009.

Speckhard, Daniel. "Provincial Reconstruction Team Leaders Discuss Progress." PRT Press Briefing. Baghdad, Iraq: Operation Iraqi Freedom, January 12, 2007. www.mnf -iraq.com/index.php?option=com_content&task=view&id=8787&Itemid=30.

Steigman, Andrew. *The Foreign Service of the United States: First Line of Defense.* Boulder, CO: Westview, 1985.

Stephenson, Barbara. Presentation at U.S. Institute of Peace. Washington, DC, February 22, 2007.

Stevens, Lory. "PRT Team Transfer of Authority Ceremony Held in Panjshir Valley." *Fort Polk Guardian, Fort Polk Louisiana.* July 24, 2009. www.fortpolkguardian.com/army _news/x2141120432/PRT-team-transfer-of-security (accessed August 8, 2009).

Stockman, Farah. "Diplomats Angry over Forced Posts in Baghdad." *Boston Globe,* November 1, 2007.

Stuart, Graham H. *American Diplomatic and Consular Practice.* New York: Appleton-Century, 1936.

Szayna, Thomas S., Derek Eaton, James E. Barnett II, Brooke Stearns Lawson, Terrence K. Kelly, and Zachary Haldeman. *Integrating Civilian Agencies in Stability Operations.* Santa Monica, CA: RAND Corporation, 2009. www.rand.org/pubs/monographs/2009/RAND_MG801.pdf.

Transition Center of the Foreign Service Institute. *Protocol for the Modern Diplomat.* Washington, DC: U.S. Department of State, 2005. www.state.gov/documents/organization/15742.pdf.

Trask, David. *A Short History of the U.S. Department of State, 1781–1981.* Washington, DC: Government Printing Office, 1981.

Tyson, Ann Scott. "Applying Diplomacy to Conflict." *Washington Post,* September 29, 2006.

United Nations. "Vienna Convention on Consular Relations, 1963." *Treaty Series,* vol. 596, p. 261. Also at http://untreaty.un.org/ilc/texts/instruments/english/conventions/9_2_1963.pdf.

———. "Vienna Convention on Diplomatic Relations, 1961." *Treaty Series,* vol. 500, p. 95. Also at http://untreaty.un.org/ilc/texts/instruments/english/conventions/9_1_1961.pdf.

U.S. Congress. Committee on Foreign Relations. *Embassies as Command Posts in the Anti-Terror Campaign.* 109th Cong., 2nd sess., 2006. Committee Print 109-52. www.fas.org/irp/congress/2006_rpt/embassies.pdf.

———. House of Representatives. Committee on Armed Services, Subcommittee on Oversight and Investigations. *Agency Stovepipes vs. Strategic Agility: Lessons We Need to Learn from Provincial Reconstruction Teams in Iraq and Afghanistan.* Washington, DC: Government Printing Office, April 2008.

———. *Embassies Grapple to Guide Foreign Aid.* 110th Cong., 1st sess., 2007. Committee Print 111-33. www.gpoaccess.gov/congress/index.html.

U.S. Congress. Senate. Committee on Foreign Relations, Subcommittee on International Operations and Organizations, Human Rights, Democracy, and Global Women's Issues. *Statement for the Record by Under Secretary for Public Diplomacy and Public Affairs Judith McHale.* Washington, DC: Government Printing Office, March 10, 2010.

U.S. Department of the Army. *Counterinsurgency.* U.S. Army Field Manual 3-24 and Marine Corps Warfighting Publication 3-33.5. Washington, DC: Government Printing Office, December 2006. www.fas.org/irp/doddir/army/fm3-24.pdf.

U.S. Department of Defense. "Report on Strategic Communication under Section 1055(b) of the Duncan Hunter National Defense Authorization Act for FY 2009." Washington, DC, February 11, 2010. www.carlisle.army.mil/dime/documents/DoD%20report%20on%20Strategic%20Communication%20Dec%2009.pdf (accessed October 10, 2010).

U.S. Department of State. *America's Overseas Presence in the Twenty-first Century: The Report of the Overseas Advisory Panel.* Washington, DC: Government Printing Office, 1999.

———. *Congressional Budget Justification, FY 2011.* Vols. 1–2. *Department of State Operations.* Washington, DC: Government Printing Office, 2010.

————. *Department of State's Goal for Arabic Speakers.* Office of the Spokesman. Question taken at the June 19, 2007, daily press briefing. www.state.gov/r/pa/prs/ps/2007/jun/86803.htm.

————. *Final Report and Recommendations of the President's Commission on Hostage Compensation.* Unpublished paper. U.S. Department of State Library, Washington, DC, September 21, 1981.

————. *Foreign Affairs Handbook.* Vol. 3, *Personnel Operations Handbook.* Washington, DC: Department of State, www.state.gov/m/a/dir/regs/fah/03fah01/index.htm.

————. *Foreign Affairs Manual.* Vol. 2, *General.* Washington, DC: Department of State, www.state.gov/m/a/dir/regs/fam/02fam/index.htm.

————. *Foreign Affairs Manual.* Vol. 3, *Personnel.* Washington, DC: Department of State, www.state.gov/m/a/dir/regs/fam/03fam/index.htm

————. "Foreign Service Assignments: The Future Is Now." State Department cable 133427, unclassified. August 15, 2006.

————. *FY 2008 Budget in Brief.* Bureau of Resource Management. February 5, 2007 . www.state.gov/s/d/rm/rls/bib/2008/html/79744.htm.

————. "New Direction for Foreign Assistance." Fact sheet, Office of the Spokesman. January 19, 2006. www.state.gov/r/pa/prs/ps/2006/59398.htm.

————. *Report of the Secretary of State's Advisory Panel on Overseas Security* [Inman Report]. Washington, DC: U.S. Department of State, 1985. www.fas.org/irp/threat/inman.

————. *Report to Congress on Implementation of Title XVI of P.L. 110-417, the Reconstruction and Stabilization Citizen Management Act of 2008.* May 9, 2009.

U.S. Department of State. Bureau of Public Affairs. "Remarks by Secretary Clinton: Remarks at the Global Philanthropy Forum Conference." Press release. no. PRN 2009/365, April 22, 2009.

U.S. Department of State. Steven Buckler, Dave Bailey, and Michael McBride. "Briefing on Reconstruction Progress in Salah ad Din." Special Briefing 2007/1069, via satellite. Washington, DC: Bureau of Public Affairs, Public Relations Office, November 30, 2007. www.state.gov/r/pa/prs/ps/2007/nov/96029.htm.

U.S. Department of State. Bureau of Diplomatic Security. *Partnerships for a Safer World.* 2006 Year in Review. Publication 11423. Washington, DC: Government Printing Office, 2007. www.state.gov/documents/organization/86789.pdf.

U.S. Department of State. Bureau of Public Affairs. "Provincial Reconstruction Teams: Building Iraqi Capacity and Accelerating the Transition to Iraqi Self-Reliance." Fact sheet. Washington, DC: Government Printing Office, March 28, 2007. ww.state.gov/documents/organization/82244.pdf.

U.S. Department of State. John E. Herbst. "Stabilization and Reconstruction Operations: Learning from the Provincial Reconstruction Team (PRT) Experience." Statement before House Armed Services Subcommittee on Oversight and Investigations. Washington, DC: Office of Reconstruction and Stabilization, October 30, 2007. www.state.gov/s/crs/rls/rm/94379.htm.

U.S. Department of State. James Knight, Steven Buckler, John Melvin Jones, and Charles Hunter. "On-the-Record Briefing with Provincial Reconstruction Team (PRT) Leaders on Iraq." Washington, DC: Digital Video Conference, March 30, 2007. www.state.gov/p/nea/rls/rm/2007/82501.htm.

U.S. Department of State. Report of the Visa Office, 2009. www.travel.state.gov/visa/statistics/statistics_4594.html

U.S. Department of State. Sean McCormack. Daily press briefing. DPB 109. Washington, DC: Bureau of Public Affairs, Public Relations Office, June 19, 2007. www.state.gov/r/pa/prs/dpb/2007/jun/86611.htm.

———. Daily press briefing. DPB 192. Washington, DC: Bureau of Public Affairs, Public Relations Office, October 31, 2007. www.state.gov/r/pa/prs/dpb/2007/oct/94402.htm.

———. Daily press briefing. DPB 193. Washington, DC: Bureau of Public Affairs, Public Relations Office, November 1, 2007. www.state.gov/r/pa/prs/dpb/2007/nov/94478.htm.

U.S. Department of State. Office of the United States Global AIDS Coordinator. *The U.S. President's Emergency Plan for AIDS Relief: Five-Year Strategy.* Washington, DC: Government Printing Office, December 2009.

U.S. Department of State. David M. Satterfield. "On-the-Record Briefing on Provincial Reconstruction Teams (PRTs) in Iraq." Washington, DC: Video Teleconference, February 7, 2007. www.state.gov/p/nea/rls/rm/2007/80216.htm.

U.S. Department of State and Broadcasting Board of Governors. *Report of Inspection, Bureau of African Affairs.* Report ISP-I-09-63. Washington, DC: Government Printing Office, August 2009.

———. *Report of Inspection: Embassy Baghdad, Iraq.* Report ISP-I-09-30A. Washington, DC: Government Printing Office, July 2009.

U.S. Department of State, Joint Center for Operational Analysis, and U.S. Agency for International Development. *Provincial Reconstruction Teams in Afghanistan: An Interagency Assessment.* Washington, DC: Government Printing Office, April 5, 2006. www.crs.state.gov/index.cfm?fuseaction=public.display&id=cbd4c378-efb3-4435-a33f-2b7a0ef0085c.

U.S. General Accounting Office. *State Department: Minorities and Women Are Underrepresented in the Foreign Service.* Report B-232884 to Congress. Washington, DC: Government Printing Office, 1989.

U.S. Government. "Executive Order 13534 of March 11, 2010: National Export Initiative." *Federal Register* 75, no. 50, 12243–45.

U.S. Government Accountability Office. *Department of State: Additional Steps Needed to Address Continuing Staffing and Experience Gaps at Hardship Posts.* GAO-09-874. Washington, DC: Government Printing Office, September 2009.

———. *Department of State: Comprehensive Plan Needed to Address Persistent Foreign Language Shortfalls.* GAO-09-955. Washington, DC: Government Printing Office, September 2009.

———. *Department of State: Persistent Staffing and Foreign Language Gaps Compromise Diplomatic Readiness.* Testimony before the Subcommittee on Oversight of Government Management, the Federal Workforce, and the District of Columbia, Committee on Homeland Security and Governmental Affairs, U.S. Senate, Statement of Jess T. Ford, Director, International Affairs and Trade, GAO-09-1046T, September 24, 2009.

———. *Staffing and Foreign Language Shortfalls Persist Despite Initiatives to Address Gaps.* GAO-06-894. Washington, DC: Government Printing Office, August 2006.

————. *U.S. Public Diplomacy: Strategic Planning Efforts Have Improved, but Agencies Face Significant Implementation Challenges.* GAO-07-795T. Washington, DC: Government Printing Office, April 26, 2007. www.gao.gov/new.items/d07795t.pdf.

U.S. National Security Council. "Management of Interagency Efforts Concerning Rconstruction and Stabilization." National Security Presidential Directive NSPD-44, December 7, 2005. www.crs.state.gov/index.cfm?fuseaction=public.display&shortcut=CK59 (accessed October 10, 2010).

————. "Staffing at Diplomatic Missions and Their Overseas Constituent Posts." National Security Decision Directive NSDD-38, June 2, 1982. www.state.gov//m/pri/nsdd/45148.htm (accessed October 10, 2010).

U.S. Senate. Foreign Assistance Revitalization and Accountability Act of 2009. S. 1524, Cong. Print 3, S. Rep. 111–22.

Vance, Cyrus. *Hard Choices: Critical Years in America's Foreign Policy.* New York: Simon & Schuster, 1983.

Weiner, Tim. *Legacy of Ashes: The History of the CIA.* New York: Doubleday, 2007.

Welles, Benjamin. "Women Winning State Department Cases." *New York Times,* February 28, 1972, 4.

White House. *The National Security Strategy of the United States of America.* Washington, DC: Government Printing Office, September 2002. www.whitehouse.gov/nsc/nss.pdf.

————. *The National Security Strategy of the United States of America.* Washington, DC: Government Printing Office, March 2006. www.whitehouse.gov/nsc/nss/2006/nss2006.pdf.

————. *The National Security Strategy of the United States of America.* Washington, DC: Government Printing Office, May 2010.

White House. Office of Management and Budget. *Historical Tables.* Table 3.1, "Outlays by Superfunction and Function." Washington, DC: Office of Management and Budget, 2010. www.whitehouse.gov/omb/budget/Historicals.

————. *The President's Budget for Fiscal Year 2011.* Appendix, Department of State and Other International Programs. Washington, DC, 2010.

Williamson, Elizabeth. "How Much Embassy Is Too Much?" *Washington Post,* March 7, 2007.

Index

About the Authors

Harry W. Kopp is a former foreign service officer and consultant in international trade. He was deputy assistant secretary of state for international trade policy in the Carter and Reagan administrations, and his foreign assignments included Warsaw and Brasilia. He is now president of Harry Kopp, LLC, a consulting company, and Venture Factors, Inc. (USA), a division of Zabaleta and Company. He is the author of *Commercial Diplomacy and the National Interest.*

Charles A. Gillespie was a foreign service officer. He was deputy assistant secretary of state for inter-American affairs; United States ambassador to Grenada, Colombia, and Chile; and special assistant to the president on the staff of the National Security Council. He was a principal of the Scowcroft Group, a consulting company, and a member of the American Academy of Diplomacy, the Business Council for International Understanding, and the Forum for International Policy. He died in 2008.